Wireless Networking

ABSOLUTE
BEGINNER'S
GUIDE

Michael Miller

que®

800 East 96th Street,
Indianapolis, Indiana 46240

Wireless Networking Absolute Beginner's Guide

ISBN-13: 978-0-7897-5078-5
ISBN-10: 0-7897-5078-3

Library of Congress Cataloging-in-Publication Data is on file.

Printed in the United States of America

Second Printing: April 2013

Trademarks

Warning and Disclaimer

Bulk Sales

Que Publishing offers excellent discounts on this book when ordered in quantity for bulk purchases or special sales. For more information, please contact

U.S. Corporate and Government Sales
1-800-382-3419
corpsales@pearsontechgroup.com

For sales outside of the U.S., please contact

International Sales
international@pearsoned.com

Editor-in-Chief
Greg Wiegand

Executive Editor
Rick Kughen

Development Editor
Rick Kughen

Managing Editor
Sandra Schroeder

Project Editor
Mandie Frank

Copy Editor
Sheri Replin

Indexer
Erika Millen

Proofreader
Kathy Ruiz

Technical Editor
Todd Meister

Publishing Coordinators
Cindy Teeters
Romny French

Book Designer
Anne Jones

Compositor
Bumpy Design

Contents at a Glance

Table of Contents

About the Author

Michael Miller is a successful and prolific author with a reputation for practical advice and technical accuracy and an unerring empathy for the needs of his readers.

Mr. Miller has written more than 100 best-selling books over the past two decades. His books for Que include *Absolute Beginner's Guide to Computer Basics, Easy Computer Basics, Windows 7 Your Way, Wireless Networking with Windows Vista, Facebook for Grown-Ups, My Pinterest,* and *The Ultimate Digital Music Guide.* He is known for his casual, easy-to-read writing style and his practical, real-world advice—as well as his ability to explain a wide variety of complex topics to an everyday audience.

You can email Mr. Miller directly at abgnetworking@molehillgroup.com. His website is www.molehillgroup.com.

Dedication

To all of my Minnesota family—you're the only network that matters.

Acknowledgments

Thanks to the usual suspects at Que Publishing, including but not limited to Greg Wiegand, Rick Kughen, Mandie Frank, Sheri Replin, and technical editor Todd Meister. Thanks also to Laura Norman for supplying some Mac-related information and screenshots as necessary.

We Want to Hear from You!

As the reader of this book, *you* are our most important critic and commentator. We value your opinion and want to know what we're doing right, what we could do better, what areas you'd like to see us publish in, and any other words of wisdom you're willing to pass our way.

We welcome your comments. You can email or write to let us know what you did or didn't like about this book—as well as what we can do to make our books better.

Please note that we cannot help you with technical problems related to the topic of this book.

When you write, please be sure to include this book's title and author as well as your name and email address. We will carefully review your comments and share them with the author and editors who worked on the book.

Email: feedback@quepublishing.com

Mail: Que Publishing
         ATTN: Reader Feedback
         800 East 96th Street
         Indianapolis, IN 46240 USA

Reader Services

Visit our website and register this book at quepublishing.com/register for convenient access to any updates, downloads, or errata that might be available for this book.

INTRODUCTION

Most homes today are networked homes. Or they should be.

That's because we all have a lot of different devices that need to connect to each other and to the Internet. It's not just desktop and notebook computers that benefit from being networked; we also have smartphones (such as the iPhone), tablets (like the iPad), videogame consoles, portable game players, and even Internet-capable TVs, Blu-ray players, audio/video receivers, and network media players. That's a lot of stuff that needs to connect.

And you need to connect them all in order to do all the things you want to do in your home. Naturally, you want to connect to the Internet, for web surfing, email checking, and social networking. But, you may also want to share files between multiple computers, view your digital photos on your living room TV, listen to your favorite music, or watch streaming movies and TV shows over the web. There's a lot you can do when all your devices are connected to a home network.

Fortunately, almost all of these devices can connect wirelessly. You don't need to run big, thick, Ethernet cable from one end of your house to the other; just install a wireless router and let all of your devices connect via Wi-Fi. (They all probably have Wi-Fi built in.)

That doesn't mean that setting up a home network is simple or even necessarily trouble proof. The complexity of today's home wireless networks can be confusing, even to the more technically adept. There are a host of questions that need answered: What kind of router should you buy? How best should you configure your network to optimize playback on all your different devices? How can you get the fastest audio and video streaming while still maintaining a decent connection on your iPhone? Should you store your music and movies on a home server or on a separate PC? Can you get your Windows and Mac computers to talk to each other? And how do you keep your neighbors from tapping into your Internet connection and home network?

That's where this book comes in. *Wireless Networking Absolute Beginner's Guide* is an easy-to-use guide for anyone installing or working with a wireless home network today. This book details how to plan, purchase, and set up a typical wireless network in your home—and then optimize that network for best performance.

Wireless Networking Absolute Beginner's Guide goes beyond simple network configuration, however. I'll show you how to connect all wireless devices to your wireless network—computers, home servers, videogames, tablets, smartphones, widescreen TVs, audio/video receivers, and the like. I'll also discuss how to get the most from these connected devices, including watching streaming audio and video over your network.

I'll also cover other types of wireless connections, both inside and outside the home, including Wi-Fi hotspots, Bluetooth in your car, and your mobile-phone carrier's cellular data service. There's even advice on how to troubleshoot network problems—because, like it or not, problems do pop up from time to time.

In short, *Wireless Networking Absolute Beginner's Guide* should give you everything you need to know to guarantee hassle-free wireless connections on all manner of devices. Everything today is wireless, and wireless is everything—you might as well get ready for it.

How This Book Is Organized

I've organized this book into five main parts, as follows:

- **Part I, "Getting to Know Wireless Networking,"** shows you how networks (wired and wireless) work, and discusses the three major types of wireless networks: Wi-Fi, Bluetooth, and mobile wireless. This is the place to start if you don't know a thing about wireless networking.

- **Part II, "Setting Up a Wireless Network,"** is where you start getting your hands dirty. This section describes, in step-by-step detail, how to plan your home network, purchase the right equipment, install and configure a wireless router, connect your network to the Internet, extend your network into larger spaces, and connect selected devices via Ethernet cable. You'll even learn why and how to employ network security. (Hint: It's to protect against unwanted intruders.)

- **Part III, "Connecting Devices to Your Network,"** shows you how to connect all sorts of different devices to your new wireless network. You'll learn how to connect notebook and desktop computers (both Windows and Mac), home servers, videogame consoles and portable game players, network media players, Internet-capable TVs and Blu-ray players, and even audio/video receivers. You'll also learn how to connect your favorite handheld devices to your network. (We're talking smartphones and tablets, folks.)

- **Part IV, "Using Your Wireless Network,"** is all about doing stuff over your network. You'll learn how to share printers and scanners, share and transfer computer files, watch streaming movies and TV shows, and listen to streaming music. You'll also learn how to troubleshoot potential network problems—just in case.

- **Part V, "Connecting Wirelessly Outside the Home,"** is where you learn how to use your wireless devices outside your home or office network. You'll learn how to connect your computer, smartphone, or tablet to public Wi-Fi hotspots, and how to access the Internet from your car. Wireless is everywhere!

Taken together, the 21 chapters in this book help you progress from an absolute beginner to experienced wireless networker. Just read what you need and, before long, you'll be connected wirelessly all over the place!

Conventions Used in This Book

I hope that this book is easy enough to figure out on its own, without requiring its own instruction manual. As you read through the pages, however, it helps to know precisely how I've presented specific types of information.

Windows or Mac?

First, know that this book attempts to be relatively platform agnostic. That is, I cover a lot of different devices on multiple operating systems; it shouldn't matter whether you're using a Mac or Windows PC, or even which version of Windows you're using; there should be ample information between these two covers for whatever device you're using. (That means there's also coverage of wireless for smartphones and tablets—so there.)

Web Page Addresses

This book contains a lot of web page addresses, because that's where you go for additional information. Technically, a web page address is supposed to start with http:// (as in http://www.molehillgroup.com). Because most web browsers automatically insert this piece of the address, you don't have to type it—and I haven't included it in any of the addresses in this book.

By the way, when it comes to web page addresses, know that they change. So if you enter a specific URL I mention in this book and get a "page not found error," don't blame me; it worked when I wrote it! (And that's why we have the Google; just search for anything you need.)

Products and Services

I mention a lot of specific products in this book, and products, like web pages, come and go. It's likely that, by the time you read this book, some of the products I mention may be discontinued or replaced by newer versions. That's life in the big city, folks. Hopefully, any newer products you find will work even better than the ones I mention in this book.

Special Elements

This book also includes a few special elements that provide additional information not included in the basic text. These elements are designed to supplement the text to make your learning faster, easier, and more efficient.

TIP A *tip* is a piece of advice—a little trick, actually—that helps you use your wireless network more effectively or maneuver around problems or limitations.

 NOTE A *note* is designed to provide information that is generally useful but not specifically necessary for what you're doing at the moment. Some are like extended tips—interesting, but not essential.

 CAUTION A *caution* tells you to beware of a potentially dangerous operation or situation. In some cases, ignoring a caution could cause you significant problems—so pay attention to them!

Let Me Know What You Think

I always love to hear from readers. If you want to contact me, feel free to email me at abgwireless@molehillgroup.com. I can't promise that I'll *answer* every message, but I do promise that I'll *read* each one!

If you want to learn more about me and any new books I have cooking, check out my Molehill Group website at www.molehillgroup.com. Who knows, you might find some other books there that you would like to read.

HOW NETWORKS WORK

Back in the dark ages of personal computing (about a decade or so ago), if you wanted to cobble together a computer network, you needed miles and miles of Ethernet cable, a couple of guys wearing white lab suits, a degree in information technology, and all the time in the world. Fortunately, that's not the case anymore; today, you can set up a home network by connecting a few cables and selecting a few options in a configuration program—so simple just about anyone can do it.

That's a good thing, because just about everyone needs a home network. At the very least, you need a network to share your single Internet connection between multiple computers. But, it's not just about computers; these days, you'll find all sorts of devices connected to a typical network, including smartphones, tablets, videogame consoles, Blu-ray players, widescreen TVs, and even whole-house automation and alarm systems.

Your home network enables all these devices to talk to one another—and for you to use them for maximum effectiveness. Heaven help you if your network ever goes down; that's when you'll realize how dependent you really are on your home network.

Why You Need a Home Network

A computer network is, simply put, two or more computers or electronic devices connected together. When the devices are connected, they can share files and other data between them.

That's all well and good, but why would you need a network in your home? Or, put differently, how can you use a home network?

Sharing the Internet

Perhaps the most common reason people set up home networks today is to share an Internet connection. That is, you have a single Internet connection coming into your house, and you want every computer and smartphone and videogame console in your home to access that connection. Well, to do this, you need to set some sort of home network—even if you never intend to do more sophisticated computer-related networking, such as sharing files or peripherals.

As you can see in Figure 1.1, sharing an Internet connection involves connecting your broadband modem to a network router, and then connecting all of your computers and devices to that router. The modem typically connects to the router via a short cable, while your computers and other devices more often than not connect wirelessly.

 NOTE   As you'll soon learn, a router is the hub for all the devices connected to a network.

With this type of setup, each device connected to your network can independently access the Internet. One computer can be checking email while another surfs the web and a third is playing games or accessing Facebook. In addition, all of your iPhones and iPads and Xbox consoles can also connect to the Internet over your network, all at the same time, all doing different things.

When you get everything connected, that single Internet connection coming from your home becomes a big pipe that transmits data to and from each of the connected computers—thanks to networking technology.

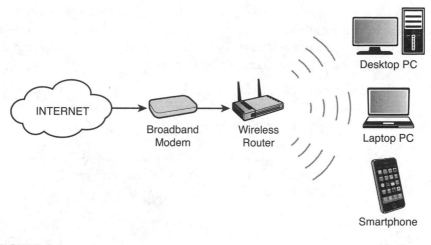

FIGURE 1.1

Sharing an Internet connection over a network.

 NOTE Learn more about Internet connection sharing in Chapter 7, "Connecting to the Internet."

Streaming Movies and Music

After you connect your network to the Internet and all of your devices to your network, you can then access anything on the Internet. You can check your email, surf a variety of websites, follow your friends on Facebook or Twitter, or even do a little online shopping.

You can also use your Internet connection to watch movies and TV shows, as well as listen to your favorite music. Streaming audio and video is the latest way to access truly personalized entertainment; you can watch your shows and listen to your music on your schedule, not at the whim of some network executive.

In terms of streaming video, we're talking services such as Hulu and Netflix, both of which offer movies and television programming for free or a low monthly subscription price. As to streaming music, services like Spotify and Last.fm provide millions of tracks that you can listen to at your choosing.

Naturally, you can use your Internet-connected computer to access streaming media. But, you're not limited to watching videos on your computer screen; many widescreen TVs and Blu-ray players are Internet-enabled, specifically for accessing streaming video services. You can also use network media players, such as Apple TV, to stream video from the Internet to your living room TV.

It's the same thing with streaming audio. Yes, you can listen through the tiny speakers in your notebook computer, but you can also use Internet-enabled A/V receivers and network media players to stream music from the Internet through the larger speakers in your home audio system.

When you're connected in this fashion, you may find yourself dropping your cable or satellite TV subscription, and getting all of your entertainment over the Internet. You couldn't do that without a home network!

 NOTE   Learn more about using your network for streaming media in Chapter 18, "Streaming Audio and Video."

Sharing Media

If you're a movie or music lover, you're not limited to just streaming audio and video from the Internet. You can also use your network to share media stored locally, on one of your home computers.

Let's say that you have your main computer or server in your office, and stored on its hard disk are thousands of digital audio files that you've ripped from CDs or downloaded from the Internet. If you want to listen to those tracks in your living room, over your home audio system, how do you do it?

The solution involves connecting that main computer to your home network, and then serving those files over the network to another computer or device connected to your home audio system. You don't have to copy the files from your main PC, or store them twice on multiple devices. As you can see in Figure 1.2, the living-room unit simply uses the network to play the files stored on the main computer.

 TIP   You can even share your audio files with multiple devices in multiple rooms, creating a multi-room audio system over your network. All you have to do is connect those devices to your network, and you can play different tunes in different rooms, at the same time.

The same concept applies to other types of digital media—movies and other videos, digital photographs, you name it. Store the movies or photos on any PC with a big hard drive, and view them on any PC or media player located in your living room (or any other room in your house, for that matter).

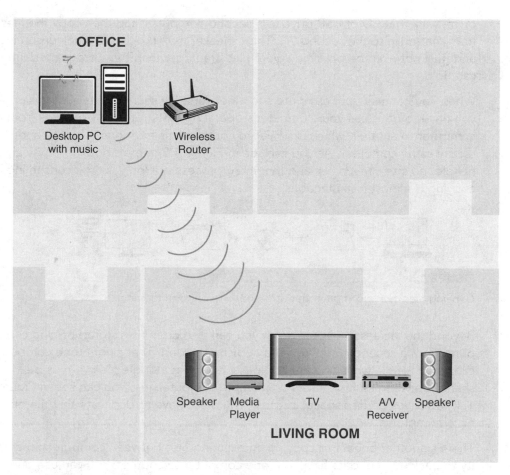

FIGURE 1.2

Using two networked PCs to play music in your living room.

 NOTE Learn more about network media sharing in Chapter 14, "Connecting Other Entertainment Devices."

Sharing and Backing Up Files

When you have more than one computer connected to your network, it's easy to share files between those computers. It's certainly a lot easier than trying to share files without a network.

If your computers aren't networked together, you'd have to copy a file from your first computer to some sort of physical media, such as a CD-ROM or USB memory drive, walk that CD or USB drive to a second computer, and then copy the files from that drive to the second PC. This "sneaker net" process is time consuming and may not even be possible if your files are larger than the storage medium can hold.

When you connect your computers to a network, file sharing gets a lot easier. All you have to do is use your computer's operating system to copy the files from one computer to another, which is similar to copying files from one folder to another on the same computer. As you can see in Figure 1.3, there's nothing physical to handle, no size constraints, and the entire process is a lot less time consuming; the copying is almost instantaneous.

FIGURE 1.3

Copying files over a computer network—nothing physical to handle.

Beyond the increased convenience, you can also open files stored on one computer from a second computer—no copying needed. That's right, one computer can store the file while another computer opens it; a single file can thus be shared between multiple users on multiple computers. As you can see in Figure 1.4, this saves on disc space, because you don't have to duplicate that file on each computer.

There's another benefit to copying and sharing files between computers: the ability to back up your data files from one computer to another. You can use one computer (or an external hard drive connected to that computer) to store the backup data from a second computer, and vice versa. It's a quick and easy way to create backup copies of all of your important data files.

 NOTE   Learn more about network file sharing in Chapter 17, "Sharing and Transferring Files."

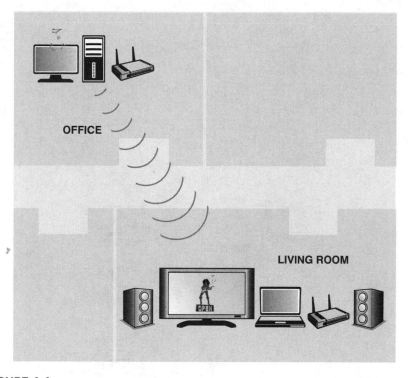

FIGURE 1.4

Sharing a file over a network.

Sharing Printers and Other Equipment

Just as a network lets you share files between multiple computers, it can also let you share computer peripherals between those same PCs. That is, you can connect a single peripheral, such as a printer or scanner, to your network and then access that peripheral from any network PC.

Let's take the most common example of this practice: the network printer. Without a network, you would have to purchase separate printers for each individual PC in your home or office. With a network, however, you only need a single printer. As you can see in Figure 1.5, connect that printer to any network PC, and then all the other PCs on the network can access and print to that printer. One printer for multiple PCs...it's a real cost saver.

FIGURE 1.5

Sharing a single printer between multiple network PCs.

 NOTE You can also use network-connected printers to print from your iPad, iPhone, or other portable wireless device.

There are variations on this theme, of course. First, you can connect more than one printer to the network, and thus let any computer print to either printer. This is a good approach if you have a black-and-white letter printer and a color photo printer, for example.

Second, you don't have to connect a printer to a networked PC. Many newer printers are so-called *network printers*, which means that they can connect directly to your network (often wirelessly), no intermediate PC required. Network printers are actually easier to set up and access from all devices connected to your network.

Finally, you're not limited to sharing printers. You can share all sorts of other peripherals over your network, including scanners and external hard disks. If you can connect it to a computer, you can share it over your network.

 NOTE Learn more about printer sharing in Chapter 16, "Sharing Printers and Other Devices."

Cutting the Cable

Remember how I previously defined a network as connecting two or more computers or similar devices? That number (two) isn't hard and fast; you can create a network with just a single computer.

The best example of this involves a portable PC and an Internet connection. Normally, you'd have to connect this single PC via a short cable to your broadband Internet modem. This type of hard-wired setup, however, significantly reduces the mobility of the PC; you're tied to the modem if you want to connect to the Internet.

To regain this lost mobility, you create a simple wireless network, like the one shown in Figure 1.6. In this simple network, the Internet connection goes into the wireless network router; the notebook PC then connects to the router wirelessly, from anywhere in the house, to access the Internet. Place the modem and router in your office, and you can sit in your living room or bedroom and surf the web. You're not using the file- or peripheral-sharing capabilities of the network, but you don't need to; all you want to do is connect to the Internet from wherever you have your laptop today.

By the way, this same type of simple network works with any wireless device, not just computers. So, if you have an iPhone or iPad in the house and want to access the Internet, set up this same type of simple wireless network—just a modem and a wireless router—and you can connect anytime you want. No cables necessary!

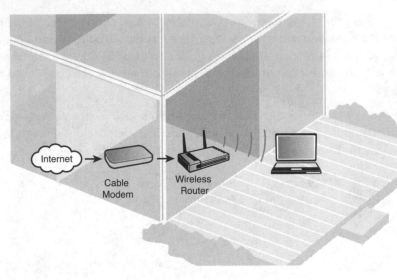

FIGURE 1.6

Sharing an Internet connection over a network.

Playing Games Online

Along the same lines, you can use your home network to connect your videogame console to the Internet. As you probably know, all current-generation videogame systems—Nintendo Wii and Wii U, Sony PlayStation 3, and Microsoft Xbox 360—have Internet-related functionality. Depending on the console, you may be able to connect to the Internet to download new games, play games with other users, or even access news and email.

To do this, of course, you need to connect your game console to the Internet. And what do you do if your Internet connection is in your office and your game console is in your living room or basement?

The answer is to set up a wireless network, of course, like the one shown in Figure 1.7. As with the notebook-based network previously described, you connect your broadband modem to a wireless network router, and then use your console's built-in wireless connection—or in some instances, connect a wireless adapter to your game console. The game console connects to your wireless network and thus gains access to the Internet—no cables to run, nothing complicated to configure.

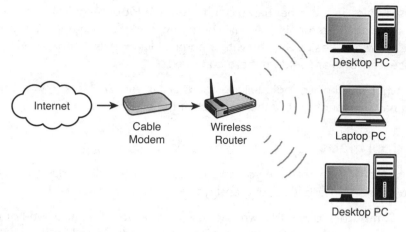

FIGURE 1.7

Playing video games over a wireless network.

Understanding Network Technology

Although setting up a home network is relatively easy, the technology that makes it work is something else. Fortunately, most of this sophisticated technology works in the background, with little or no human intervention needed. Still, there's value in knowing a bit about this technology in order to better understand how networks work.

LANs and WANs

First, know that there are different sizes of networks. A simple, small network in a single location—home networks, small office networks, and the like—is called a *local area network*, or LAN. A larger network that encompasses computers in multiple locations (such as in several different offices of a corporation) is called a *wide area network*, or WAN.

 NOTE The biggest WAN in the world is a little thing known as the Internet. With hundreds of millions of device connected worldwide, it's the ultimate wide area network!

As you might suspect, a WAN is considerably more complex to set up and manage than is a LAN. WANs typically require network administrators to keep everything working on a day-to-day basis.

Most LANs, on the other hand, don't require a lot of technical expertise, either to set up or to keep running. A basic home network, for example, can be set up in just a few minutes by anyone with a nominal level of skill and experience. Small office networks are seldom more complex.

So, when you hear people talking about LANs and WANs, know that the network you have in your home is the simplest of the two: a basic LAN.

Connecting Things to Your Network

What types of devices can you connect to a home or small business network? You'd be surprised; it's a long and growing list, and includes the following:

- **Computers**, obviously, whether desktop or portable, all-in-one or netbook. (They are referred to as "computer networks," after all.)

- **Modems**, which are devices that connect your network to the Internet.

- **Printers and scanners** and other computer peripherals, so that a single device can be shared by multiple computers. (That's a lot cheaper than buying and connecting separate printers to each PC in your home.)

- **Home servers**, which is a fancy term for a dedicated computer used for file storage and backup. All the computers on your network can share files stored on the home server and back up their important files to the same device.

- **Smartphones**, such as iPhones or Androids or Windows phones. When you want to surf the Internet with your phone, connecting via your home wireless network is both faster and cheaper (no data charges) than connecting through your phone's cellular network.

- **Tablets**, such as the iPad, rely on an Internet connection to do much of anything.

- **Ebook readers**, such as the Kindle and Nook, who need to connect to the Internet to download new ebooks.

- **Videogame consoles**, such as the Xbox 360, PlayStation 3, and Wii, which connect to the Internet for multi-player gaming and other services.

- **Portable videogames**, such as the Nintendo 3DS and PlayStation Vita, which use your home network for multiplayer gaming and connecting to the Internet.

 NOTE You can also connect Apple's iPod touch—a portable music player that doubles as a portable game machine—to your network, for all sorts of games and apps.

- **Widescreen TVs**, many of which let you connect to the Internet to view movies and television programming via streaming video services, such as Netflix and Hulu.

- **Blu-ray players**, which connect to the Internet to download movie updates and special features—and, with some models, to view streaming video.

- **Audio/video receivers**, many of which let you listen to streaming music from the Internet.

- **Network media players**, such as the Apple TV box, which let you stream music and video from the Internet to your home theater system—or to multi-room systems throughout your home.

- **Internet appliances**, which connect to your home network for Internet use. For example, Samsung and LG both "smart fridges" that include a touchscreen LCD monitor in the door that enables you to access online recipes, check the news and weather, manage your family calendar, listen to music, and even Skype with friends, all from the comfort of your kitchen.

Most of these devices connect to your network wirelessly, although some (such as desktop computers and home servers) can also connect via a wired Ethernet connection. It's the wireless connections that are most flexible, because you can use those devices anywhere in your home without having to worry about keeping a cable connected.

Connecting Everything Together

How do you get all these devices to talk to each other over the network? The physical connections themselves may be relatively simple, but the technology involved is complex.

First, know that the devices on your network do not connect or communicate directly to each other. That is, the computer in your living room doesn't communicate directly with the one in your office, nor does your smartphone connect directly to your modem to access the Internet.

Instead, each and every device on your network connects directly to a central hub, called a *router*. As you can see in Figure 1.8, all transmitted data passes through the router en route to another device on the network. Even Internet signals from your modem pass through the router and then stream to all the other connected devices.

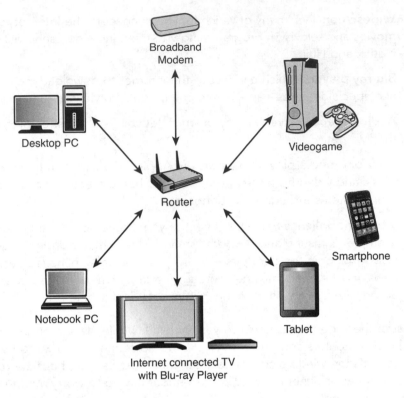

FIGURE 1.8

All networked devices connect through a central router.

In a wireless network, the router is a wireless router, and devices connect to the router using wireless technology. In a strictly wired network, devices connect to the router via Ethernet cables. That said, most network routers today offer both wired and wireless connections. A typical wireless router might have four to six Ethernet connections on the back. This enables you to connect devices both wirelessly and via Ethernet to the same network.

Transferring Data over the Network

The physical part of connecting a network is as simple as setting up your network router and then connecting all of your devices to the router, either wirelessly or with Ethernet cables. What happens next is more complex.

All data transferred over the network is broken into smaller pieces. That is, you don't transfer a complete file at once or stream a complete television show from the Internet. That file or video stream is broken into multiple smaller data packets, which enables large amounts of data to be transferred without clogging the connection. The data packets are then reassembled at the receiving end by the appropriate networked device, as shown in Figure 1.9.

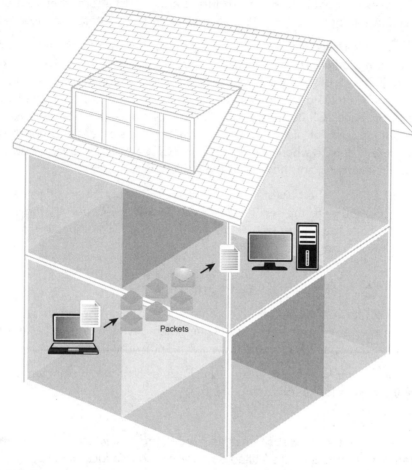

FIGURE 1.9

Transmitting multiple data packets over a network.

To enable this disassembly/transmittal/reassembly process, your networked hardware must work in tandem with a predescribed set of networking transfer protocols. These rules determine how data is transmitted across the network.

Your network could use several different network protocols, but the one most used in home and small business networks is called TCP/IP. This stands for *Transmission Control Protocol/Internet Protocol*, and it's also the transport protocol used by the Internet.

The IP part of this protocol provides the standard set of rules and specifications that enables the routing of data packets from one network to another. The TCP part of the protocol supports the necessary communication between two computers; it takes network information and translates it into a form that your network can understand. In other words, IP sets the rules and TCP interprets those rules.

Here's how it works in practice. Let's say that you want to copy a file from the PC in your home office to the PC located in your basement. When you click the Copy button, TCP establishes a connection between the two computers, and then IP lays down the rules of communication and connects the ports of the two computers. Because TCP has prepared the data for transmittal, IP then takes the file, breaks it into smaller pieces (data packets), and puts a header on each packet to make sure it gets to where it's going. The TCP packet is also labeled with the kind of data it's carrying and how large the packet is.

Next, IP converts the packet into a standard format and sends it on its way from the first computer to the second. After the packet is received by the second PC, TCP translates the packet into its original format and combines the multiple packets back into a single file.

Understanding Network Addresses

For TCP/IP to work, each device on a network needs to be properly configured with the proper information. In particular, each device needs to be assigned a local IP address, which is how the device is known by the network.

An IP address is kind of like a street address, except that it's all numbers. A typically IP address looks something like this:

```
192.106.126.193
```

On the Internet, each website has its own IP address, which is tied to an easier-to-remember web address (called a *uniform resource locator* [URL]), in the form of www.url.com. In the case of computer networks, an IP address is the software address of an individual PC; every computer on your network has its own individual IP address.

 NOTE Each computer on your network may also need to be assigned a *subnet mask*, which identifies which part of the network the computer belongs to. In essence, a subnet mask is a number that is overlaid onto the computer's IP address.

It may sound complicated, but all these addresses are necessary for the network router to know which data goes to which connected device. As you can see in

Figure 1.10, TCP/IP broadcasts data to the router, with a particular IP address identified as the recipient of that data. The router reads the IP address and then routes the data to the computer with that address.

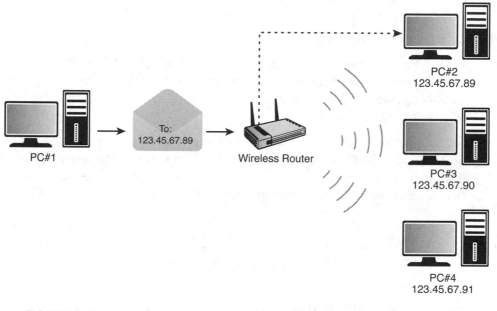

FIGURE 1.10

Sending a file to a specific network address.

Fortunately, all this happens pretty much in the background. It didn't used to be this way; with older networking equipment, you had to manually configure all these addresses for each computer on your network. Today, however, this configuration is done automatically when you set up your router and connect your computers and other devices, thanks to Dynamic Host Configuration Protocol (DHCP), a technology that enables client devices to acquire the necessary configuration information from the network server. This has made networks easy for even technical novices to set up and led to the profusion of home networks—especially wireless networks.

Different Ways to Connect

Networking protocols define how data is transmitted from one computer to another; the actual transmission of that data can be done via wired or wireless technology.

It's not giving anything away to say that most home networks today are wireless networks, using Wi-Fi technology. But, there are other connection technologies available; you may end up using different technologies to connect different types of devices to a single network.

Connecting via Ethernet

Ethernet is a cabling protocol for transmitting data across LANs. To construct an Ethernet network, each computer in the network must have a network interface card (NIC) installed. You then use Ethernet cables to connect each computer/NIC to a central network router.

An Ethernet connection can transmit data at one of three standard speeds. So-called *Gigabit Ethernet* is the fastest, transferring data at 1 gigabit per second (Gbps); Fast Ethernet operates at a tenth that speed, or 100 megabits per second (Mbps); and older 10Base-T Ethernet is a tenth of that, at 10Mbps.

 NOTE Network-connection speed is measured in terms of bits per second. A thousand bits per second is a kilobit per second (Kbps). A thousand Kbps is one megabit per second (Mbps). A thousand Mbps is one gigabit per second (Gbps).

Exempting the older 10-Mbps Ethernet standard, today's Ethernet networks are faster than most wireless networks, more stable (you don't have to worry about the wireless signal cutting in and out), and more secure. Because there are no signals sent through the airwaves (everything's contained within the Ethernet cables), there's no way to intercept the signals and steal the data—through the air, anyway.

Because of the enhanced security, Ethernet connections are recommended for your most important and private data. The stability of an Ethernet connection also makes it ideal for high-volume streaming, such as streaming high-definition movies from the Internet.

Connecting via Powerline

Ethernet isn't the non-wireless way to network. You can also, in some instances, connect your networked devices via your home's power circuits.

What we're talking about here is a *powerline network* (PLN). The concept is simple: You connect each networked device via an adapter to a free power outlet, and the networking signal runs through your home's power circuitry to other networked devices. The connection is simple—just plug each device into a wall outlet—and there are no new wires to run. (Figure 1.11 shows typical powerline networking equipment.)

FIGURE 1.11

A powerline network adapter—plug it into a power outlet, then connect to your computer via Ethernet cable. (Photo courtesy TRENDnet.)

As appealing as it may be, powerline networking has a few significant issues. First, it's still a wired technology, which means it's no good for connecting your smartphones, tablets, and portable game devices. Second, connections are problematic if the wiring in your house or apartment is anything less than straightforward. For example, you may have trouble networking between outlets connected to different circuits in your house. That is, if the outlets are powered by different circuit breakers, the network signal may not cross those circuits.

Finally, powerline networking has been slower than other types of connections, although that's changing. Just a few short years ago, powerline connections were limited to just 50Kbps, which isn't much faster than a dialup connection. More recent powerline standards have upped the theoretical maximum speeds to 500Mbps or so, which is fast, but circuitry in older homes can significantly knock down that speed.

For all these reasons, powerline networking hasn't really taken off—although it still may be an option if you have relatively simple networking needs.

Connecting via Wi-Fi

If you want to be able to connect *all* the devices in your home—not just computers—to the network or Internet, you need to cut the cables and go with a wireless network. A wireless network uses radio frequency (RF) signals to connect all of your devices together and is the only way to connect your smartphones, tablets, and other handheld devices to the network.

The most popular wireless technology for home networks is called Wi-Fi, which stands for *wireless fidelity*. There are actually multiple Wi-Fi protocols, each operating at different frequencies and speeds and distances, but they're pretty much compatible with each other. As all computer and handheld devices are Wi-Fi-compatible, this is the type of home wireless network you'll want to build.

 NOTE   Learn more about wireless networks in Chapter 2, "How Wi-Fi Works."

To set up a wireless network, each computer or other device must have a *wireless adapter* installed or connected to it. This adapter is essentially a miniature transmitter/receiver for those RF signals. Data is then transmitted from each device's wireless adapter to a wireless network router. The wireless router, like the wireless adapters, functions as both a transmitter and receiver for the wireless signals.

 NOTE   For computers, a wireless adapter can be a small external device that connects to a PC via USB, an expansion card that installs inside a desktop PC's system unit, or circuitry built into the computer itself. Most notebook computers and handheld devices have built-in wireless circuitry.

The main advantage of a wireless network, of course, is that you don't have to run any cables, which is a big plus if you have a large house with computers on different floors. It's also the only way that most handheld devices, such as smartphones and tablets, can connect. For this reason, wireless networks are the most popular type of home network today.

 NOTE   There are two other types of wireless technology that you may use with various devices. We discuss Bluetooth wireless in Chapter 3, "How Bluetooth Works," and cellular wireless in Chapter 4, "How Mobile Networks Work."

What Type of Network Is Best for You?

For most home users, wireless networking is the way to go. Not only do you get to connect all types of devices, including smartphones and tablets, you also don't have to run a lot of expensive cable throughout your house; a wireless network is definitely the easiest type to set up.

There are occasions, however, where a wired network makes more sense. If your house is very, very large, a wireless network may not be able to broadcast a strong signal all the way from one end to another; in this instance, Ethernet will be more reliable. In addition, if security is your thing, an Ethernet network is much more secure than a wireless one.

In reality, you can combine wired and wireless technologies. As a personal example, my home network consists of a wireless router that connects most of my computers and devices wirelessly, but I also have several computers connected to my router via Ethernet, for a faster, more secure connection. (Most network routers, remember, have both wireless and Ethernet capability.) It's the best of both worlds.

THE ABSOLUTE MINIMUM

Here are the key points to remember from this chapter:

- Home networks enable you to share data across multiple devices and connect all of your devices to the Internet.

- You can connect all manners of devices to a network, including computers, printers, smartphones, tablets, ebook readers, videogame consoles, TVs, receivers, and network media players.

- All devices on your network connect to a central network router that functions as a hub for all communication and data transmittal.

- Devices can connect to a network via Ethernet cable, powerline (through your home's power circuitry), or wirelessly, using Wi-Fi technology.

- Most home networks are wireless, although you can also connect devices via Ethernet to a wireless router.

2

HOW WI-FI WORKS

Wireless networking is so ubiquitous today that we tend to take it for granted. We have wireless networks in our homes, coffee shops, hotels, airports, and most college campuses. In fact, many towns and cities have become giant wireless networks in and onto themselves.

As common as wireless networks are, there's a lot of sophisticated technology behind the connections. In fact, there are actually several different types of wireless technologies in play, and they each have their own unique performance characteristics.

Want to know more about how wireless networking works? Read on to find out.

Understanding Wireless Network Technology

Today's wireless networks make it relatively easy to connect your computer or smartphone or tablet and get busy working. Behind this connectivity, however, is some advanced technology.

Bands on the Radio

Setting up a wireless network is much like building a mini radio station in your home or office. That's because wireless devices transmit and receive radio frequency (RF) signals at a specific frequency, the same signals used in AM and FM radio. The big difference is that an AM/FM radio only receives signals, whereas wireless networking devices both send and receive.

How exactly do RF signals work? It all starts with a single radio wave, which is nothing more than a pulse of electromagnetic energy. As you can see in Figure 2.1, radio waves are generated when a transmitter oscillates at a specific frequency. The faster the oscillation, the higher the frequency. An antenna is used to amplify and broadcast the radio signal over long distances.

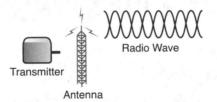

Radio Wave

Transmitter

Antenna

FIGURE 2.1

How a radio transmitter works.

To receive a radio signal, you need a radio receiver. The receiver is tuned to a specific frequency to receive signals oscillating at that rate. If the receiver is not tuned to that frequency, the radio waves pass by without being received.

NOTE In a wireless network, each device (such as a router or wireless adapter) functions as both a transmitter and receiver.

RF transmissions are spread over a broad range of frequencies, which are measured in cycles per second. For example, 93.5MHz is a frequency of 93,500,000 cycles per second. (MHz is shorthand for megahertz, or millions of cycles per second; GHz is shorthand for gigahertz, or billions of cycles per second.)

Different frequency ranges are used for different types of communications. The range of frequencies between 88MHz and 108MHz, for example, is known as the FM range, and it's where you find all of your favorite FM radio stations.

Current wireless networks use two distinct RF frequencies. Earlier equipment works in the 2.4GHz band (frequencies between 2.4GHz and 2.48GHz), while newer equipment can also utilize the 5GHz band (frequencies between 5.15GHz and 5.85GHz).

The 2.4GHz band is free for anyone to use, for any purpose. That's both good and bad—good because it can be used at no cost (without potentially expensive licensing fees), but bad because space within the band is finite, and several other types of devices also use this band.

 NOTE The 2.4GHz frequency range is alternately called the ISM band—for instrumentation, scientific, and medical usage.

Currently, the 2.4GHz band is used by

- 802.11 Wi-Fi wireless networks (of course)

- Bluetooth wireless networks

- HomeRF wireless networks

- 2.4GHz cordless telephones

- Baby monitors (newer models)

- Garage-door openers (newer models)

- Urban and suburban wireless communications systems, including many emergency radios

- Some local government communications in Spain, France, and Japan

- Microwave ovens

 NOTE Regarding microwave ovens, 2.4GHz is the resonating frequency of water molecules; because microwave ovens work by exciting the water molecules in organic materials (such as food), they transmit their microwaves at this 2.4GHz frequency. Although microwave ovens are theoretically shielded against microwave leakage, in practice, they all leak to some degree—older models more so than newer ones. If you're using a wireless device near a microwave oven, the oven can effectively "jam" your device's transmissions; this can cut your device's throughput by up to 75 percent.

The 5GHz band, on the other hand, is relatively unused—and a lot wider, with more frequencies that can be used. (It stretches from 5.15GHz to 5.85GHz, remember.) Some cordless phones use this band, but not too many, so there's not a lot of competition for frequencies. Like the 2.4GHz band, it's unregulated, which means that it's free for any device to use.

 CAUTION   As noted, the 2.4GHz RF band is used by many different types of electronic devices, any of which can create interference with a wireless network, typically in the form of data or signal loss. If you run into this type of interference, choose network equipment that operates on the less cluttered 5GHz band.

Routing the Signals

In the case of a wireless network, those radio signals get sent between each connected device and the central hub of the network, the wireless router, as shown in Figure 2.1. The router, of course, functions as both a transmitter and receiver, so signals go back and forth. Signals do *not* move from one device to another, however; everything gets transmitted to and from the router.

Desktop PC with Wireless Adapter   Laptop PC

Wireless Router

Smartphone   Videogame

FIGURE 2.2

A typical wireless network.

The wireless router not only routes the network data (files, Internet signal, and so on), but can also broadcast the name of the network (called a Service Set Identifier [SSID]) over a beacon signal. This beacon is broadcast every 100 milliseconds and enables nearby wireless devices to recognize and communicate with the wireless network.

When you power on a wireless device, whether it's a computer or a smartphone, it picks up all the beacon signals in the immediate vicinity and displays the SSIDs for each of the available wireless networks. You can then select which network to connect to.

If you're connecting to a public wireless network, that may be all you have to do—select the network's SSID from a list and get connected. Many private networks, however, are protected by some form of wireless security. This typically requires you to enter a password for the selected network; without the correct password, your device can't connect.

Once connected to the wireless router, the individual wireless device transmits and receives selected data in the form of small data packets via RF signals, over the selected frequency band.

Alphabet Soup: The Different Wi-Fi Standards

Today's wireless networks use a type of RF transmission called *Wi-Fi* (short for *wireless fidelity*), which is the consumer-friendly name for the IEEE 802.11 wireless networking standard. All of today's wireless networks are technically Wi-Fi networks and use Wi-Fi-certified products.

 NOTE The IEEE is the Institute of Electrical and Electronics Engineers, and it does things like ratify different technology standards. In the case of Wi-Fi, the technology is now regulated by a subgroup called the Wi-Fi Alliance. Learn more about it at the Wi-Fi Alliance website (www.wi-fi.org).

But, here's the thing. There isn't a single Wi-Fi protocol. Instead, there are multiple 802.11 protocols, each designated by a one- or two-letter suffix. Different versions of Wi-Fi offer different levels of performance; which Wi-Fi standard you choose for your wireless network depends on your needs and the equipment currently available for purchase.

Table 2.1 summarizes the specifications of the most popular 802.11 protocols for consumer use. More details on each version follow.

TABLE 2.1   Wi-Fi Protocols

Wi-Fi Protocol	Release Date	Frequency Range	Number of Data Streams	Maximum Bandwidth	Data Transfer Rate (Max)	Transmission Range (Indoor)
802.11 (no suffix)	1997	2.4GHz	1	20MHz	2Mbps	66 feet
802.11b	1999	2.4GHz	1	20MHz	11Mbps	115 feet
802.11a	1999	5.0GHz	1	20MHz	54Mbps	115 feet
802.11g	2003	2.4GHz	1	20MHz	54Mbps	125 feet
802.11n	2009	2.4/5GHz	4	40MHz	600Mbps	230 feet
802.11ac (draft)	2012	5GHz	8	160MHz	1.3Gbps	230 feet
802.11ad (proposed)	2014*	60GHz	4	2.16GHz	7Gbps	NA

*2014 is the projected year for the release of 802.11ad equipment, but things may change.

NOTE   The stated data-transfer rates for each Wi-Fi protocol are the theoretical maximum; actual transfer rates typically average half of the maximum.

Now, Table 2.1 contains a lot of data, so let's examine what it means:

- **Wi-Fi protocol.** This is the specific version of Wi-Fi, each of which has its own performance characteristics. Generally, newer versions are fully compatible with older ones. So, for example, if you buy a newer 802.11n router, it will work with older 802.11b and 802.11g adapters.

- **Release date.** This is the date (year, actually) when each protocol was originally released to the market. This is *not* the date the protocol was officially ratified; in most cases, ratification came a few years after initial release.

NOTE   Before a wireless protocol is officially ratified, it's said to be in "draft" format. So, for example, you can now find draft 802.11ac routers for sale, even though that particular protocol has not yet been officially ratified.

- **Frequency range.** The RF band used by the specific wireless signals. This compares to the frequency bands used by AM and FM radio; signals are broadcast at the given frequency. For what it's worth, there is no inherent benefit to operating at either 2.4GHz or 5GHz, other than the 5GHz band is less crowded with other devices, and thus less prone to interference.

- **Number of data streams.** More data streams mean that more data can be transmitted. Each stream carries its own set of data or can be combined into a single larger virtual stream that creates a larger "pipe" for heavier data loads, such as streaming video.

 NOTE   The combination of multiple data streams into a single virtual stream is called *spatial multiplexing*. Data is split into multiple parts and broadcast in separate multiple streams, then recombined (multiplexed) at the receiving end.

- **Maximum bandwidth.** Bandwidth is essentially the size of each data stream. The greater the bandwidth, the wider the "pipe"—and the more data that can flow.

- **Data transfer rate.** The maximum amount of data that can be transmitted over the wireless connection, measured in either megabits per second (Mbps) or gigabits per second (Gbps). Naturally, more data transferred per second means faster file transfers and smoother streaming audio and video.

- **Transmission range.** This is the maximum theoretical indoor range of the wireless connection. Actual transmission range will probably be shorter, due to factors that interfere with the wireless signal.

A quick note about that transmission range: Radio signals don't suddenly stop when they get out of range; they weaken as you get farther away from the transmitter. So, an 802.11n network, for example, won't go dead when you get 230 feet away from it. Instead, the data-transfer rate decreases as the signal decreases. Get 250 or 300 feet away from an 802.11n transmitter, for example, and you're likely to find your transfer rate decreasing from 450Mbps to something like 54Mbps. To maximize data speeds, keep your equipment closer to the wireless router.

 CAUTION   The data-transfer rates listed in this table are the maximum rates either promised by the specification or trumpeted by manufacturers. It's likely that the rates you experience will be lower than these maximum rates. It's a case of reality intruding on the theoretical; there are lots of physical obstacles to achieving that top rate. So, if you buy yourself a brand-new 802.11n router expecting to experience 450Mbps or 600Mbps rates and only achieve 300Mbps, that's completely normal.

802.11 (Legacy)

The original Wi-Fi protocol, plain old 802.11 (no suffix), was released back in 1997, and officially ratified in 1999. This version of Wi-Fi didn't really impact the consumer market, as it was quickly supplanted by the more ready-for-prime-time 802.11b standard. It did, however, set the benchmark for all future versions of the protocol.

802.11b

Released in 1999, 802.11b was the first form of Wi-Fi intended for general consumers. 802.11b equipment operated in the 2.4GHz RF band and transferred data at a rate of 11 megabits per second (Mbps). Although this is obviously slower than 100Mbps Ethernet, it was more than fast enough for most home and small office uses of the time, especially when compared to a typical 3Mbps (or less) broadband Internet connection.

 NOTE   Several years after the introduction of the original 802.11b equipment, some manufacturers introduced equipment using what they called 802.11b+ technology. This proprietary equipment operated in the same 2.4GHz band, but transferred data at twice the normal 802.11b rate: 22Mbps.

802.11a

A common problem with 802.11b equipment was that these devices often suffered from interference from other devices using the same 2.4GHz RF band, such as baby monitors, cordless phones, and the like. The same situation sometimes occurs with the later 802.11g protocol, which also operates in the 2.4GHz band.

To solve that problem, 802.11a was developed as an alternate Wi-Fi standard, using the less-crowded 5.0GHz RF band. This standard makes for reduced interference with other wireless devices, while still transferring data at 54Mbps rates.

802.11g

Wi-Fi 802.11g was released about four years after 802.11a and 802.11b, in 2003. Like the older 802.11b equipment, 802.11g equipment also operates in the 2.4GHz band. This is a faster standard, however, transferring data at a rate of 54Mbps.

 NOTE   Some manufacturers sold what they called "Extreme G" equipment, which upgraded the standard 802.11g firmware to achieve data transfer rates of 108Mbps—twice the normal 802.11g rate.

802.11n

The next generation of Wi-Fi, 802.11n, hit the market in 2009, and is the standard used by most wireless equipment sold today. This was a major improvement over previous versions of Wi-Fi, employing four data streams, each twice as wide as the single data stream in the previous 802.11g standard. That, combined with dual-band operation (in both the 2.4GHz and 5GHz ranges), increased data rates almost ten-fold, to 450Mbps. (There's even a new theoretical top speed of 600Mbps, not that you'll find equipment actually operating at this speed.) It also doubled the effective network range, from 125 feet to 230 feet, with less interference (when operating at 5GHz, anyway).

Part of this performance improvement is due to the use of *multiple-input, multiple-output* (MIMO) technology, the optional use of which is written into the 802.11n standard. MIMO technology utilizes multiple antennas at both the transmitting and receiving end of the wireless signal, which enables more aggressive transmittal of data than a single-antenna system. Most 802.11n MIMO routers employ three or four antennas, either inside the router casing or outside, as shown in the router in Figure 2.3.

FIGURE 2.3

Buffalo's three-antenna model N450 wireless router. (Photo courtesy of Buffalo.)

The result is Wi-Fi equipment that does a good job transmitting dense streaming media to multiple devices in a network, even in fairly large houses. It's the best solution for most of us today.

802.11ac (Gigabit Wi-Fi)

Technology does not stand still, however, and there's a new Wi-Fi standard on the horizon, dubbed 802.11ac, or *Gigabit Wi-Fi*. Actually, equipment conforming to draft versions of this standard is already on the market, so you can get a sample of this new high-performance Wi-Fi.

Here's what you get with 802.11ac:

- Operation in the 5GHz band for less interference with other wireless devices.

- Eight data streams instead of the current 4

- Much larger "pipes," in the form of 160MHz-wide streams

- Increase in data rates to at least 1.3Gbps (that's more than 1 gigabit per second, hence the "Gigabit Wi-Fi" moniker) or more

These are all significant performance improvements, even if the effective transmission range remains pretty much the same as with 802.11n equipment.

This improved performance will be especially noticeable with streaming video, particularly high-definition (HD) video. HD video needs all the bandwidth it can get for those really high-resolution pictures and can sometimes clog a crowded 802.11n network. With 802.11ac, you should have more than enough bandwidth to stream multiple HD video transmissions to different devices on your network, which you're probably going to want to do, sooner or later.

 CAUTION Most 802.11n and 802.11ac routers adhere to a "good neighbor" policy that can result in lower data-transmission rates. To avoid having two or more routers operating in the same vicinity from interfering with each other (as can sometimes happen in an apartment building or even with nearby suburban houses), channel bonding is minimized, thus limiting transmission to individual channels as opposed to larger virtual channels combined via spatial multiplexing.

Another benefit of 802.11ac equipment is the implementation of *beamforming*. Current wireless routers and adapters transmit and receive in an omnidirectional fashion—that is, the signal beams in concentric circles outward in all directions, much like the ripples that result when you throw a rock into a lake. With beamforming, the router and the adapter actively exchange information that creates a simpler, more direct signal path between the two. This concentrated signal is theoretically faster than the traditional omnidirectional one.

To take advantage of these performance improvements, you have to buy both an 802.11ac router and 802.11ac wireless adapters. You can use an 802.11ac router with older 802.11n adapters (the new standard is compatible with older equipment), but you'll only get 802.11n performance.

802.11ad (WiGig)

There's another new Wi-Fi standard on the horizon, set for release sometime in 2014. This new 802.11ad protocol, also known as *WiGig*, operates in the much higher 60GHz frequency band, with data speeds up to a theoretical 7Gbps—more than six times faster than 802.11ac equipment.

Here's the thing, though. 802.11ad is not necessarily designed for traditional router-based wireless networks. Instead, it's a protocol for short-range peer to peer connectivity; it's ideal for streaming HD video from one device to another.

As such, you may find 802.11ad technology used to beam signals between equipment in your home audio/video system—say, to replace today's HDMI cable between a Blu-ray player and widescreen TV. It's unlikely—but not impossible— that you'll find 802.11ad wireless routers and adapters anytime in the near future.

Wide-Area Wi-Fi

Then, we have wide-area Wi-Fi, or wireless coverage that covers an entire college campus or small city. This sort of campus-wide and city-wide Wi-Fi extends well beyond a normal router's 230-foot range to cover an area of several square miles.

These municipal wireless networks can employ one of several different technologies. One approach is to employ hundreds of traditional 802.11n routers throughout the covered area, typically outdoors on utility poles. These routers work together in a type of *mesh network*, where each router functions as a relay for the signal transmitted by other routers in the network. In effect, the signal streams from router to router, and then ultimately to individual receiving devices.

Another approach is to move beyond Wi-Fi to a different wireless technology called *WiMAX*. WiMAX is designed specifically for use in metropolitan area networks (MANs), using the 802.16 wireless standard. It's similar to Wi-Fi, but provides coverage over much greater distances.

Whatever technology is used, wide-area wireless networks are designed to offer Internet connectivity to a mass population. In some instances, access is offered free of charge, with costs offset with browser-based advertisements; other municipalities charge monthly subscription fees for access.

Which Wi-Fi Is Right for You?

Okay, that's lots of numbers and letters. With all these available options, which type of Wi-Fi is best for your home network?

Obviously, you want the greatest range and the highest data-transfer rate possible—all other things (such as cost) being equal, of course. To that end, Figure 2.4 compares the ranges of the different Wi-Fi standards; Figure 2.5 compares the data transfer rates.

This data would convince you to choose from either 802.11n or 802.11ac equipment—which is, in effect, my recommendation. Look, when dealing with technology products in general, you always want to go with the latest stuff available. That's easy enough to do when we're talking wireless network equipment, as (in most cases) equipment based on older standards simply is no longer available. You choose from what's on the shelves.

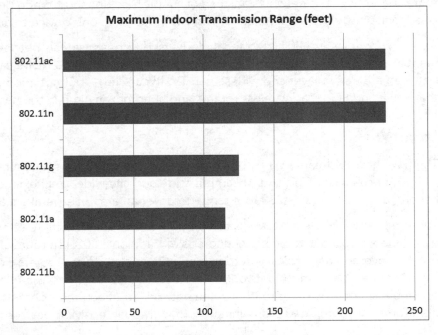

FIGURE 2.4

Comparing transmission rates for the various Wi-Fi standards.

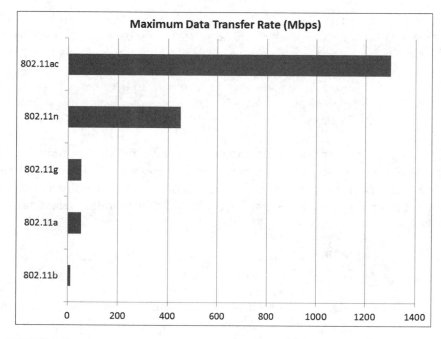

FIGURE 2.5

Comparing data transfer rates for the various Wi-Fi standards.

 NOTE Wireless equipment that is compatible with multiple Wi-Fi protocols is often identified with multiple suffixes. For example, it's not uncommon to see a notebook PC announced as having "802.11b/g/n wireless;" this simply means that this machine will work with 802.11b, 802.11g, and 802.11n routers.

So, now you're choosing from current 802.11n equipment or newer "draft" 802.11ac units. Not surprisingly, there are a lot more 802.11n choices out there; the n standard has been around longer, and manufacturers have had more time to perfect their offering. Although there will certainly be more 802.11ac units introduced as time goes by, the choices out there today are few and expensive.

In terms of both cost effectiveness and compatibility, you probably want to stick to 802.11n equipment. Chances are any piece of 802.11n equipment you buy will be fully compatible with any other wireless equipment you have or plan to purchase. It'll even be compatible with newer 802.11ac equipment, when the time comes.

TIP Not all 802.11n equipment offers the same performance. Lower-priced routers will typically offer data rates in the 300Mbps range, while you have to spend a bit more to get the faster 450Mbps or 600Mbps transfer rates promised by the full n standard. In addition, most lower-end 802.11n routers only offer single-band (typically 2.4GHz) networking, where higher-end models will offer dual-band (2.4GHz and 5GHz) performance.

That said, if you want the latest and greatest, with the most potential upside in terms of performance, make a bet with 802.11ac—especially an 802.11ac router. This future-proofs your network, to some degree, even if all of your other equipment (notebook computers, smartphones, and other wireless adapters) are still 802.11n.

TIP Don't expect your Internet speeds to increase just because you buy a router that uses a faster Wi-Fi protocol. Most broadband Internet connections in the U.S. transmit data at well under 30Mbps; at 54Mbps, even older 802.11b routers are faster than that. (Which means that the bottleneck will be your Internet connection, not your router.)

THE ABSOLUTE MINIMUM

Here are the key points to remember from this chapter:

- Wireless networks function much like mini radio stations, broadcasting and receiving radio frequency (RF) signals.

- All wireless devices on a network connect directly to a central wireless router, which also broadcasts a beacon signal that identifies the network to nearby devices.

- All home wireless networks today use Wi-Fi technology and compatible equipment. (Wi-Fi is the consumer-friendly name for the IEEE 802.11 wireless networking standard.)

- There are actually multiple 802.11 protocols. The current version is 802.11n, although 802.11ac is in "draft" use with prototype equipment already on the market.

- 802.11n equipment is probably the best choice for most home users today, although 802.11ac equipment will deliver faster speeds over the same distance, which makes it better suited for streaming HD video.

3

HOW BLUETOOTH WORKS

Wi-Fi isn't the only wireless technology found in most homes today. There's also another wireless technology you've probably heard about— Bluetooth—which is used in more ways and places than you might suspect.

Understanding Bluetooth Wireless

Bluetooth is a wireless technology similar to Wi-Fi in many respects, but also different. It's similar in that it operates via radio frequency (RF) transmission, and even in the same 2.4GHz frequency range as some forms of Wi-Fi. But, it's different in that it isn't intended for use in hub-and-spoke networks; instead, it's designed for direct communication between devices—what's called *peer-to-peer networking*.

Technology-wise, Bluetooth is a global standard that bridges the worlds of computers and communications. As such, it has been adopted by all the major players in both the computer and telecom industries, as well as an interesting cross-section of companies in other industries—including the home entertainment, automotive, healthcare, industrial automation, and toy industries. (Yes, that's right—Bluetooth technology can be used in children's toys!)

As to how Bluetooth is used, it's all about connecting different devices together—without wires. In this sense, Bluetooth is more a cable-replacement technology than a local area networking one.

What Bluetooth Does

Put simply, Bluetooth technology enables short-range wireless communication—both data and voice—between all sorts of electronics devices. Bluetooth can do the following:

- Eliminate wires and cables between both stationary and mobile devices over short (30 foot) distances. For example, Bluetooth can provide a wireless connection between a computer and a mouse or between a smartphone and a car-audio system.

- Facilitate both data and voice communication. (Hence the ability to handle voice calls over a car's audio system.)

- Enable ad-hoc networks and provide automatic synchronization between multiple Bluetooth devices. This means that you can connect multiple slave devices to a single master device (such as both wireless mouse and keyboard to a desktop PC) via multiple Bluetooth connections.

This wireless communication takes place without the explicit manual intervention of the user; whenever one Bluetooth-enabled device detects another Bluetooth-enabled device, the two devices automatically synch up and a type of ad-hoc wireless network is created.

How Bluetooth Does It

For two devices to communicate with each other, both devices must contain Bluetooth radios. These radios are extremely small (the radio built into a computer chip, which also contains the link controller that establishes and manages the individual connections) and consume little power.

NOTE Every Bluetooth radio conforms to the exact same specifications for both transmitting and receiving signals, so they can be used anywhere in the world without modification. It's not a country-specific technology.

Bluetooth radios operate in the same 2.4GHz radio band as do 802.11a/b/n Wi-Fi devices. When one Bluetooth device senses another Bluetooth device (within about a 30-foot range), they automatically set up a connection between themselves—once the initial manual configuration is complete, of course. This connection is called a *piconet*, which is a kind of mini-network—a *personal area network* (PAN), to be specific.

In a piconet, one Bluetooth device is assigned the role of master, while the other device—and any subsequent devices, up to eight in total—is assigned the role of slave. The master device controls the communication, including any necessary transfer of data between the devices. Each piconet can contain up to eight different devices.

NOTE Because Bluetooth radios are incorporated into small computer chips, they have a small form factor and can be produced at relatively low cost. The combination of small size and low cost helps make Bluetooth technology ubiquitous in a variety of electronics devices—especially in those with portable applications.

Synchronizing, Automatically

Bluetooth is more than just a cable-replacement technology. It also enables any electronics device to automatically communicate with any other electronics device.

This means that, over short distances, a device such as a smartphone can connect to, synchronize with, and even control the other electronic devices in your home, office, or car—such as your personal computer, printer, television set, home-alarm system, or car-audio system. All this communication takes place in an ad-hoc fashion, without your being aware, totally automatically.

Consider this scenario. You have a smartphone that contains your contacts list. You need to synchronize this contacts list, which includes phone numbers, with your car's built-in dialing system. Instead of connecting your phone to your car via an unwieldy cable and synchronizing your data manually, all you have to do is carry your smartphone with you when you enter your car. When you're close enough (and your car is powered on), your phone automatically connects to your car's system via Bluetooth, and then automatically synchs the contact data between your phone and the car. If you've added a new contact to your phone, it's also added to your car's system. You can then dial any of your contacts from your car's dashboard; all the communication is synchronized via the Bluetooth connection.

It's a no-fuss, no-muss connection, no cables necessary. Just automatic smart communication, enabled by Bluetooth technology.

Bluetooth in Action

Let's look at an example of how Bluetooth technology might be employed in your home office. In this hypothetical office, Bluetooth technology is embedded in multiple devices—a desktop PC, wireless keyboard, and wireless mouse. For good measure, let's also include a Bluetooth-capable mobile printer.

Each of these Bluetooth-enabled devices is assigned a specific electronic address by its manufacturer. In addition, each device is programmed to automatically look for other devices within a predefined range, so that all similar devices automatically recognize each other—and automatically establish their own private piconet. This is done when each device, as it powers up, sends out a signal asking for responses from other devices within the predefined range; any responding devices are automatically added to the first device's Bluetooth piconet.

 NOTE Each type of Bluetooth device is assigned a particular range of addresses—so that all wireless keyboards, for example, have addresses that fall within a predefined range.

As each device in our wireless office is powered on, a new piconet is established, like the one shown in Figure 3.1. Data is then routinely exchanged between all the devices within the piconet. For example, when you press a key on your wireless keyboard, that instruction is beamed to the Bluetooth radio embedded in or attached to your desktop PC.

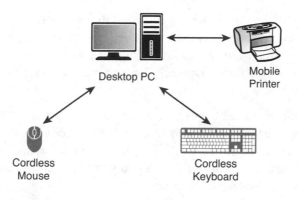

FIGURE 3.1

A home office Bluetooth piconet.

Now, let's add to the complexity and say that you have an iPhone in your pocket and a Bluetooth headset sitting in your ear. These two devices automatically find each other when they're powered up and establish their own separate Bluetooth piconet, as shown in Figure 3.2. Voice data is then sent over this connection from the phone to the headset, and back again.

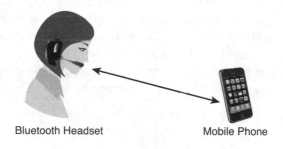

FIGURE 3.2

A simple phone-based Bluetooth connection.

NOTE The automatic connection between Bluetooth devices happens only after the two devices are initially associated with each other—which must be done manually. All subsequent connections, however, happen automatically, without need for manual interaction.

Interestingly, Bluetooth technology is such that these two individual piconets can operate in close proximity without interfering with each other. The phone and headset are on their own Bluetooth network, and the computer, keyboard, mouse, and printer are on another network. No communication is enabled between the two Bluetooth networks.

The neat thing about all this is that these connections take place relatively invisibly. There's little you have to do to configure the devices to work together; it's a lot less setup required than with a typical Wi-Fi network. This makes Bluetooth technology ideal for situations where you want to replace connecting cables between devices—either in your home, car, or on the go.

How Bluetooth Is Used Today

Chances are, you already have one or more Bluetooth-enabled devices in your possession, and those devices are connected right now in one or more wireless piconets. Let's quickly look at the many ways that Bluetooth is used today.

Computer Equipment

If you have a wireless keyboard or mouse connected to your desktop or laptop computer, chances are they're connected via Bluetooth. Bluetooth-enabled keyboards and mice are common and easy to connect; in most cases, all you have to do is plug in a Bluetooth receiver to your computer (via USB), and the connection is automatically established. You can then type and mouse to your heart's content, and not worry about being tethered to your computer. (Figure 3.3 shows a typical Bluetooth cordless mouse, with an accompanying USB dongle/receiver.)

FIGURE 3.3

Logitech's V470 Cordless Laser Mouse for Bluetooth. (Photo courtesy of Logitech.)

NOTE Some smaller Bluetooth keyboards are designed specifically for use with iPhones and other smartphones and enable wireless keyboarding with your handheld device.

Some printers, particularly those designed for mobile use, also come with Bluetooth wireless connectivity. This lets you print directly from any Bluetooth-enabled device, such as a smartphone, without connecting any cables or even connecting to a home Wi-Fi network.

Cell Phones

Bluetooth is a standard feature with most cell phones today. The primary function for this capability is to connect your phone to a wireless headset, like the one shown in Figure 3.4. This provides hands-free operation of your phone, which is required by law in many states when driving. It's also just more convenient to stick one of those little bugs in your ear than it is to hold your phone up against your face all day.

FIGURE 3.4

Plantronics' Voyager Pro HD Bluetooth wireless headset. (Photo courtesy of Plantronics.)

Automobiles

The Bluetooth radio in your smartphone can also be used in your car. Many cars come equipped with built-in Bluetooth capability, so that you can connect your phone to the car to make hands-free calls. You speak into a microphone (typically somewhere on your dash or visor) and listen through your car's audio system.

Many new car models offer built-in Bluetooth capability as an included feature or option. If you have an older car or one without Bluetooth capability, you can add Bluetooth to your car with an add-on kit, like the one shown in Figure 3.5. Connecting one of these kits probably requires professional installation; it's not a plug-and-play situation, although it's easy to use once it's installed.

FIGURE 3.5

The Parrot MKi9100 Bluetooth Car Kit. (Photo courtesy of Parrot USA.)

Some newer cars also offer Bluetooth connectivity for music playback. That is, if you have an iPhone, you can beam music via the Bluetooth connection to your car's audio system and listen to it via your car's built-in speakers—no messy cables required. It's a nice feature, especially if you like to listen to tunes while you drive.

 CAUTION Because of limited bandwidth for the Bluetooth signal, Bluetooth wireless audio may not offer sufficient fidelity to critical ears. In most instances, Bluetooth audio sounds more like FM radio than it does listening to a CD. For better quality sound, you may need to connect your iPhone the old-fashioned way—using a cable.

How Do Bluetooth and Wi-Fi Compare?

As noted, both Bluetooth and Wi-Fi are RF-based technologies that enable wireless communication over the 2.4GHz band. The similarities end there, however.

Bluetooth is designed specifically for direct communication between devices. It replaces traditional cable connections with short-range wireless ones, and thus is perfect for cordless keyboards, smartphones, and the like.

Wi-Fi is more ambitious. It's not designed for simple peer-to-peer communication and control; instead, its focus is on creating larger wireless networks that beam all manner of data to and between connected devices.

In other words, you use Bluetooth when you want to replace a short cabled connection between two devices, either at home, in your car, or when you're just walking around. You use Wi-Fi when you want to connect multiple devices for large-scale sharing and communication in your home or office.

Fortunately, Bluetooth and Wi-Fi can—and do—co-exist. That is, you can establish any number of Bluetooth connections in the same space where you have a Wi-Fi network set up. They won't interfere with each other, and they'll both do their own things—just as they were designed to do.

THE ABSOLUTE MINIMUM

Here are the key points to remember from this chapter:

- Bluetooth is a wireless technology that operates in the same 2.4GHz RF range as does Wi-Fi.

- Bluetooth is designed as a cord-replacement technology to establish direct communications between two devices over a short range (30 feet maximum).

- Bluetooth is typically used to connect cordless keyboards and mice to personal computers, hands-free headsets to cellular phones, and mobile phones to car audio systems.

- Bluetooth and Wi-Fi are complementary technologies; they don't compete or interfere with one another.

4

HOW MOBILE NETWORKS WORK

There's one last type of wireless network we need to discuss, and it's one with which you're probably intimately and constantly familiar. I'm talking about the ubiquitous wireless network employed by the humble cell phone—or, more common today, the high-tech cellular-data network used by iPhones and other smartphones to connect not only to each other, but also to the Internet.

How does cellular networking work—and what does it have to do with the other wireless networking you employ on a daily basis? Good questions, and two of many that are answered in this chapter.

Understanding Cellular Phone Technology

Cellular phones work much the same way as do the other wireless devices we've been discussing. Signals carrying voice, text, and digital data are transmitted via radio waves from one device to another. In the case of cellular networks, the data is transmitted not to a central hub in a small network of devices (as it is with Wi-Fi) or even directly from device to device (as it is with Bluetooth), but through a global network of transmitters and receivers.

Cells in a Network

What's interesting about mobile phone networks is their cellular design. (Hence the terms "cellular network" and "cellular phone.") By that, I mean that a mobile phone network is divided into thousands of overlapping geographic areas, or *cells*. A typical cellular network can be envisioned as a mesh of hexagonal cells, as shown in Figure 4.1, each with its own *base station* at the center. The cells slightly overlap at the edges to ensure that users always remain within range of a base station. (You don't want a dropped call when you're driving between base stations.)

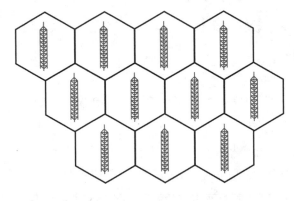

FIGURE 4.1

Cells in a cellular network.

NOTE   The cells in a cellular network vary in size, depending on how many calls are conducted within that geographic area. The smallest cells, which might cover only a few city blocks, are those where there's the heaviest population density, and thus the largest demand for service. The largest cells are most often in rural areas with a smaller population per square mile.

The base station at the center of each group of cells functions as the hub for those cells—not of the entire network, but of that individual piece of the network. RF signals are transmitted by an individual phone and received by the base station, where they are then re-transmitted from the base station to another mobile phone. Transmitting and receiving are done over two slightly different frequencies.

Base stations are connected to one another via central switching centers which track calls and transfer them from one base station to another as callers move between cells; the handoff is (ideally) seamless and unnoticeable. Each base station is also connected to the main telephone network, and can thus relay mobile calls to landline phones.

Carrying a Two-Way Radio

All this transmission within a cellular network originates with the handheld cell phone. A mobile phone is actually a two-way radio, containing both a low-power transmitter (to transmit data) and a receiver (to receive data).

When I say low power, I mean low power—really low power. The typical cell phone includes a dual-strength transmitter, capable of transmitting either 0.6-watt or 3-watt signals. In comparison, a larger AM radio station will typically broadcast a 50,000-watt signal; even smaller AM stations broadcast 5,000-watt signals. A cell phone's 3-watt signal is puny in comparison.

The reason mobile phones can get by with such low-power transmitters is that they're transmitting within a relatively limited range—within the current network cell. It's not necessary or desirable for a phone's signal to extend beyond the current cell; this way, the same broadcast frequencies can be used by multiple cells without danger of interference.

Pulling Some Gs

If you're a mobile phone user (and you are, of course), then you've probably heard talk about something called 3G, and maybe even something called 4G. Each "G" is a generation of technology, which means we're currently in the middle of the third generation and moving into the fourth. Let me explain.

1G

Before the age of digital mobile networks, all cell phones broadcast analog signals. In the U.S., this meant using the Advanced Mobile Phone System (AMPS) standard, which operated in a range of frequencies between 824MHz and 894MHz, dubbed the 800MHz band.

This type of analog transmission was the first generation of cellular phone technology, or what some refer to as 1G. Because analog phones could transmit only analog voice data, not digital data, they couldn't be used to access the Internet or transmit text messages. Fortunately, there were more Gs to follow.

2G

Moving past the analog age, the cell-phone carriers needed to cram more calls into each frequency they were assigned. The way to do that was to move beyond inefficient analog signals into more efficient digital ones. That is, the original analog voice signal is digitized into a series of 0s and 1s; the resulting digital signal is then compressed and transmitted across the assigned frequency band.

 NOTE   Because of the digitization and compression, a digital system can carry about ten times as many calls as an analog one.

In this second generation of cellular transmission (dubbed 2G, of course), several competing standards came into play, and different cellular carriers adopted different standards. There are two of these standards used in the United States:

- **Code Division Multiple Access (CDMA).** This standard operates in the same 800MHz band used by the previous analog transmissions and is employed by Sprint and Verizon.

- **Global System for Mobile Communications (GSM).** This standard operates in the 1,900MHz band and is used by AT&T and T-Mobile.

That's just in the United States, of course. Other standards and frequency bands are used in other countries.

 NOTE   CDMA and GSM are mutually exclusive technologies. A CDMA phone will not work on a GSM network, and vice versa.

2G networks and phones could also be used to transmit non-voice data. This ushered in the era of text messaging, in the form of Short Message Service (SMS) and, later, Multimedia Message Service (MMS). It also enabled access to the Internet, for email, web browsing, and the like.

 NOTE   SMS transmits text-only messages. MMS transmits text messages with multimedia attachments (photo, video, and so on).

3G

The next generation of cellular transmission was developed with the smartphone in mind. So-called 3G networks feature increased bandwidth and transfer rates that better accommodate the transfer of digital data necessary for Internet access and the use of web-based applications.

How much faster is 3G? A lot. Today's 3G networks boast transfer speeds up to 2Mbps; in contrast, 2G phones can only transfer data at around 144Kbps. That's a 13-fold increase in speed, more or less, if you're doing the math.

Just as with 2G digital networks, there are several different 3G standards in use in the U.S. (and a few more in use overseas):

- **CDMA2000** is an evolution of the previous CDMA standard. It's used by Sprint and Verizon.

- **Universal Mobile Telecommunications System** (**UMTS**) is an evolution of the GSM standard used by AT&T and T-Mobile.

If you use your smartphone for anything other than voice calls and text messages, you need to be on a 3G network. In those areas where you're forced to use a 2G connection, accessing the Internet is painfully slow. In this respect, 3G is the de-facto minimum requirement for using a smartphone today.

4G

Now, we get to the fourth generation of cellular networking. Carriers are just start-ing to roll out 4G networks, and suppliers are just starting to produce 4G smart-phones. 4G promises data transmission rates in excess of 1Gbps, which is more than 30 times the rate of 3G networks. (That should make it a lot easier to watch streaming video on your iPhone!)

Naturally, competing 4G standards are in play. Look for the following protocols used by U.S. carriers:

- **Long Term Evolution (LTE).** This standard promises data download rates to mobile users up to 300Mbps. It's used by AT&T and Verizon.

- **Evolved High Speed Packet Access (HSPA+).** This standard promises data download rates up to 168Mbps, although current rates top out at 42Mbps. It's used by T-Mobile.

- **Worldwide Operability for Microwave Access (WiMax).** This standard prom-ises data download rates of 128Mbps. It's used by Sprint.

To put all these Gs into perspective, see Figure 4.2. This chart compares the data-transmission (download) rates of 2G, 3G, and 4G networks. (Remember, 1G was analog, not digital, and thus couldn't transmit non-voice data.) There's been a lot of improvement over the years!

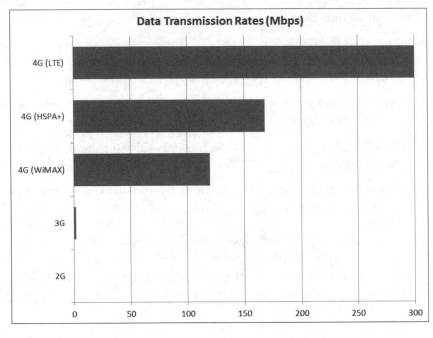

FIGURE 4.2

Comparing 2G, 3G, and 4G data download speeds.

Sharing a Mobile Data Connection with Your PC

With the advent of 3G cellular technology, it suddenly became feasible to use your cell phone to access the Internet. Before 3G, rates were just too slow; loading a simple web page could take minutes, not seconds.

3G's maximum 2Mbps data download speed is close to that offered by many home Internet service providers (ISPs); DSL, for example, typically delivers speeds in the same 2Mbps range. Naturally, when we're talking 4G networks with speeds approaching 300Mbps, cellular Internet is suddenly faster than what you get at home—or sitting in your local Wi-Fi hotspot.

With that in mind, why not use your smartphone to provide Internet access for your computer? Well, you can—and there are two different ways to do it.

External Data Modems

Most cellular providers offer external data modems that provide access to their 3G or 4G cellular-data network. These modems are small and portable and connect to your computer via USB; they let you access the cellular network with your PC, just as you do with your phone.

What this means is that you can now connect to the Internet anywhere you can receive a cellular connection. This lets you surf the web in places where you can't get Wi-Fi, such as when you're driving your car.

Figure 4.3 shows a typical USB modem from AT&T. You'll want to purchase the right modem for the connection you want; most carriers offer separate 3G and 4G modems. Expect to pay anywhere from $30 to $300, depending on the unit, the carrier, and which service plan you subscribe to. Oh, and you'll have to pay for a data service plan; the more data you use, the more you'll pay each month.

FIGURE 4.3

AT&T's USBConnect Force 4G USB modem.

Tethering Your Smartphone

Some carriers let you connect your computer to their data networks without pur-chasing a separate modem for your PC. Instead, you connect a cable between your computer and your smartphone; you connect to the data network with your smartphone and then share the Internet connection with your PC.

This process is called *tethering*, and it's a great way to share a connection and an existing data service plan. Not all carriers support this type of tethering, however, and those that do may charge extra for it—in addition to the normal data usage plan. For example, T-Mobile has a $15/month tethering charge, Verizon charges $20/month, and Sprint charges $30/month, all in addition to your normal data plan; AT&T includes tethering in its $45/month 4GB data plan.

 NOTE Check with your cellular carrier to see what's available and what you have to do to use it.

Tethering can be done both physically or via Wi-Fi. We'll look at both methods.

A physical tether requires the use of a USB cable or special data connection kit. Essentially, you connect one end of the cable to your smartphone and the other to your PC, as shown in Figure 4.4. Once everything's connected, you run a special tethering app to pipe the Internet signal from your phone to your computer.

FIGURE 4.4

Sharing a cellular data signal via physical tether.

A Wi-Fi tether turns your smartphone into a portable Wi-Fi hotspot. You establish an ad-hoc Wi-Fi network with your phone as the router, and then connect your computer to that network to share the phone's Internet connection. It's easier than it sounds, especially when facilitated by using the appropriate tethering app on your phone.

CAUTION Some technically adept users try to get around carriers' tethering charges by jailbreaking their phones and using third-party tethering apps. This is breaking the rules, however, as most carriers like to charge you extra for the privilege of tethering—not that there are any technical reasons to do so. If your carrier detects the tethering, you'll get charged for that usage—or, perhaps, kicked off the service entirely.

Powering Your Home Network with Your Cellular Signal

Here's something else you may not have considered. Some manufacturers make what they call *mobile broadband routers* that receive a 3G (or, in some instances, 4G) mobile signal and then convert it into Wi-Fi. The Wi-Fi signal is then broadcast throughout your home, same as with a wireless router, and all of your Wi-Fi-enabled devices can connect to it to access the Internet.

Figure 4.5 shows one such device from NETGEAR. The little receiver on the right is what picks up your cellular signal; it's connected to the big unit on the left, which is essentially a wireless router. The router provides the Wi-Fi signal for your network of devices.

FIGURE 4.5

NETGEAR's MBRN3000 Mobile Broadband Router. (Photo courtesy of NETGEAR.)

 CAUTION The big problem with using a mobile broadband modem in your home is that, unless you have an unlimited data plan from your cellular provider, you're going to pay through the nose for all the data downloaded by all the devices on your network.

Mobile Data Versus Wi-Fi: Choosing One or the Other

You've just seen one way that cellular networking and Wi-Fi networking can work together—by tethering your smartphone and computer together, via Wi-Fi, to share the cellular data signal. In most other aspects, these two wireless technologies work side-by-side, offering similar Internet-based functionality, but in different ways.

Here's the deal. Your smartphone can connect to the Internet either via Wi-Fi or via your cellular service's network. Most phones are configured to use the nearest Wi-Fi signal by default, as Wi-Fi is both faster than 3G data connections and doesn't rack up charges against your phone's data plan. So, if you're near a Wi-Fi network, your phone tries to connect to that network; if there's not Wi-Fi nearby, then your phone switches to the standard cellular data network.

This default-to-Wi-Fi behavior makes a lot of sense, especially if you consume a lot of media online. Checking your email won't necessarily eat up your available data plan, but viewing a lot of photos on web pages or consuming streaming music or video will. If you use your phone to watch a lot of streaming movies or TV shows, chances are you'll blow through your data plan much sooner than you'd like, and be liable for costly overage charges.

Naturally, you can, at any time, switch off your phone's Wi-Fi, which then forces your phone to connect to the cellular network to access the Internet. In most instances, however, you probably want to use Wi-Fi when it's available and fall back on your 3G network only when you have to.

 NOTE   Some smartphones won't let you perform certain functions, such as updating your existing iPhone apps, over cellular. To access these functions, your phone needs to be connected to a Wi-Fi network.

Mobile Service and Bluetooth: Learning to Co-Exist

Then, there's the issue of Bluetooth wireless, which is also built into most smartphones. Bluetooth is typically used to connect your phone to cordless headsets and your car's built-in phone/audio system. In this respect, Bluetooth and cellular wireless co-exist quite nicely; in fact, you can easily flow one wireless connection through the other.

You can see this co-existence in action when you connect to your phone's data network while your phone is connected to another Bluetooth-enabled device. The Bluetooth connection then carries your cellular voice call to your headset or car system, in a nice little flow that looks something like the one in Figure 4.6. One wireless stream flows into the other.

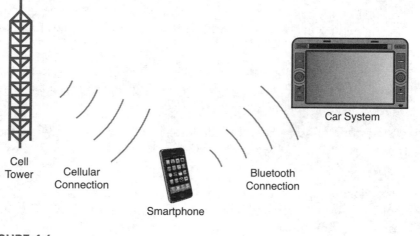

FIGURE 4.6

Flowing a cellular connection through a Bluetooth connection.

THE ABSOLUTE MINIMUM

Here are the key points to remember from this chapter:

- Cellular telephone networks are so-named because they're built from a series of adjoining cells; as a phone travels from one point to another, its signal is handed off from cell to cell.

- There have been four generations of cell phone technology: 1G (analog), 2G (original digital), 3G (faster digital), and 4G (even faster digital, designed specifically for smartphone and streaming video use).

- Using a smartphone to access the Internet is painful on older 2G networks, acceptable on 3G networks, and downright enjoyable on the latest 4G networks.

- Most smartphones can connect to the Internet via either Wi-Fi or cellular data networks; Wi-Fi is faster than 3G cellular (but not as fast as 4G) and doesn't use up your monthly data plan.

- Smartphones can connect to cellular and Bluetooth networks simultaneously, in order to beam cellular voice calls to a Bluetooth-enabled device.

5

PLANNING YOUR NETWORK AND PURCHASING EQUIPMENT

You don't have to know how wireless networking works to set up your own home or small business network. You do need to know, however, what your network should look like—and what equipment you need.

Shopping for the right equipment, of course, requires the necessary advanced planning, as well as a bit of knowledge as to what's out there. You also need to set and work within a budget. Fortunately, even this equipment planning and shopping is easier than it used to be; a lot of what used to be optional wireless equipment is now built into most devices.

Put all these parameters together, and it's time to put together your equipment wish list. So get out your credit card and get ready to shop!

Planning Your Network

Let's start by thinking through just what you need your network to look like. That's right, we're talking network planning—which is actually quite easy.

Making a List

The first step is to list all the devices you have that you want to connect to the network. I'll make this step easier by providing a checklist that you can use; just copy the checklist and note which and how many of these devices you currently own.

Network Device Checklist

Quantity	Devices
1	Wireless router
	Desktop computers
	E-readers (for ebooks)
	Home server
	Internet connection (modem)
	Internet-capable Blu-ray players
	Internet-capable televisions
	Network attached storage (external hard disks)
	Network-enabled audio/video receivers
	Network media players
	Non-smartphone Internet-capable phones
	Notebook computers
	Portable videogame devices
	Printers
	Scanners
	Smartphones
	Tablet computers
	Videogame consoles
	Other devices

For example, you might have one desktop computer, two notebook computers, a broadband Internet connection, two printers (one inkjet and one color photo printer), a scanner, an Xbox 360 videogame console, three smartphones, and a tablet. Write down all those devices that you intend to connect to your network.

Mapping the Network

The next step is to take all these devices, add a network router, and then draw a simple map of how these devices will be connected. You want to distinguish between the following:

- Devices that must be connected to each other via USB cable—that is, those that must be in physical proximity to each other, such as printers and scanners

- Devices that must be connected via Ethernet cable

- Devices that will connect to the network wirelessly

At this point, some explanation is in order.

The first type of device is typically a peripheral, such as a printer or scanner, that physically connects to a single computer on the network via USB. That is, the peripheral doesn't directly connect to the network; it connects to a computer, which can then make its own connection to the network.

The second type of device, one that must connect to another via Ethernet cable, might seem out of place in a wireless network. Although it's true that every computer on a wireless network can connect to the network router wirelessly, you might not want to go *completely* wireless. For example, you may want to connect a computer via Ethernet if it contains a lot of sensitive information, as an Ethernet connection is more secure than a wireless one. Or you may want to connect a media player or television via Ethernet if you watch a lot of streaming videos; Ethernet is faster and more reliable than Wi-Fi.

The third category describes any device that is not physically connected to the network router. This type of device has to connect to the network wirelessly.

With this information in hand, sketch out a rough diagram of your network. In general, follow this general flowchart:

Internet connection > Modem > Wireless router > Connected device

Figure 5.1 shows a typical network diagram, with a mixture of wired and wireless devices, along with a few connected peripherals.

Desktop PC

Notebook PC 1

Notebook PC 2

Cable
Modem

Smartphone 1

Smartphone 2

xbox

FIGURE 5.1

A network map for a typical mixed network.

Adding the Necessary Network Equipment

With the first iteration of your network map in hand, you now need to note the network equipment necessary to implement the network. You're probably looking at some or all of the following:

- **Wireless router.** Typically one for the entire network.

- **Wi-Fi adapters.** One for each computer or device that you want to connect wirelessly but does not have built-in Wi-Fi capability. An adapter can be an external device that connects to the PC via USB, or an internal PC expansion card.

NOTE Some videogame consoles, televisions, and Blu-ray players require the purchase of proprietary Wi-Fi adapters sold by the device's manufacturer. Others can use any Wi-Fi adapter on the market.

- **Network interface cards.** One for every computer that you want to connect via Ethernet but does not have an existing Ethernet port.

- **Ethernet cables.** One to connect between every wired device and your network router. (Unless your house is pre-wired for Ethernet, in which case you'll need Ethernet cables to connect between each device and the nearest wall jack.)

You need to add these devices to the network map you previously created. For example, Figure 5.2 shows a notated version of the network map that was created in Figure 5.1, with the appropriate equipment added.

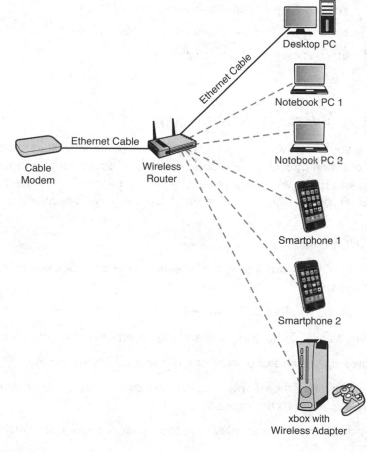

FIGURE 5.2

Our first network map with network equipment added.

You'll use this network map to create your equipment shopping list, which we discuss momentarily.

Creating Your Network Equipment List

With your network properly mapped out, you now need to make a list of the network equipment you need to buy. Work through the equipment you just added to the network map, and write it all down. You can use the following checklist.

Network Equipment List

Quantity	Equipment
1	Wireless router
	Wireless adapters (external, USB)
	Wireless adapter cards (internal for desktop PCs)
	Network interface cards (for desktop PCs)
	Ethernet cables (indicate length for each)

Choosing a Wireless Router

Now that you know what equipment you need, it's time to start shopping. There are lots of different options available, in terms of equipment configuration, functionality, and price. We'll look at each type of equipment separately, starting with the wireless router, which is the central hub of any Wi-Fi network.

What a Router Does

As you probably already know, the wireless router provides key several functions for your network:

- Creates the wireless Wi-Fi network
- Serves as a Wi-Fi hotspot to share your Internet connection wirelessly
- Routes signals and data from one network device to another
- Offers several Ethernet ports to connect computers or other devices directly (non-wirelessly) to the network
- Provides firewall functionality to protect your network from outside attack

NOTE   Some Internet service providers (ISPs) offer combination modem/routers, which combine those two types of units into a single box. A combo modem/router may be easier for a novice to set up and certainly eliminate one piece of equipment from your shelf. Learn more about these combo devices in Chapter 7, "Connecting to the Internet."

Understanding the Nomenclature—And the Specs

The first decision you have to make when choosing a wireless router is which Wi-Fi protocol you want to use. As you recall from Chapter 2, "How Wi-Fi Works," a number of different Wi-Fi protocols are in use today. Most common are routers that employ the 802.11n protocol, although you'll find some equipment running the "draft" 802.11ac protocol, which can be considerably faster—when used with other devices and adapters also running 802.11ac.

Now, you may not see the "n" or "ac" suffix on the front of the router box. (It's in the detailed specs, however—which you should always familiarize yourself with.) Instead, you may see manufacturers referring to 802.11n routers as Wireless-N models, and 802.11ac routers referred to as Wireless-AC or Gigabit Wi-Fi models. I guess they think that makes the technology more accessible to the masses.

There's some more nomenclature you'll need to wade through. Within the 802.11n family of products, you'll see models specified as N300, N450, N600, and N900. These numbers refer to the data-transfer rates achieved by the router—sort of. It's actually kind of a cheat, in that manufacturers add together the transfer rates for each of the bands in a dual-band router (one that can connect at both 2.4GHz and 5GHz frequencies); it's not the true real-world connection speed.

For example, a dual-band router that offers 300Mbps performance in each band gets to call itself an N600 router. It's not that this particular router delivers 600Mbps performance; it's that you get simultaneous 300Mbps performance over two bands. (300 + 300 = 600—even though the actual data-transfer rate for each connection is still 300Mbps.)

I'm not sure whether this is meant to be deliberately misleading or it's just lazy, but you need to watch out for it. Likewise, watch out for equipment reviews that talk about "900Mbps routers"—it's the same thing, adding together performance specs from two simultaneous bands. Don't believe the shorthand; look at the more accurate detailed specs instead.

TIP   Always examine the detailed specifications provided by the manufacturer. Look at the data-transfer rates for each band, not the phony knocked-together numbers on the front of the box or the bullet points in the online copy.

Examining 802.11n Routers

For most users, an 802.11n router is the way to go; it'll be compatible with all older equipment and is fast enough for most of the things you want to do on your network. The thing is, there's more than one type of 802.11n router available.

First, you need to look at the router's maximum speed. Some older and/or lower-priced 802.11n routers only deliver 150Mbps, which is not state-of-the-art these days. More common are those that deliver 300Mbps, which is good but not great. Some higher-end routers deliver 450Mbps, which is what you want if you're doing a lot of video streaming. Naturally, you'll pay more for higher-speed routers.

Also, know that 802.11n enables operation in both the 2.4GHz and 5GHz frequency bands. So-called single-band routers only operate at 2.4GHz; dual-band models operate at both 2.4GHz and 5GHz. A dual-band router lets you connect some devices at 2.4GHz and others at 5GHz, all at the same time, thus alleviating any congestion in the more crowded lower range. (Figure 5.3 shows a higher-end dual-band model from Linksys.)

FIGURE 5.3

The Cisco Linksys EA4500 dual-band 802.11n wireless router.

TIP   One popular strategy is to connect older 802.11g or less-demanding devices at 2.4GHz and reserve the 5GHz connections for those true 802.11n devices that utilize streaming video. This turns your 5GHz connection into a faster, more reliable media stream for your most demanding devices.

Use the following checklist to help determine what type of 802.11n router to shop for.

802.11n Router Shopping Guide

Feature	Your Choice
Speed (150Mbps, 300Mbps, 450bps)	
Single-band or dual band	
Number of Ethernet connections and speed	
Additional features	
Desired price range	

Let's make it simple. If you're on a budget, look for a slower single-band router operating at 150Mbps or 300Mbps. If you watch a lot of streaming video, however, or do a lot of real-time online gaming, you need the additional throughput and reliability of a dual-band router—ideally, one that delivers the fastest 450Mbps performance. Given the slight difference in prices (both single- and dual-band routers can be found for under U.S. $100), it's worth the investment to go with the highest performance model you can afford.

NOTE   All 802.11n routers should be fully compatible with older 802.11a/b/g equipment.

Examining 802.11ac Routers

As I write this in the fall of 2012, the 802.11ac protocol has yet to be officially ratified, so the only equipment on the market conforms to the draft standard. This is fairly common, however; there were a lot of "draft" 802.11n routers on the market before that standard was officially ratified.

What this means, however, is that there aren't a lot of 802.11ac routers available yet, and those that are (such as the NETGEAR model shown in Figure 5.4) are on the expensive side. These draft 802.11ac routers aren't for everyone, but they will have some appeal to early adopters.

FIGURE 5.4

The NETGEAR R6300 802.11ac wireless router.

If you choose an 802.11ac router, know that you won't necessarily get the promised 802.11ac speeds—at least not yet. That's because there are relatively few 802.11ac devices out there to connect to your 802.11ac router. Most notebook computers today, for example, are 802.11n models; most smartphones run 802.11n; and almost all external wireless adapters (which you can use to upgrade a slower network device) are also of the 802.11n variety. You only get 802.11ac speeds when you connect an 802.11ac device to an 802.11ac router; when an 802.11ac router is used with 802.11n equipment, those devices connect at the slower 802.11n speeds.

Why, then, would you purchase an 802.11ac router now? It's a matter of future-proofing your network. You're betting that you will have 802.11ac devices connected to your network at some point in the future, and your 802.11ac router will be ready for them. Until then, it'll work just fine as an 802.11n-compatible router—even if it does cost a little more.

 NOTE If you purchase a "pre-802.11ac" router, you'll probably need to upgrade the router's firmware once the protocol is officially ratified. This is typically an easy thing to do through the router's advanced settings menu.

Evaluating Ethernet Performance

It's important to remember that a wireless router, while providing wireless network connections, also provides *wired* network connections. As you can see in Figure 5.5, most wireless routers have at least four Ethernet connections on the back; you'll use one of these to connect your broadband modem, but the rest are open to connect any network computer via Ethernet cable.

FIGURE 5.5

The connections on the back of the D-Link DIR-835 wireless router—one Ethernet connector for a broadband modem and four (labeled LAN 1 through 4) to connect to other wired devices.

You'll want to consider not only the number of Ethernet connections on the back of a router (make sure you have enough for all the devices you don't want to connect wirelessly) and the speed of those connections. Most routers today offer Gigabit Ethernet, which delivers 1Gbps speeds. Be wary of any routers that only provide the slower Fast Ethernet (100Mbps) or 10Base-T (10Mbps) speeds connections.

Considering Other Features

Many manufacturers offer proprietary features on their wireless routers that may be worth considering. For example, you may find these features interesting:

- **Automatic quality of service (QoS).** This technology recognizes and gives priority to streaming video signals, thus ensuring (in theory, anyway) a more stable video viewing experience.

- **Beamforming.** This technology enables the router to make a more direct connection with a single device, as opposed to one formed from the wider wireless waveform. The result, theoretically, should be a slightly faster and more stable connection with that individual device.

- **Cloud connections.** This feature connects your home network to additional file storage in the Internet cloud.

- **Guest network.** Many routers let you configure two separate networks from the same router—a full-featured network protected by passwords and a limited-function Internet-only network for guest users.

- **Hard disk storage.** A router with a built-in hard disk lets you store files (data, music, photos, whatever) for access over the network. You can also use a built-in hard drive for network backup—that is, you can back up data from networked computers to your router's hard drive.

- **Pushbutton setup.** Many routers today offer so-called pushbutton setup, typically between devices from the same manufacturer. To connect a device, such as a wireless adapter, you just press a button on the adapter and a similar button on the router; all the necessary connections and configurations (including wireless security) are then made automatically.

- **USB ports.** These let you connect additional peripherals, such as printers or external hard drives, to your network through the router.

 NOTE   Some of these proprietary features only work when all the devices on your network are from the same manufacturer. They may also require special software to be installed on your networked computers.

Ultimately, you want a router that delivers the necessary performance and functionality, and is easy to set up and configure. Examine the available features to make sure that you're getting what you need.

Choosing Wireless Adapters

Most handheld devices today come with built-in Wi-Fi capability. That is, your notebook computer, tablet, e-reader, and smartphone all have built-in Wi-Fi radios and the accompanying technology necessary to make a connection to a Wi-Fi network.

Other less-portable devices, such as desktop PCs and videogame consoles, may not have this Wi-Fi functionality built in. For these devices, you'll need to add a Wi-Fi adapter to connect to your wireless network.

USB Adapters

Most wireless adapters today, like the one shown in Figure 5.6, connect to your device via USB—and, in fact, resemble a USB flash drive in appearance. Most of these adapters are compatible with the current 802.11n Wi-Fi standard.

FIGURE 5.6

Belkin's N300 USB Wireless N Adapter. (Photo courtesy of Belkin.)

The typical wireless adapter offers 300Mbps performance over the 2.4GHz band. Dual-band adapters also exist that work in either the 2.4GHz or 5GHz bands. With this type of dual-band adapter, you have to select which band you want to use. It won't (in fact, can't) connect to both bands simultaneously.

 NOTE Most videogame consoles can use any third-party wireless adapter—assuming Wi-Fi isn't built in, of course. Some consoles, such as the Xbox 360, recommend their own proprietary adapters which, although not absolutely necessary, may offer additional functionality.

Depending on the brand, configuration, and functionality, expect to pay between U.S. $40–$100 for an external wireless adapter.

 TIP Make sure that you can place an external wireless adapter in a position away from other electrical equipment to minimize interference and establish a stronger signal. In this regard, connecting a keychain Wi-Fi adapter to the rear of a desktop PC often results in disappointing performance—it's too low and too near your PC to work effectively.

Internal Adapters

If you don't want an external wireless adapter cluttering your office desktop, you can always add an internal adapter to your desktop PC. This is a wireless adapter on an internal expansion card, like the one shown in Figure 5.7, that you install inside your PC's system unit. For optimal reception, these cards have either an antenna sticking out of the back or an external antenna on a short cable.

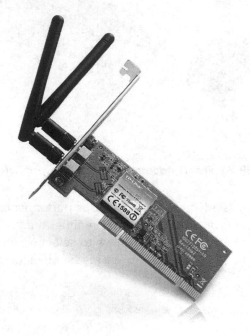

FIGURE 5.7

A 300Mbps wireless adapter card from TP-LINK. (Photo courtesy of TP-LINK.)

There are two downsides to using an internal wireless adapter card, however. First, you have to open up your PC's system unit and install the thing, which might be somewhat daunting to the technically inexperienced user. (And, if you have an all-in-one PC, this sort of expansion may not be possible.) Second, this type of configuration typically places the Wi-Fi antenna low to the ground, which might not provide optimal reception. For these reasons, I usually recommend an external adapter over the internal type.

If you decide to go with an internal wireless adapter card, expect to pay between U.S. $35 and $90.

Choosing Network Interface Cards and Ethernet Cables

Most desktop and notebook PCs today have built-in Ethernet ports, in case you want to connect them via Ethernet instead of wirelessly. On the offchance that a given PC *doesn't* have an Ethernet port available, you can add one—either internally or externally.

To add Ethernet capability to a desktop PC, you need to install a network interface card (NIC). This type of expansion board is typically priced from U.S. $15 to $40. Make sure you go with a model that offers a Gigabit Ethernet connection.

To add Ethernet to a notebook PC, you need to connect an external Ethernet adapter via USB. You can also use an external USB Ethernet adapter with a desktop PC; if you have a free USB port, it's easier than installing an internal card. Expect to pay from U.S. $20 to $40 for an external Ethernet-to-USB adapter.

If you're connecting one or more devices via Ethernet, you'll need to purchase the necessary Ethernet cables to make the physical connection. You can purchase Ethernet cables in various lengths; expect to pay between U.S. $10 and $20 for a 10- or 25-foot cable.

 TIP   You can purchase Ethernet cables that conform to either the Cat-5 or Cat-6 standard. Cat-6 is a newer standard that can offers transmission bandwidth of 200MHz, compared to CAT-5's 100MHz bandwidth. This means you can send more data faster over longer distances. In most instances, Cat-5 is more than sufficient, but you may want to go Cat-6 just to future-proof your network.

Upgrading Your Current Network

All this talk of 802.11n this and 802.11ac that might mean nothing to you if you already have a wireless network installed in your home. Well, it *should* mean something—in that your older network might not be quite state-of-the-art in terms of performance.

If you have an 802.11g (or older) router in your home, you may want to replace it with a newer 802.11n model. You'll know it's time to upgrade when you start asking your router to perform more demanding tasks, such as streaming video over the Internet, and find that it's not up to the job. (You'll know what I mean; watching streaming video on an older router often results in unwanted pauses, blips, and even disconnections.)

Fortunately, upgrading an existing network is relatively easy to do. We discuss the installation process in Chapter 6, "Installing a Wireless Router," but, for now, know that the main piece of equipment you need to replace is your router. It's likely that you've connected newer wireless devices since you purchased your router, and these devices likely adhere to the newer (and faster) 802.11n standard. However, they can't connect at 802.11n speeds if your router is still an 802.11g model, so that's what you need to change.

 TIP Your new router does not have to be from the same manufacturer as the router you're replacing.

Use the information presented in this chapter to choose the right 802.11n or 802.11ac router for your needs, and then swap out your old one for the new one in your network. It's actually quite easy to do.

Where to Buy Networking Equipment

You can find consumer-grade networking equipment from a number of reputable manufacturers, including the following:

- Apple (www.apple.com/wifi/)

 NOTE Apple's AirPort wireless routers (called "base stations") can work with any type of computer—Windows and Mac alike.

- ASUS (www.asus.com)
- Belkin (www.belkin.com)
- Buffalo (www.buffalotech.com)
- Cisco Linksys (home.cisco.com)
- NETGEAR (www.netgear.com)
- TP-LINK (www.tp-link.com)
- TRENDnet (www.trendnet.com)
- Western Digital (www.wdc.com)
- ZyXEL (www.zyxel.com)

Most major electronics retailers, such as Best Buy and Fry's, sell wireless networking equipment. You can also find equipment online, from Amazon.com and other online retailers.

 TIP You should be able to mix-and-match wireless equipment from different manufacturers. That is, an 802.11n wireless adapter from Belkin should connect just fine to an 802.11n wireless router from NETGEAR. You're not locked into equipping your entire network from a single manufacturer.

THE ABSOLUTE MINIMUM

Here are the key points to remember from this chapter:

- Do the proper planning before you put your network together; determine what equipment you need and where it should be installed.

- The centerpiece of your network is the wireless router. Most users today will choose 802.11n routers, although you can future-proof your network with a (more expensive) 802.11ac model.

- When selecting an 802.11n router, you need to look at speed (300Mbps or 450Mbps) and whether to go with a single-band or dual-band unit. You'll pay more for a faster dual-band unit, but also get better performance for high-bandwidth tasks, such as watching streaming video.

- If a given device doesn't have Wi-Fi built in, you need to connect it to a wireless adapter, either internally (for desktop PCs) or externally (for just about everything else).

- When you want to improve the speed and range of an older network, the only piece of equipment you probably need to replace is the wireless router; upgrading to a newer 802.11n or 802.11ac router should provide better performance for all of your newer wireless devices.

INSTALLING A WIRELESS ROUTER

After you select and purchase your wireless router, it's time to install it and get your network up and running. This used to be a somewhat daunting task, full of arcane settings that needed configured, but that's changed of late; today, router setup and configuration is pretty much a matter of connecting a few cables, clicking a few buttons, and letting the automatic setup program do its thing.

Before You Start

Before you start the installation process, you need to do some prep work. In particular, you need to assemble everything you need to get things up and running—including a few Ethernet cables.

The first items you need to assemble are all of your networking equipment—the wireless router, notebook computers, and handheld devices, wireless adapters for non-wireless PCs and game consoles, and the like—pretty much everything you identified in Chapter 5, "Planning Your Network and Purchasing Equipment." Don't connect anything as yet, but do place each piece of external equipment next to the computer to which it belongs. In the case of your wireless router, place it next to what you consider your main PC—the computer you'll be using to configure the router—and near your broadband Internet modem. (Figure 6.1 shows a typical setup.)

 NOTE   The main PC for your network can be either a desktop or notebook model, running either Windows or Mac OS.

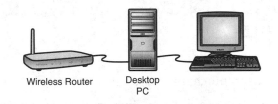

Wireless Router   Desktop
                      PC

FIGURE 6.1

Place your wireless router next to the main PC and broadband modem.

In your house or apartment, it's best to place your router as near as possible to the center of all of your wireless devices. That probably means near the center of the main floor of your house; you want to minimize the distance from the router to the furthest point in the network.

Of course, since you need to place your router near your broadband modem, you may be limited where you can place your router. Most of us have the main Internet connection entering somewhere in the home office area, which may or may not be in the center of your house.

 CAUTION   Trying to stretch a Wi-Fi signal too far will result in degraded performance for the most distant wireless devices. That's why the middle of the main floor is recommended. Trying to transmit/receive from one end of your basement to the opposite end of your top floor may simply be too far to ensure networking success.

Next, because the wireless router requires power, make sure that you place it next to a free power outlet—or, even better, next to a surge-suppressor power strip. You'll also want to arrange power for any other AC-powered devices; most wireless peripherals, however, get their power from the USB connection to the host computer.

For all the wireless equipment, make sure that each device is relatively out in the open, not buried in a cabinet or behind other equipment, as shown in Figure 6.2. Although Wi-Fi signals can travel through most solid objects, such placement rapidly degrades the signal. It's better to place all equipment where it can be seen, so you maximize the signal strength over the necessary distance.

FIGURE 6.2

Don't bury your equipment!

In addition, you probably want to place the wireless router away from other electronic equipment, as shown in Figure 6.3. That means moving it away from your cordless phone, PC, or computer monitor. Any and all of these devices emit electronic signals that can interfere with the router's radio frequency transmission.

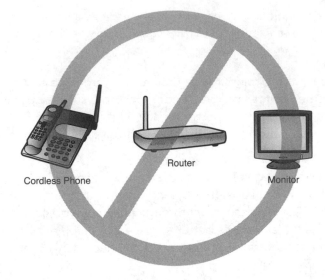

FIGURE 6.3

Avoid close encounters with other electronic equipment.

Finally, make sure that you have all necessary cables to complete your network. Although you don't have to deal with a lot of cables in a wireless network (that's one of the advantages, after all!), you probably need a few Ethernet cables. You'll need one to connect between your router and broadband modem; you may also need another to connect between your router and your main PC. Make sure the cables are of adequate length—not too short, of course, but also not too long.

 TIP   I like having a foot or so of extra play in my Ethernet cables, just in case I need to scoot things around at some point.

Making the Physical Connections

Almost all routers today come with a setup/installation program on CD; you run this program from the main computer you first connect to the router. How you connect your router depends to some degree on the specifics of this installation program.

Here's the deal. Some router setup programs require the router to be physically connected to the main computer during the installation process. After the initial installation, this computer can be disconnected (physically) and reconnected wirelessly.

NOTE Why might you need to initially connect your router to your main PC via Ethernet? It's because not all setup routines can remotely sense and configure the main PC's wireless connection; in this situation, the direct wired connection is necessary to access the PC and then configure its wireless functionality.

Other router setup programs are completely wireless. That is, they can (theoretically) connect to the main computer via its wireless connection, and perform the entire network setup process wirelessly. When this works, it's great; if you have trouble establishing this initial wireless connection, you may need to punt and go the Ethernet route, instead.

Obviously, you'll need to follow the instructions of your specific router installation program. But, in general, here are the steps you'll take to get everything connected:

 NOTE Some routers require you to run the setup/installation CD before making any physical connections—essentially putting step 9 and 10 before step 1. Always read and follow the instructions for your particular router to make sure you get the steps right.

1. Make sure your broadband modem is connected to the incoming Internet connection, but disconnect it from its power supply.

2. Connect one end of an Ethernet cable to the "out" port on the back of your broadband modem, as shown in Figure 6.4.

FIGURE 6.4

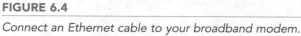

Connect an Ethernet cable to your broadband modem.

3. Connect the other end of the Ethernet cable to the "Internet" or "Modem" port on the back of your wireless router, as shown in Figure 6.5. If the router doesn't have a dedicated "Internet" port, connect to the cable to the first Ethernet port ("Ethernet 1").

FIGURE 6.5

Connect the other end of the Ethernet cable to your wireless router.

4. If your router has automatic wireless setup (check the router's installation instructions to make sure), proceed to step 6. Otherwise, connect one end of another Ethernet cable to the first free Ethernet port on the back of your router, as shown in Figure 6.6.

5. Connect the other end of this Ethernet cable to the Ethernet port on your main computer, as shown in Figure 6.7.

6. If your router has external antennas, rotate them into the "up" position (toward the ceiling), parallel to each other.

FIGURE 6.6

Connect another Ethernet cable to your wireless router.

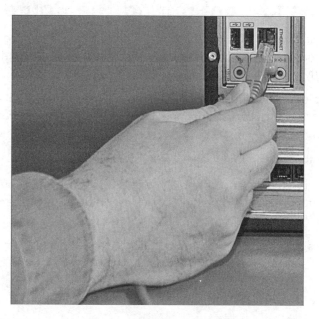

FIGURE 6.7

Connect the other end of the Ethernet cable to your main computer.

7. Plug in the modem's power supply and wait 60 seconds or so for the modem to turn on and settle itself in.

8. Plug in router's power supply and wait for it to cycle through the startup process and its lights to go green. This should take no more than 30 seconds.

9. Insert the router's setup/installation CD into your main computer.

10. When the setup/installation wizard launches, follow the onscreen instructions to complete the setup process.

CAUTION Note all routers come with installation CDs. If your router lacks an installation program, follow the manufacturer's instructions to complete the installation manually using the router's web-based advanced setup utility.

After the installation process is complete, you can disconnect the Ethernet cable running between the router and your main computer, and then establish a new wireless connection for this computer. Alternately, you can leave the main computer connected via Ethernet, if it's close enough to be convenient.

Setting Up and Configuring the Router

What happens when you run the router's setup/installation program? Well, it differs from manufacturer to manufacturer and from router to router; everybody does it differently.

For example, Belkin offers the following setup procedure for its newer 802.11n routers; note that no physical connection between the main computer and router is necessary:

1. When the CD menu appears, click the Setup icon.

2. After a brief installation period, the setup software asks you to enter the network name (SSID) and password printed on the side of the router, as shown in Figure 6.8.

3. There's another pause as additional software is installed and things are configured. Then, you see the Success screen, which is shown in Figure 6.9.

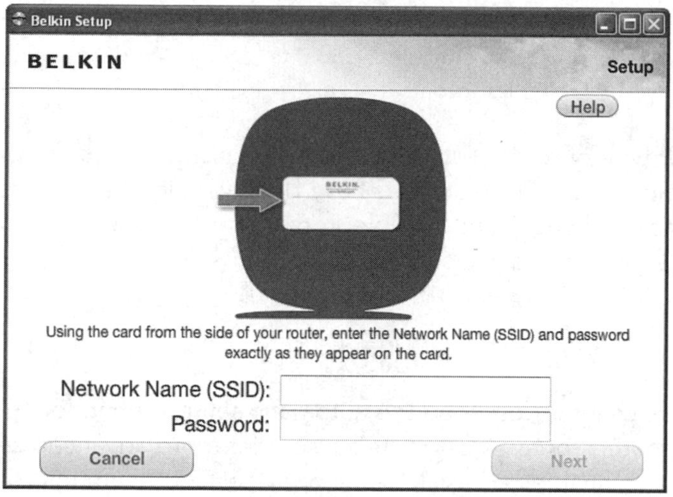

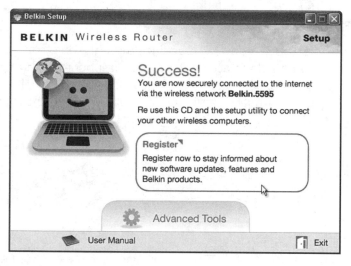

FIGURE 6.8

Entering your router's SSID and password.

FIGURE 6.9

Congratulations—your router is set up!

That's a simple procedure, and one I particularly like. Other setup/installation programs may be somewhat different, of course. For example, NETGEAR's Smart Wizard Setup walks you through a series of questions designed to determine what type of network you're setting up, and then directs you to connect the various cables in the proper order.

TIP   You can use your router's configuration dashboard, discussed in the next section, to change the default network name and password if you like.

Whatever type of router you're installing, I think you'll find the process fairly quick and simple. Router manufacturers have been working hard to make the setup process less painful and more "troubleproof," with the result that all you have to do is follow the instructions you see onscreen.

Advanced Router Setup

So far, this chapter described the automatic setup routine found with most new wireless routers today. Most routers also offer more advanced setup and configuration, which enables access to some more technical settings you may need to access in some situations. You can also use this advanced setup to change the default network name and password you entered during the initial installation process.

Opening the Dashboard

You access your router's advanced settings through some sort of web-based dashboard. You may be able to access this router dashboard from a desktop shortcut or Start menu item on your computer, or you can do it manually. Launch your web browser (any browser will do) and enter the following into the Address bar:

```
192.168.0.1
```

or

```
192.168.1.1
```

or

```
192.168.2.1
```

CAUTION   The exact numeric address you need to enter should be listed in your router's instruction manual. You may have to enter "http://" in front of the numeric address, depending on your router or web browser; consult the router's manual for specific instructions.

This should open the router dashboard in your web browser. You'll probably be prompted to log into the dashboard and enter a password; the default password should be listed in your router's instruction manual or on the back or bottom of the router.

Navigating the Dashboard

The router dashboard you see is manufacturer- (and perhaps router-) specific. That is, you'll probably see something different than what is presented here. In any instance, the dashboard is a web page (actually, a series of tabbed web pages) that display a variety of router and network settings. (Figure 6.10 shows the Genie dashboard for a NETGEAR wireless router.)

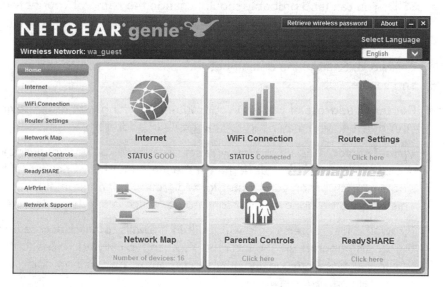

FIGURE 6.10

Configuring advanced network settings from the NETGEAR Genie dashboard.

There are lots of settings referenced here. Most dashboards let you display specific types of settings by clicking tabs or buttons along the top or left side of the dashboard. To change a specific setting, open that particular page and click or double-click the setting you want to change. You can then enter and save a new value for that setting.

I can't go into the particulars of what you can or can't configure, or exactly how you go about doing that, because each router's dashboard is different. When in doubt, consult and follow the router's instruction manual for more details.

Key Settings

There are a lot of advanced settings you can tinker with, but few that most users have to consider. Most of these settings are for administrators of larger and more complex networks, or if you're experiencing select problems with your network. The average user on the average home network won't have to deal with these at all.

NOTE   Learn more about using these advanced settings to fix pesky network problems in Chapter 19, "Troubleshooting Network Problems."

So, which of these settings might you need to configure at some point in time? Focus on these:

- **SSID.** You can (and probably should) change the name of your network from the default name provided by the manufacturer. You typically do this from the advanced settings utility.

- **Password.** Change the default network password to something more unique and secure.

- **Router IP address.** If you find your router conflicting with other devices on your network, you may need to change its IP address.

- **Virtual server.** This setting lets you set up a server on your network and access it from outside your home via the Internet. This works by defining a single public port on your router for redirection to an external LAN address. This can also be done via *port forwarding*, which is another advanced option.

- **Firewall.** Most routers come with built-in firewalls to block access from unauthorized computers via the Internet. You can typically add rules to this firewall to allow access from specific outside computers or block outgoing data from computers on your network.

NOTE   Learn more about firewalls in Chapter 10, "Securing Devices on Your Network."

- **Filters.** In addition to the firewall rules, many routers employ filters that block specific types of Internet usage. For example, you may be able to keep devices on your network from accessing specific undesirable URLs or even complete domains.

- **Application rules.** Similarly, some software applications need to send data over the Internet. You can create rules to open one or more outgoing ports on your router when data is sent from selected applications.

Where you find these settings depends on your specific router and configuration utility. Some basic settings, such as SSID and password, may be located in the utility's Setup section. Other settings are probably in the Advanced section of the utility. As always, consult your router's instruction manual for specific details.

Upgrading from an Existing Router

As you can see, installing a new router is a relatively painless process. But, what if you already have a wireless network in your home, and you want to trade out your old router for a newer, faster model?

Fortunately, most router manufacturers make it easy to upgrade to a new router by automatically detecting your existing network when you power up the new router. The new router can then be configured to use similar settings (such as the network name and password) as your old one—pretty much automatically.

 CAUTION   If you're using an all-in-one router/modem pro-vided by your ISP, you don't have the option of upgrading your router. You'll need to switch to a separate router and modem if you want to upgrade.

For this to work, you have to have both your old and new routers working simul-taneously. That means power up your new router before you disconnect anything from your old one, including the broadband Internet connection. You'll want to run the setup/installation program for the new router from your main PC, of course, and follow the onscreen instructions you see there. (There's probably an option for using an existing network; choose that one.)

If you do need to manually configure the new router, here are some tips for mak-ing things go as smoothly as possible:

- Give the new router the same name (SSID) as the old one. This way, all of your existing devices will connect automatically to the new router. (If you give the new router a different name, you'll have to establish new connections with your existing devices.)

- Similarly, assign the same password you used with your old router to your new router. You may want to change this (ideally, to a stronger password) at some future time, but by using the old password, you can connect all of your exist-ing devices without any manual reconfiguration.

- In addition, make sure the new router is using the same type of wireless secu-rity as the previous router.

- After you have the new router up and running, disconnect your Internet modem from your old router and reconnect it to the new one. Likewise, move any Ethernet connections from the old router to the new one.

- If you've upgraded to a dual-band router, assign a slightly different network name to the new 5GHz band. Then, select which devices you want to connect at 5GHz; you should probably assign devices that require high bandwidth, such as streaming video, to the upper band.

 NOTE   If you configure your new router with a different SSID and/or password, you'll need to reconnect all of your existing devices to the new router using these new settings.

After you have everything connected, you should notice an improvement both in speed and range. That is, you should be able to get further from your new router and still receive a strong signal—assuming that your wireless devices also support the new 802.11n standard. If you have older 802.11g devices on your network, they'll exhibit the same range and performance as they did with your older router; a connection is only as fast as its slowest link.

THE ABSOLUTE MINIMUM

Here are the key points to remember from this chapter:

- Place your router next to your broadband modem and close to your main computer.

- Position your router as near as possible to the center of all the devices that will be connecting to it—typically in the middle of your home's main floor.

- You'll need to connect your broadband modem to your router with an Ethernet cable; you may also need to connect your main computer to your router via Ethernet, at least for the initial installation. (Many routers don't require this physical connection to the main computer; they perform the entire setup process wirelessly.)

- To set up your router, insert and run the router's installation CD from your main computer.

- If you're upgrading from an existing router, many routers will detect your existing network and configure the new router appropriately. If you need to manually configure the new router, use the same network name (SSID) and password as the old router.

7

CONNECTING TO THE INTERNET

The main reason most people set up a wireless home network is to share an Internet connection. We depend on the Internet for just about everything these days, from basic communications (via email and instant messaging) to social networking (with Facebook and Twitter) to being entertained (with streaming movies and music)—and we do so on a variety of different devices. It's not just a single computer doing email and web browsing; these days, we connect our smartphones and videogame consoles, and even our TVs and Blu-ray players, to the Internet.

It's important, then, that you not only have an Internet connection, but that you have the right type of connection—and then use your home network to share it among all of your home's wireless devices. If your Internet connection isn't working, there isn't much worth doing at home.

Understanding Internet Connections

To connect to the Internet at home, you must sign up with an Internet service provider (ISP). This company, as the name implies, provides your home with a connection to the Internet. Your Internet provider might be your phone company, your cable company, or your satellite TV company; they all offer Internet access, typically for a low monthly subscription rate.

Most ISPs offer some form of what we call *broadband* Internet access. Broadband is the fastest type of Internet connection available to homes today, and it comes in many flavors—cable, DSL, FiOS, and even satellite. Whichever type of broadband connection you choose, the Internet comes into your home via a wire or cable and connects to a device called a *modem*, which then connects either directly to a single computer or, more often, to a wireless router, so you can share the connection with all the computers and wireless devices in your home.

 NOTE In some rural areas, broadband access may not be available. If you don't have access to broadband Internet, you need to connect via a *dial-up connection*—that is, by dialing in through your normal telephone line. Unfortunately, dial-up connections are much, much slower than broadband connections, which means it takes longer to download music and photos—and make watching online videos problematic.

Broadband DSL

DSL is a phone line-based technology that operates at broadband speeds. DSL service piggybacks onto your existing phone line, turning it into a high-speed digital data connection.

Not only is DSL faster than dial-up (up to 3Mbps, compared to 56Kbps for dial-up), you don't have to surrender your normal phone line when you want to surf; DSL connections are "always on." Most providers offer DSL service for U.S. $30–$50 per month. Look for package deals that offer a discount when you subscribe to both Internet and phone services.

Broadband Cable

It's likely that your local cable company offers broadband Internet in addition to those hundreds of television channels you seldom watch. Broadband cable Internet piggybacks on your normal cable television line, providing speeds up to 30Mbps, depending on the provider.

Most cable companies offer broadband cable Internet for U.S. $30–$50 per month, which is about the same as you pay for a similar DSL connection. As with DSL, look for package deals for your cable company, offering some sort of discount on a combination of Internet, cable, and (sometimes) digital phone service.

FiOS Broadband

The newest type of broadband connection is called Fiber Optic Service (*FiOS*). As the name implies, this type of service delivers an Internet connection over a fiber-optic network.

FiOS connection speeds are similar to those of broadband cable, with different speeds available at different pricing tiers. Most ISPs offer download speeds between 3Mbps and 50Mbps. Pricing is also similar to broadband cable (in the U.S. $30–$50 per month range).

In the home, the FiOS line connects to a modem-like device called an optical network terminal (ONT), which can split the signal to provide a combination of Internet, television, and telephone services. You typically connect the ONT to your wireless router via Ethernet. In the U.S., FiOS Internet service is available through AT&T and Verizon, in limited areas.

Broadband Satellite

If you can't get DSL, cable, or FiOS Internet in your area, you have another option: connecting to the Internet via satellite. Any household or business with a clear line of sight to the southern sky can receive digital data signals from a geosynchronous satellite at speeds between 10–15Mbps.

The largest provider of satellite Internet access is HughesNet. (Hughes also developed and markets the popular DIRECTV digital satellite system.) The HughesNet system (www.hughesnet.com) enables you to receive Internet signals via a small dish that you mount outside your house or on your roof. Fees range from U.S. $50 to $100 per month.

 NOTE   Almost all ISPs have different download and upload speeds—with downloads being faster than uploads. That is, you can download stuff from the Internet faster than you can upload it. That's probably okay for most users, who do a lot more downloading (of emails and music and movies) than they do uploading.

Choosing the Right Internet Connection for Your Network

Given the options of DSL, cable, FiOS, and satellite Internet, which should you choose?

Looking just at the raw numbers, you might think cable and FiOS offer the fastest connections—and you'd probably be right. Even though your cable company might not deliver on the promised 30Mbps top speed, your cable Internet connection is likely to be faster than your phone company's comparable DSL connection.

That's if, of course, you have both DSL and cable Internet available to you. (I'm going to write off FiOS right here for most readers, as its availability is much more limited than either DSL or cable Internet.) Not all phone companies offer DSL, and those that do don't offer it to all customers; you have to be within a minimum distance (5,000 feet or so) from the phone office to receive DSL coverage. And not all cable companies offer cable Internet, either. (Although most do.)

Even if you have both DSL and cable Internet available, you still need to consider price as part of the equation. Cable Internet may be faster than DSL, but it may also be more expensive. Or not. Pricing varies from company to company and from location to location, so shop carefully to find the best compromise between speed and price. That might be cable, it might be DSL, or (in some locations) it might be FiOS. See what's out there and then make your choice.

Connecting the Internet to Your Network

Because wireless Internet sharing is so ubiquitous, the various ISPs and networking companies make the process as painless as possible. In most cases, sharing an Internet connection is no more difficult than connecting your Internet modem to your wireless router.

Connecting with a Wireless Router

Your ISP runs a cable into your home, which then connects to a broadband modem. A broadband modem, like the one in Figure 7.1, converts the incoming signal (from either your phone line—for DSL—or your cable line) into a digital signal that can be fed to a computer or router. (In the case of FiOS, the box is an optical network terminal, which functions pretty much like a modem but with fiber-optic signals instead of electrical ones.)

 NOTE The word "modem" stands for *modulator/demodulator*, as it modulates an analog signal to digital format, and then demodulates the digital signal back to analog.

FIGURE 7.1

A typical cable modem from Motorola. (Photo courtesy of Motorola.)

The broadband modem then connects either to a single computer (if you don't have a network) or to a network router. The connection is typically via Ethernet, although some modems let you connect via USB, instead. Figure 7.2 shows how it all works; the Internet signal from the modem is broadcast to all the wired and wireless devices connected to your router.

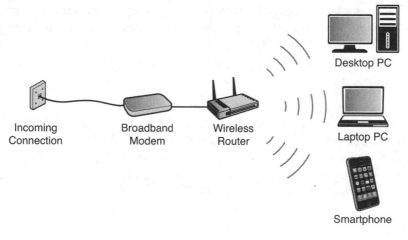

FIGURE 7.2

A home network utilizing a separate broadband modem and wireless router.

Connecting with a Combination Modem/Router

Some ISPs offer their own proprietary networking equipment. Having your ISP supply your networking equipment can be attractive, especially if the equipment is offered at low or no cost.

Obviously, your ISP supplies you with a broadband modem; that's standard operating procedure. But, some ISPs combine the broadband modem and a wireless router into a single modem/router device, like the one shown in Figure 7.3.

FIGURE 7.3

NETGEAR's DGN1000 ADSL2+ Modem Router. (Photo courtesy of NETGEAR.)

Many users like this combination device, sometimes called a wireless gateway, as the one unit replaces two pieces of equipment. It also simplifies the hookup and configuration to some degree; you don't have to worry about the router not recognizing or working with the modem, for example. And many of these gateway units include a built-in hardware firewall, which increased your network and Internet security.

If you have the option of using modem/router gateway, you don't have to buy a separate wireless router; this single piece of equipment serves as both your broadband modem and your wireless network router. Connect your incoming Internet cable to this unit and it both beams the Internet connection to all your wireless computers and manages all network data transfer and communications. (Figure 7.4 shows how this works.)

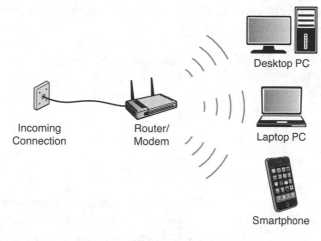

FIGURE 7.4

A home network utilizing a combination router/modem gateway.

Setting Up a Public Wi-Fi Hotspot

So far, we focused our attention on sharing an Internet connection on traditional home or small business networks. But, you can also configure your modem and wireless router to create a public Wi-Fi hotspot, just like the kind you find at your local Starbucks or public library.

First, a definition. A Wi-Fi hotspot is nothing more than a wireless network with no wireless security set up. Because users don't have to enter a password or network key, any wireless device within range can access the network, and thus the Internet connection.

Turning your wireless network into a Wi-Fi hotspot is as easy as turning off wireless security on your router—although there are other ways to do it, too.

Turning Your Wireless Router into a Wi-Fi Hotspot

Let's look at the easy way first. Because a Wi-Fi hotspot is nothing more than a wireless network with no security enabled, it's simple to convert your private network for public use. Just follow these steps:

1. Set up your broadband modem and wireless router as normal.

2. When prompted to enable wireless security, choose not to.

That's that. Without wireless security enabled, your network and Internet connection are now completely public.

CAUTION   If you choose to share your Internet connection publicly, you should enable password protection and disable file sharing for your network to protect your private data files. See Chapter 11, "Connecting Home Computers," for more instructions.

Setting Up a Wi-Fi Hotspot with a Wireless Access Point

If you're creating a public Wi-Fi hotspot for commercial use—that is, with no need for typical networking functions—you don't need or particularly want a fully featured wireless router. Instead, a better choice might be a single-function wireless access point, like the one shown in Figure 7.5. A wireless access point of this type is kind of like a wireless router without the network router functions. (And without any Ethernet connections.)

FIGURE 7.5

TRENDnet's TEW-637AP wireless access point. (Photo courtesy of TRENDnet.)

NOTE A wireless router is a single unit that combines network router and wireless access point functions. Remove the router functions, and you're left with a wireless access point.

The advantage of using a wireless access point instead of a wireless router is simplicity. It's pretty much a plug-and-play affair: Connect an Ethernet cable between your broadband modem and the access point, power everything up, and you're good to go. There are configuration settings to tweak if you want to, but they're seldom necessary—unless you're using the device for commercial use. (When you're running a public Wi-Fi hotspot, you may want some control over how the access point is used.)

 NOTE Wireless access points aren't limited to Wi-Fi hotspot use. Many large businesses use wireless access points to provide wireless access to their Ethernet-based corporate networks.

Security Matters: To Share or Not to Share?

Sharing an Internet connection over a wireless network involves broadcasting that connection over the airwaves. When broadcasting an Internet signal in this fashion, you can choose to make the connection public, so anyone can use it, or private, so that only devices with the proper password have access.

As just noted, to create a public wireless Internet hotspot, you simply don't enable wireless security on your network. With no password required to log on, anyone within Wi-Fi range can access your wireless signal and connect to the Internet over your connection.

Conversely, to keep others from leeching onto your Internet connection, all you have to do is enable wireless security on your router. Unless your neighbors know your network security key or passphrase, they can't log on and connect.

 NOTE Learn more about wireless security in Chapter 10, "Securing Devices on Your Network."

The question of whether or not to publicly share your Internet connection is both social and technical in nature. The social aspect comes from the notion, embraced by many, that the Internet should be freely available for as many people as possible. If you have an Internet connection, the thinking goes, you're morally obligated to share that connection with others. (Or, at least, you see no harm from such sharing.) Of course, this argument conveniently ignores the fact that you're paying $30 or so a month for that Internet connection, and anyone tapping into your connection is getting it for free; you're not getting compensated for sharing your connection. That said, perhaps you don't care that your neighbors across the street are using your connection to access the Internet. Maybe you're just being a good neighbor.

The technical aspect concerns security. If someone can tap into your unsecured Internet connection, that also means they can tap into your unsecured home network. If they can access your Internet connection, they can also access files stored on your networked computers, which is not necessarily desirable—for you, anyway. If you choose to share your Internet connection in this fashion (by not enabling wireless security), you should at least disable file and folder sharing on your network, and perhaps enable password protection to access network files. Sharing your Internet connection doesn't mean you have to put your own valuable data at risk.

There's an additional risk involved in publicly sharing an Internet connection. What happens if one of your neighbors uses your Internet connection to perform an illegal activity, such as sending out a raft of spam messages or illegally downloading music files from a file-sharing site? Because it's your Internet connection that was used, you may be liable for damages related to that illegal activity—even though you yourself didn't participate. You're in fact an accessory to the crime and, because there may be no way to determine whether or not your PC was involved in the activity, you may be presumed guilty until proven innocent.

These are all good reasons *not* to publicly share your Internet connection—which argues in favor of enabling wireless security to keep your connection private. On the flip side, you may want to keep your network open, in spite of these risks, if you often have visitors that need to access the Internet. Instead of constantly fiddling with network settings on your guests' computers (typically involving the entering of that long and difficult-to-remember network security key or pass-phrase), you may want to keep your network public instead. With a non-protected network, any guest can easily connect to the Internet simply by making a connection to your network's wireless signal. It's the equivalent of establishing your own public Wi-Fi hotspot, just like the one in your local coffeehouse.

THE ABSOLUTE MINIMUM

Here are the key points to remember from this chapter:

- There are four primary types of always-on broadband Internet connections: DSL (through your phone company), cable broadband (through your cable company), FiOS (using fiber-optic cable), and satellite Internet (fed through an orbiting satellite).

- All other things being equal, cable and FiOS provide faster Internet connections than DSL or satellite Internet. (But, things are not always equal; you may not have access to all the different types of connections.)

- To share an Internet connection, connect your ISP's broadband modem to your wireless router—or use a combination modem/router, which is offered by some ISPs.

- A public Wi-Fi hotspot is nothing more than a wireless network with password security disabled—although you can also use a simpler wireless access point in place of traditional wireless router.

8

EXTENDING YOUR NETWORK IN A LARGER HOME OR OFFICE

As you've seen, setting up a wireless home network is relatively easy—unless, that is, you have a particularly large house or office. If you're trying to connect a device on one end of your house to a router located at the opposite end (and perhaps on a different floor), you may find that your devices are too far away to consistently connect. That is, it's possible for your home to be too big for your network.

For example, I have my wireless router in my home office at one end of the main floor of a 4,000-square-foot house. My wireless signal gets pretty weak (or sometimes non-existent) at the other end of the house, especially upstairs or in the basement. Wireless routers, after all, have a limited range; get too far away, or put too many obstacles in the way, and connecting to the router becomes difficult.

How, then, can you extend the range of your router to cover a larger area? There are several things you can do, from moving your existing router to installing a second one.

Revisiting Transmission Range

Let's start by taking another look at the transmission range of a wireless network. As you know, all wireless routers transmit data using radio frequency (RF) signals. What you may not know is that these signals don't suddenly stop when they get out of range; they simply weaken as you get further away from the transmitter.

If your 802.11n router has a theoretical 230-foot range, its signals don't go dead when you get 231 feet away. Instead, the network's data-transfer rate decreases as the signal strength decreases over distance. Get 240 or 250 feet away from that 230-foot router, and you're likely to find your transfer rate decreasing from 450Mbps to 300Mbps or even 150Mbps. It's not an immediate drop off; it's something more gradual.

Wireless range can also be affected by geography. That is, if your wireless router or the wireless device you're using is located too near the ground, you may experience lower-than-expected signal strength. For that matter, locating a router or device too close to other electronic equipment, including older CRT computer monitors, can also reduce the transmission range.

 TIP If you're experiencing difficulty connecting distant devices to your network, try locating the router up higher and away from other electronics. You want to provide more of a straight shot from your wireless devices to your router.

Upgrading to a More Powerful Router

If you have an established network with an older router, you may be able to fix your range problems with a new router. In particular, 802.11g routers have an average indoor range of about 125 feet. Newer 802.11n routers have an average indoor range of 230 feet. Upgrading to a newer router will almost double your effective network range.

If you have an older 802.11g router that isn't delivering a strong enough signal at long distances, try upgrading to an 802.11n model. Just make sure that all of your wireless devices—your notebook PC, Wi-Fi-enabled mobile phone, and wireless adapters connected to desktop PCs—are capable of receiving 802.11n signals; otherwise, they'll still be limited to the shorter 802.11g range.

Here's another thing: Not all 802.11n routers are created equal. Some 802.11n routers have a longer range than do others. (Typically, it's the less expensive routers that have a shorter range.) Compare the specs of one router to those of another; you may find that upgrading to a higher end router will give you the needed range boost.

Connecting a More Powerful Antenna

If you're receiving a weak signal over your wireless network, you can try boosting that signal. This is most commonly done by replacing your router's existing antenna with a larger, more powerful one.

 NOTE Most replacement antennas work only with 2.4GHz wireless networks. If you're utilizing the 5GHz frequency in a 802.11n or 802.11ac network, make sure a given antenna supports 5GHz Wi-Fi.

Now, you probably can't do this if your router has an internal antenna—unless there's an "antenna" connector on the back of the unit. But, if your router has one or more external antennas, you should be able to unscrew them and replace them with larger, high-gain models, like the one shown in Figure 8.1.

FIGURE 8.1

ALFA Network's APA05 booster antenna. (Photo courtesy of ALFA Network.)

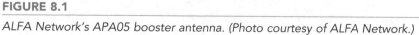

You can find replacement antennas from a number of different companies, including ALFA Network (www.alfa.com.tw) and Hawking Technology (www.hawkingtech.com). Many router manufacturers also offer higher-gain antennas for their products.

Connecting a Wireless Range Extender

Another approach to extending wireless network range is to boost the signal when it starts to drop off. This is accomplished by means of a *wireless range extender* (sometimes called a *repeater*), which you position somewhere between your wireless router and the farthest wireless adapter or device in your home.

A wireless range extender is essentially a "repeater" device that takes the original Wi-Fi signal and bounces it further down the line. The extender does not physically connect to any computer or to your main router; it only needs AC power and to be in range of the main wireless router.

For example, if you have your router at one end of a large house and a notebook PC way at the other end, install a range extender somewhere in the middle of the house. The extender will receive a still-strong wireless signal from the router and then re-transmit it from there, effectively doubling the range of the original signal. (Figure 8.2 shows how this works.)

In practice, then, a range extender functions as both a wireless adapter (to receive the original signal) and a wireless router (to re-transmit the signal). Installing a range extender is relatively simple, although not as simple as adding a booster antenna; there's some network configuration stuff you have to do.

Most networking-equipment companies offer range extenders, such as the one shown in Figure 8.3, typically under U.S. $100. Some (but certainly not all) extenders include one or more Ethernet connections, so you can establish wired connections to devices that aren't close to your main router.

 CAUTION   Make sure that your wireless range extender matches the Wi-Fi protocol used by your wireless router. You don't want to use a 802.11g extender with an 802.11n router or a single-band extender with a dual-band router.

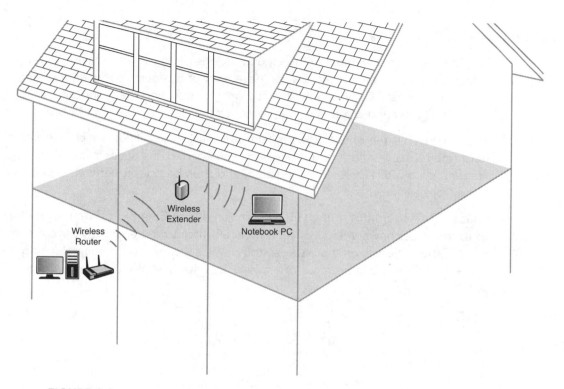

FIGURE 8.2

A network in a large house that requires the use of a wireless extender.

FIGURE 8.3

Linksys' RE1000 802.11n wireless range extender. (Photo courtesy of Linksys by Cisco.)

Connecting a Second Wireless Router

Sometimes, even a wireless range extender doesn't do the job. Maybe your house is just really, really big, or maybe you have a lot of obstacles between the router and your wireless PCs. Whatever the reason, you may find that your only solution is to install a second wireless router, closer to the other end of your house.

This approach is the one used by most hotels and large offices, which need at least one router per floor of the building. You connect the second router to the first one via a wired Ethernet connection, and then broadcast network signals wirelessly from each router.

That's right—to go this route, you have to run a long Ethernet cable from router 1 to router 2, as shown in Figure 8.4. Almost all wireless routers today have a number of Ethernet ports on the back, so the physical connection is easy. Running the cable, however, might be more of a hassle, but that's what you have to do.

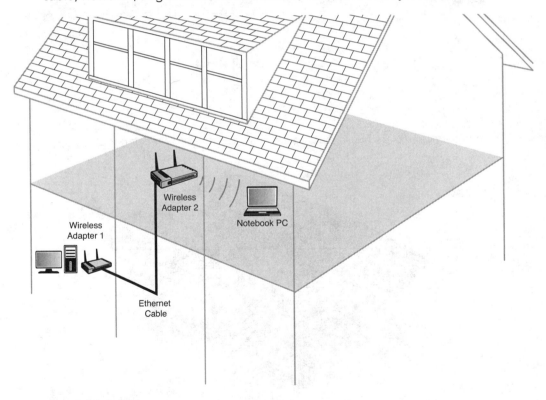

FIGURE 8.4

Connecting two routers together to cover a large range.

Once you have the two routers physically connected to each other, the tricky part of this approach is configuring things so that your PCs and other network devices see only one network, not multiple networks from multiple routers. Here's what you have to do.

First, get your main router set up and configured as you like it. That means, of course, giving the router a unique name (SSID) and network password.

Next, install and configure the second router per the manufacturer's instructions. This should include connecting the Ethernet cable from the first router to the second one. As part of this setup, you'll give the second router its own SSID, which is different from that of the first router.

With this initial setup complete, disconnect the second router from the first one and launch the router's manual configuration utility. You now want to change the SSID of the second router to that of the first; that is, you want both routers to have an identical SSID. So, if your first router's SSID is "My Main Router," you want to assign the second router's SSID "My Main Router," too.

You also want the second router to have the same network password assigned to the first router. Effectively, you want your wireless devices to be indifferent as to which router they connect to. A device should connect to the nearest router and, thus, receive the strongest possible signal.

To keep the two routers from interfering with each other, however, you need to assign the second router a unique static IP address. Otherwise, it's possible (likely, actually) that both routers will try to use the same IP address, and thus knock each other off your Internet connection. So, you need to manually assign an IP address to the second router.

Save your changes and then reconnect the Ethernet cable from the first router to the second one. You should now have one big, happy wireless network, broadcast from two different wireless routers. Any computer or wireless device in your household should connect to whichever router is nearest; they see both routers as a single network.

THE ABSOLUTE MINIMUM

Here are the key points to remember from this chapter:

- If wireless devices are too far away from your wireless router, they may receive weak or no network signal.

- If you're using an older 802.11g router, you can effectively double your network range by upgrading to a newer 802.11n model.

- Additional range boost can come from replacing your router's stock antenna with a more powerful booster antenna.

- To cover even more distance, install a wireless range extender at the far end of your current router's range.

- To cover large distances, run an Ethernet cable to a second wireless router and assign that router the same SSID and password as the first.

CONNECTING DEVICES VIA ETHERNET

Even though we're talking about wireless networks in this book, not all devices on your network should be connected wirelessly. A wired (Ethernet) connection makes more sense if you want the maximum possible speed, or if you're networking particularly sensitive data.

What is this Ethernet thing, then, and how does it work? If anything, networking via Ethernet is even easier than connecting via Wi-Fi; in most instances, getting up and running is as simple as connecting an Ethernet cable to your computer or other devices and letting your PC's operating system do the rest.

How Ethernet Works

As you're no doubt aware by now, Ethernet is a network-cabling protocol that enables you to connect computers and other devices to wired hubs and routers. The Ethernet protocol was developed by Xerox, DEC, and Intel, and it's been in widespread use for the better part of three decades. It is a tried-and-proven technology.

Speeds Vary

As you learned in Chapter 1, "How Networks Work," there are three different Ethernet protocols, each capable of transmitting data at different speeds. Table 9.1 outlines the differences, but if maximum speed is your need, you'll want to go with the fastest Gigabit Ethernet, which transmits data at a blazing 1Gbs. (That's 1,000Mbps, in case you misplaced your slide rule—or, if you want to get technical, exactly 1,024Mbps. There's rounding involved.)

TABLE 9.1 Ethernet Speeds

Protocol	Speed (Mbps)
Gigabit Ethernet	1,024
Fast Ethernet	100
10Base-T Ethernet	10

Ethernet Routers

What Ethernet does is transmit digital signals from one device to another over the network. Or, more accurately, it transmits signals from each connected device to the central network router or hub. The router does as its name implies—it routes data packets from one network computer to another, as shown in Figure 9.1.

NOTE In wired-network terms, a *router* (sometimes called a *broadband router*) is used to both manage your LAN and connect it to the Internet. A simpler *network switch* or *network hub* only connects local devices together in a network; it cannot connect your network to the larger network we call the Internet.

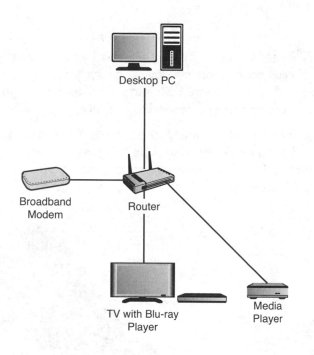

FIGURE 9.1

A typical Ethernet network.

This wired network router can be a freestanding device, like the one in Figure 9.2, or part of the package you get with a wireless router. That is, Ethernet-only routers function as a hub for wired devices, without any wireless access point functionality; a wireless router, on the other hand, combines a wired network router with a wireless access point, providing four or more Ethernet connections in addition to the Wi-Fi transmitter/receiver.

FIGURE 9.2

D-Link's EBR-2310 Ethernet Broadband Router. (Photo courtesy of D-Link.)

NIC's Picks

The network router serves as the central hub of your Ethernet network. On the other end of each connection is a device, typically a computer, with its own Ethernet port. That port can be built into a device (as it is with most desktop or notebook computers today) or added to a device, either internally or externally.

To add internal Ethernet capability to a computer, you have to install a network interface card (NIC) inside the system unit. Figure 9.3 shows a typical NIC; in most instances, installation is as simple as inserting the card into an open expansion slot inside the computer.

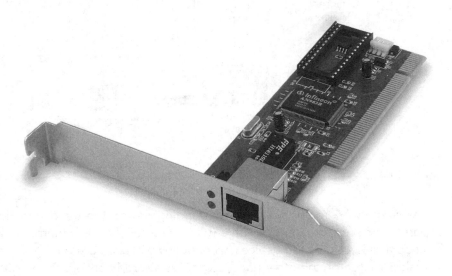

FIGURE 9.3

A generic NIC—before installation.

You can also go with external Ethernet adapters, such as the one shown in Figure 9.4. These units connect to your PC via USB, which is a lot easier to deal with than opening up your PC's system unit. (It's also the only way to add Ethernet to a notebook or tablet PC; you can't open up those babies like you can desktop PCs.)

FIGURE 9.4

An external USB-to-Ethernet adapter from Apple. (Courtesy of Apple.)

Cable Time

To connect a NIC to a network router, you use an Ethernet cable, like the one shown in Figure 9.5. This type of cable, sometimes called a Category 5 (or Cat-5) cable, looks a little like an old-school telephone cable, but with a slightly larger connector (called an RJ-45 connector) at either end. Inside the cable are eight smaller cables twisted into four pairs, which is why a Cat-5 cable is sometimes called a *twisted-pair* cable (lots of different names for the same thing).

FIGURE 9.5

A twisted-pair Ethernet cable.

NOTE Why are the wires inside of an Ethernet cable twisted together? To protect against interference and noise, of course. When two wires are wrapped around each other, they cancel out each other's noise.

By the way, there's also a newer type of Ethernet cable, dubbed Category 6 (or Cat-6). Cat-6 cables have the same connectors on either end, but can handle twice the bandwidth of the older Cat-5 cables. For most home networks, Cat-5 is just fine; however, if you want to future-proof your network for any coming technologies, feel free to go with Cat-6. Physically, the cables are interchangeable.

Unlike USB or HDMI cables, you can run Ethernet cables over a fairly long distance—up to 300 feet or so. (Past that distance, you can connect two cables with an Ethernet switch.) The rewards, in terms of speed and security, may be worth it—as we'll discuss next.

When an Ethernet Connection Makes Sense

Connecting wirelessly to a network is the utmost of convenience; no wires to run, nothing to physically connect, just click your mouse or tap your screen, enter a password, and you're forever connected. Connecting via Ethernet, on the other hand, is anything but convenient; you have to run those Ethernet cables through your walls and ceilings or along your baseboards, and then try to make them as unobtrusive as possible.

Why, then, would you want to connect something via Ethernet when you could more easily connect it via Wi-Fi? There are three possible reasons: you need the speed, you need the reliability, or you need the security.

Speed Matters

When it comes to ensuring the fastest possible speed over your network, nothing beats Ethernet. (Well, Gigabit Ethernet, anyway.) The fastest 802.11n Wi-Fi network is less than half as fast as a 1GB Ethernet connection, and even the new 802.11ac standard is only *theoretically* as fast as wired Ethernet.

NOTE In reality, most wireless connections are somewhat slower than the theoretical maximums, due to distance, interference, and such.

So when you need the speed, Ethernet is the way to go. Consider Ethernet, then, for any or all of the following tasks:

- Streaming video

- Downloading or uploading large files, such as video, high-resolution digital photos, or big PowerPoint presentations

- Playing high-performance real-time online games

Not that you *have* to go Ethernet with any of these tasks, but you will experience faster performance if you do.

Reliability Matters

In addition, the speed you get from an Ethernet connection is reliable speed. Wi-Fi, let's be honest, can have its hotspots and cold spots in any given house; metal objects can obstruct the signal, electrical devices can interfere with it, and distance can degrade it. That won't happen when your signal is moving through Ethernet cabling; the data courses through that cable at 1 gigabit per second, and nothing will stop it or delay it.

Security Matters

Ethernet also creates a more secure network than you get with Wi-Fi. Although there are ways to secure a wireless network from outside intrusion, those methods are not foolproof; you are, after all, broadcasting your data over the public air-waves, and those signals can be intercepted.

Keeping your data off the air makes it more secure. When your data moves only over the cables that are inside the walls of your house, there's really no way for someone to break in and steal that data. There's a reason why big corporations and banks use Ethernet-only networks; they don't trust their data to be transmitted over the air.

So, if you deal in extremely secure data—big financial dealings, corporate secrets, CIA black ops, and the like—disconnect that wireless router and keep your data secured via an Ethernet connection.

 CAUTION   Even if you have a completely wired network, your data can still be intercepted at the point you connect your network to the external Internet. For ultimate security, keep your LAN thoroughly local—and sever all connections to the outside world.

There's No Wireless Option

Some of the devices you want to connect to your network may not have Wi-Fi capability. I've found that some Internet-capable audio/video receivers, televisions, and Blu-ray players, for example, come with only Ethernet ports and no built-in Wi-Fi. If that's the case, guess how you'll be connecting. (It won't be wirelessly….)

In addition, Ethernet is the way to go if you can't establish a reliable wireless signal to a given device. For example, if you just can't get a fast connection to a computer located in your basement or the far end of your house, string some Ethernet cable instead.

Connecting via Ethernet to a Wireless Network

Connecting via Ethernet to a Wi-Fi network is one of the easiest things you can do in this networked world. Pretty much all you have to do is connect one end of an Ethernet cable to the device's Ethernet port, and the other end of the cable to an Ethernet port on the back of your wireless router. (Virtually all wireless routers include a handful of Ethernet ports just for this purpose.)

 TIP   If you're connecting more than one device via Ethernet, label both ends of each cable so you'll know which device is connected to which cable.

This only becomes complicated if the device you're connecting via Ethernet also has built-in wireless capability. In this instance, you'll need to deactivate the device's wireless connectivity. (Or, in the case of a device with an external Wi-Fi adapter, disconnect the adapter.) If you don't deactivate the wireless functionality, the device may try to connect via Wi-Fi instead of Ethernet, which is not what you want.

 NOTE   Some computers and wireless devices let you turn off the built-in Wi-Fi by flipping a switch or pressing a keyboard shortcut. Other computers may require you to enter the operating system's network settings to deactivate the wireless adapter. (Learn more about these settings in Chapter 11, "Connecting Home Computers.")

Most devices you connect via Ethernet will automatically detect the new network connection and perform any necessary configuration automatically. Other devices may need to be configured for the new Ethernet connection. Follow the instructions for your particular device.

THE ABSOLUTE MINIMUM

Here are the key points to remember from this chapter:

- Ethernet is a cabled network-connection technology that utilizes twisted-pair cable over distances up to 300 feet.

- Gigabit Ethernet is faster and more consistent than current Wi-Fi connections, making it a viable option for streaming video and downloading large data files.

- An Ethernet connection is also more secure than a wireless connection, and thus ideal for private or sensitive information.

- If your network device has a built-in Ethernet port, connecting to your network is as simple as running an Ethernet cable between your device and your wireless router, which should have a handful of Ethernet ports on the back.

10

SECURING DEVICES ON YOUR NETWORK

A wireless network is particularly vulnerable to intrusion. Not only do you have the expected gateway to the Internet, where all sorts of malware and attacks can enter (even on wired networks), the wireless signal itself can be intercepted and your data observed or stolen.

What you need to do, then, is secure your network from intrusion and attack, by whatever means possible. Fortunately, there are several things you can—and should—do in this regard.

Facing the Potential Dangers of Wireless Networking

One of the issues with a wireless network is that all of your data is just out there, broadcast over the air via radio waves, for anyone to grab. When you connect your computer to a network or the Internet, not only can your PC access other computers, but other computers can also access *your* PC. Unless you take precautions, malicious hackers and crackers (other network users, individuals on the Internet, or even someone with a Wi-Fi receiver driving by your neighborhood) can access your PC and steal important data, delete files and folders, or use your computer (via remote control) to attack other computers.

 NOTE   A *hacker* is someone who finds weaknesses in computer systems and networks, often for fun. A *cracker* is a hacker who exploits the weaknesses found, either for profit or to do harm.

Different Types of Intrusions

Your PC can be attacked in several different ways. These different types of attacks—more accurately called *intrusions*—include the following:

- **Data theft.** In this type of intrusion, the attacker steals valuable data stored on your computer—user names, passwords, credit-card numbers, bank-account numbers, and so on. This can lead to the crime known as *identity theft*, where the person who stole your data uses that information to impersonate you online, using your personal and financial data to steal money from your bank account, use your credit card to make large purchases, and even use your Social Security number to establish a false identity.

- **Data destruction.** This type of intrusion is damaging, because after the attacker gains access to your computer, he starts deleting things. The attacker deletes data files, program files, even the system files necessary to keep your computer up and running.

- **Denial of service (DoS).** A DoS attack is designed to crash your system, typically by inundating it with hundreds and thousands of electronic requests from other computers on the Internet. As your system receives more and more of these requests, it begins to slow, then crawls to a halt. (To be fair, DoS attacks are typically aimed at larger public websites, not home networks.)

- **Hijacking.** Many attackers don't want to do harm to your PC, but rather to use your PC to do harm to other computer systems or websites. In a hijacking attack, the attacker surreptitiously installs backdoor software on your PC, so that he can operate it via remote control. With your PC under his control, the attacker then uses it—and thousands of other "zombie" computers—to initiate a larger denial of service attack on another system, or to send out thousands of spam messages.

- **Signal leeching.** This intrusion isn't an attack per se, but rather a theft of services—in particular, your Internet connection. If your wireless network is configured for public access, with no security key or password required, anyone with a wireless PC in range of your wireless router can tap into your network and your wireless Internet connection. Although this type of intrusion causes no immediate harm to your computer or network, it does steal part of your Internet bandwidth—which you're paying for.

How to Tell If Your Network Has Been Breached

What are the signs that your network is under attack or has been otherwise compromised? Here are some behaviors to look out for:

- On a PC, an unusual amount of hard disk activity—especially when the computer isn't being used.

- An unusual amount of Internet access—especially when you're accessing the web yourself.

- Your Internet connection appears to slow down, taking longer to load web pages and download files.

- Missing or edited files on your hard disk.

- Unusual behavior—lots of pop-up windows, programs launching of their own accord, sluggish performance, and the like.

How to Protect Your PC from Intrusion

If the threat of unwanted intrusion scares you, that's good—you should be scared. Fortunately, you can do several things to reduce your risk of attack and minimize the impact if an intrusion does occur.

The key to protecting a network is to create as many obstacles as possible for a potential cracker. Although no network can be 100 percent secure, the more effort an attacker has to make, the more likely he'll give up and try a network that's easier to break into.

So, how can you protect against unauthorized access to your wireless network? By using a little common sense, along with enabling basic security procedures, including

- Activate the wireless security technology built into your Wi-Fi router. This wireless security, in the form of encrypted or password access, should keep all but the most dedicated hackers from accessing your wireless network.

- Change the default password for your wireless router. (You'd be surprised how many wireless networks can be accessed by entering the default password "password.")

- Change the default network name (SSID) of your wireless access router.

- Disable broadcast SSID function on your wireless router (if possible), so that the name of your network isn't publically broadcast to the world at large.

- Physically locate your wireless router toward the center of your home or office—not near the windows, where it can extend the range of your network well outside your building.

- Install and activate a firewall program on every computer on your home network to block attacks from outside your network.

- Install and regularly update anti-virus and anti-spyware utilities on each of the computers on your network.

- Deactivate file sharing on your PCs, so attackers won't be able to access your personal files.

- Make regular backup copies of your important data—just in case.

We discuss most of these steps throughout this chapter.

Protecting Against Internet Intrusions with a Firewall

There are two main points from which intruders can infiltrate a wireless network: via the network's wireless signal and via the network's gateway to the Internet. We'll talk about stopping wireless intrusion in a moment, but first, we focus on stopping the bad guys from getting into your system from the Internet.

The best way to protect your system against Internet-based attack is to block the path of attack with a *firewall*. A firewall is either a piece of hardware or a software program that forms a virtual barrier between your computer and the Internet. The firewall selectively filters the data that is passed between both ends of the connection and protects your system against outside attack.

OS-Based Firewalls

If your computers are running Microsoft Windows, pretty much any version, you already have a firewall built into the operating system. This firewall, imaginatively dubbed the Windows Firewall, is activated by default, which is a good thing. Although you can deactivate it if you want, it's better to just leave it on and let it do its thing.

Similarly, Apple includes the Application Firewall utility in its Mac OS operating system. If you're using a Mac, leave the Application Firewall on for best protection.

Using Third-Party Firewall Software

For most users, the Windows Firewall or Mac Application Firewall is more than enough protection against computer attacks. That said, there are also a number of third-party firewall programs you can employ, most of which are more robust and offer more protection than either of the firewalls built into Windows and the Mac OS. Some of these programs are freestanding firewalls, others offer firewall functionality as part of a more inclusive security suite.

The best of these programs include

- Agnitum Outpost Pro Firewall ($39.95, www.agnitum.com)
- Comodo Firewall (free, personalfirewall.comodo.com)
- Norton Internet Security ($79.99, www.symantec.com)
- ZoneAlarm Free Firewall (free, www.zonelabs.com)
- ZoneAlarm Pro Firewall ($29.95, www.zonelabs.com)

Using Router-Based Firewalls

Most wireless and Ethernet-only routers include their own internal firewalls. These router-based firewalls block any computer outside your network from accessing computers inside the network; the router itself functions as the firewall, as shown in Figure 10.1.

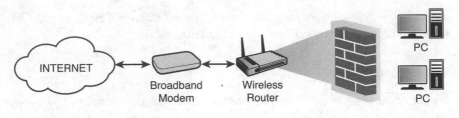

FIGURE 10.1

How a router-based firewall works.

What a router-based firewall does *not* do is protect any computer or device on your network from improperly accessing other devices on the network. So, while your router will keep outsiders from getting in, you'll still need computer-based firewall utilities to protect each individual computer from unauthorized access from other users on your network.

 NOTE   To protect other users from accessing files on a given computer, you need to turn off file sharing for that computer—or at least limit sharing to specified users. Learn more in Chapter 11, "Connecting Home Computers."

Enabling Wireless Security on Your Router

If you have a 100 percent wired network, a firewall is just about all you need to block unauthorized outside access. But, if you have a wireless network (and you do, or you wouldn't be reading this book), you still need to take precautions against unauthorized RF signal intrusion or interception.

This extra layer of precaution is necessary, because when you're transmitting network signals via radio waves, anyone within range can receive your signals. You need to secure those signals to keep outsiders from listening in or breaking in to your network.

 CAUTION   Without some form of wireless security, anyone with a nearby wireless device can tap into your wireless network. At the very least, they can steal bandwidth from your Internet connection. Worst case, they might be able to access the personal files stored on your computers.

To keep outsiders from tapping into your wireless network, you can assign to your network a fairly complex encryption code, called a *network key*, via your wireless router's configuration settings. To access your network, a device must know the code—which, unless it's officially part of your network, it won't.

Fortunately, all wireless routers today come with built-in wireless security. It's a relatively easy matter to enable this security during your router's initial setup procedure, or at any later time.

Different Types of Wireless Security

There are four primary types of wireless security in use today. All these security protocols require the use of a network key. This network key may be generated automatically by your wireless router, or you may have to specify the key by typing it yourself during the configuration process. The longer the network key, the more powerful the encryption—and the more secure your wireless network will be.

The four types of wireless security include the following, with the most secure listed first:

- **WPA2.** WPA stands for Wi-Fi Protected Access, and the new WPA2 standard offers the strongest level of security available today. With WPA2 (and the older WPA standard), network keys are automatically changed on a regular basis.

- **WPA.** This is the older, slightly less secure version of Wi-Fi Protected Access security.

- **WEP 128-bit.** WEP stands for Wired Equivalent Privacy. There are two levels of WEP protection: the stronger 128-bit and the weaker 64-bit.

- **WEP 64-bit.** This is the weakest level of wireless protection available. If you have an older (re: ancient) laptop PC or wireless adapter, you may have to use this level of protection instead of WEP 128-bit or WPA/WPA2.

 NOTE WPA2 is supported by most wireless equipment sold in the past few years.

You should choose the highest level of protection supported by all the equipment on your network—your wireless router, wireless PCs, smartphones, and so forth. If just one piece of equipment doesn't support a higher level of security, you have to switch to the next highest level; the security level you choose has to fit the lowest common denominator, as defined by the wireless equipment in use.

So, if your wireless router and all of your wireless devices support WPA2 encryption (and they probably do), you should switch to that method because it provides the strongest protection. Otherwise, choose either WPA, WEP 128-bit (preferred), or WEP 64-bit encryption—in that order.

Configuring Your Network for Wireless Security

To set the wireless security for your network and assign network keys, you can use the setup utility that came with your wireless router. Some routers come with a default passkey assigned, which you can then change at any later time; other routers require you to enter your own passkey. However it works, enter a password or password phrase of sufficient length and complexity to ensure the maximum security—but be sure you can also easily remember it.

 CAUTION   You can also write down your wireless passphrase, but make sure that you keep that piece of paper well hidden—otherwise, someone could break into your home to steal your password and gain network access.

Limiting Access to Your Network

Enabling wireless security for your network is a good first step. There's more you can do, however, to both hide and protect your network from unwanted intruders.

Changing the Router's SSID

As you know, every wireless network has a name, otherwise known as its SSID (Service Set Identifier). The SSID is assigned by your wireless router.

Many router companies use their company names as the default SSID. For example, a Linksys router might have a SSID labeled "LINKSYS." This type of common SSID could give your network the same name as other wireless networks in your neighborhood, which makes it easy for hackers to locate (and then gain access) to your network.

Fortunately, most router manufacturers have gotten smarter about this and now create random SSIDs for the equipment they sell. Although a random SSID is better than a generic one, you probably still want to override this default SSID and assign a more unique name to your wireless network. It's going to be tougher for a hacker to guess that your network is named "GREATWHALEINABOTTLE-9057" than if it was generically named "LINKSYS."

You should be able to change the SSID from your router's configuration utility, as discussed in Chapter 6, "Installing a Wireless Router." If you're not sure how to do this, refer to your router's instruction manual.

CAUTION If you change your SSID after you set up or connect other computers and devices on your network, you need to reconfigure all of them to find and use the new SSID.

Changing the Password

Along the same lines, you should also change the default password for accessing your network. Most routers come from the factory with a simple network password assigned—often, the password is "PASSWORD." (Although, as with SSIDs, many manufacturers now randomly generate this password.)

As you might suspect, it's relatively easy for a hacker to access a network if the default password is still in use. So, when you go to change the router's SSID, also change the password to something more difficult to crack.

You see, the longer and more complex your password is, the harder it is crack. All you need to do is increase the password's length (8 characters is better than 6—and way better than 4) and use a combination of letters, numbers, and special characters (such as !, @, #, $, and %). You should also use a combination of uppercase and lowercase letters, if your router lets you use case-sensitive passwords. (Most do.)

You also need to be smart about the passwords you create. Avoid using real words that you might find in a typical dictionary; any standard dictionary cracker will crack that password faster than it takes you to type it. Also, don't use easily guessed words, like your middle name, your wife's maiden name, or the name of your pet. It's better to use nonsense words or random combinations or letters and numbers—anything that won't be found in a dictionary.

CAUTION As tempting as it is to use the same password for multiple devices and websites (I know, I have too many passwords to remember, too), each function that requires a password should receive its own unique password. You don't want a cracker to obtain one password and then be able to break into multiple accounts or devices.

Most importantly, remember that your password should never be shared—with anyone. As blatantly obvious as that sounds, many people feel no compunction about providing guests with their network passwords; after all, what's the harm of letting your Uncle Jim access the Internet while he's visiting?

The problem is that if Uncle Jim has access to the Internet, it's through your network—which also means he has access to all the unsecured computers and data on your network, too. Although Uncle Jim might be trustworthy (or not—you know your relatives better than I do), the risk is that someone else will get your password from your Uncle, by hook or by crook. The fewer people who know your network password, the better.

This is why I like the option of setting up a separate "guest" account for your network, which many routers now let you do. You can let Uncle Jim access this guest account, either with or without a (different) password, and all Jim can access is the Internet; the guest account is blocked from the rest of your network. It's the best of both worlds for both you and Uncle Jim.

 TIP   You should change your password with some regularity, so that any cracked password has a short shelf life.

Disabling SSID Broadcasting

Most wireless routers, by default, constantly broadcast the network's SSID, so that all nearby wireless devices will know that the network is there and ready to be connected to. The downside of this is that when an SSID is broadcast, anyone with a notebook PC or smartphone receives notice of your network's name—which makes your network a more obvious target for hackers.

For this reason, you can configure your router to disable SSID broadcasting. If the SSID is not broadcast, your wireless network will be less visible to outsiders. When a hacker doesn't immediately see your network on his list of nearby wireless networks, he'll likely find another network to tap into.

As with changing the SSID, you should be able to turn off SSID broadcasting from your router's configuration utility.

 CAUTION   When you disable SSID broadcasting, your own wireless devices won't be able to see your network in the list of available networks, either. This means you'll have to enter the SSID manually when you initially go to connect.

Protecting Against Malware

Someone breaking into your network isn't the only thing you have to worry about. There's also the risk of your networked devices contracting a computer virus or spyware infection—both of which can be damaging.

NOTE At present, most malware affects only personal computers, not smartphones, tablets, and other devices. That's not to say that some enterprising youth won't someday devise spyware for phones and tablets, but that's not where the bulk of the problem is today.

Understanding Viruses and Spyware

Computer viruses and spyware are two different types of malicious software programs—what we call *malware*. Although these are two different types of infections, they're both to be avoided.

A *computer virus* is a malicious software program designed to do damage to a computer system by deleting files or even taking over a PC to launch attacks on other systems. A virus attacks your computer when you launch an infected software program, launching a "payload" that oftentimes is catastrophic. You want to avoid virus infections at all costs—and cleanse viruses from your system if it happens to become infected.

Similar to but slightly different from computer viruses is a type of malicious program called *spyware*. This type of malware installs itself on your computer and then surreptitiously sends information about the way you use your PC to some interested third party. Although spyware is not technically a computer virus, having spyware infect your system is almost as bad as being infected with a virus. Some spyware programs will even hijack your computer and launch pop-up windows and advertisements when you visit certain web pages. If there's spyware on your computer, you definitely want to get rid of it.

NOTE Spyware typically gets installed in the background when you're installing another program. One of the biggest sources of spyware are peer-to-peer music-trading networks (*not* legitimate online music stores, such as the iTunes Store); when you install the file-trading software, the spyware is also installed.

Practicing Safe Computing

How do you protect your computers against computer viruses and spyware? The only surefire way to avoid infection is to disconnect each individual computer from your network and from the Internet, and never introduce any shared media (USB memory drives, CDs, external hard drives, and so on) into your system. That's right—the only guaranteed prevention against malware is total isolation.

Because you're not going to completely isolate your computer from the outside world, you'll never be 100 percent safe from the threat of computer viruses and spyware. There are, however, some steps you can take to reduce your risk:

- Don't open email attachments from people you don't know—or even from people you *do* know, if you aren't expecting them. Most viruses today are transmitted via infected email attachments—and some viruses can hijack the address book on an infected PC, thus sending out infected email that the owner isn't even aware of.

- Don't accept any files sent to you via instant messaging or on social networks.

- Download files only from reliable file archive websites, such as Download.com (download.cnet.com) and Tucows (www.tucows.com), not from anonymous downloading or peer-to-peer file sharing sites.

- Don't visit peer-to-peer file sharing or BitTorrent sites, and don't install file sharing software.

- Don't execute programs you find posted to web message boards, blogs, or Usenet newsgroups.

- Don't click links sent to you from strangers via instant messaging or in a chat room.

- Don't click links that appear in unexpected pop-up windows—even (and especially) if these windows appear to be warnings that your system is infected with a computer virus. (That's an old trick!)

- Share USB drives, disks, and files only with users you know and trust.

- Use anti-virus and anti-spyware software.

These precautions—especially the first one about not opening email attachments—should provide good insurance against the threat of computer viruses.

Using Anti-Virus Software

One of the primary lines of defense against computer viruses is to install an anti-virus software program on each computer in your network. Anti-virus programs are capable of detecting known viruses and protecting your system against new, unknown viruses. These programs check your system for viruses each time your system is booted and can be configured to check any programs you download from the Internet. They're also used to disinfect your system if it becomes infected with a virus.

NOTE Pricing for most anti-virus software is actually for a one-year subscription. You'll end up paying this amount every year to keep the software and its virus definitions up to date.

The most popular anti-virus programs include

- AVG AntiVirus Free (free, www.avg.com)

- AVG AntiVirus ($39.99, www.avg.com)

- Kaspersky Anti-Virus ($59.95, www.kaspersky.com)

- McAfee AntiVirus Plus ($49.99, www.mcafee.com)

- Microsoft Security Essentials (free for Windows Vista/7 PCs, windows.microsoft. com/en-US/windows/products/security-essentials)

- Norton AntiVirus ($49.99, www.norton.com)

- Trend Micro Titanium AntiVirus+ ($39.95, www.trendmicro.com)

- ZoneAlarm Free Antivirus+Firewall (free, www.zonelabs.com)

- ZoneAlarm PRO Antivirus+Firewall ($29.95, www.zonelabs.com)

 NOTE Windows 8 has its own built-in anti-malware utility, called Windows Defender. This program is probably adequate for most users.

Whichever anti-virus program you choose, you'll need to go online periodically to update the virus definition database the program uses to look for known virus files. As new viruses are created every week, this file of known viruses must be updated accordingly. Remember this: Your anti-virus software is next to useless if you don't keep it updated. An outdated anti-virus program won't be capable of recognizing—and protecting against—the very latest computer viruses.

 CAUTION All these anti-virus programs do a good job—sometimes *too* good. I have personally had problems with Norton and McAfee anti-virus products being too aggressive in protecting my system, resulting in system slow downs and numerous program crashes. If you find your computer slowing down or freezing up after installing an anti-virus program, you may need to uninstall that program and try another.

Using Anti-Spyware Software

Unfortunately, many anti-virus programs won't catch spyware, because spyware isn't a virus; the inherent technology involved is different. To track down and uninstall spyware programs, you need to run an anti-spyware utility.

Here are some of the more popular anti-spyware programs:

- Ad-Aware Free Antivirus+ (free, www.lavasoftusa.com)
- Spybot Search & Destroy (free, www.safer-networking.org)
- Webroot SecureAnywhere ($39.99, www.webroot.com)

 TIP Some of the major Internet security suites also include anti-spyware modules. Check the program's feature list before you buy.

THE ABSOLUTE MINIMUM

Here are the key points to remember from this chapter:

- Wireless networks can be broken into via the wireless signal or via the gateway from the Internet.

- To stop Internet-based intrusions, install and activate firewall software on each of your personal computers; you should also activate your router's firewall functionality.

- To protect against a cracker breaking into your network's wireless signal, activate wireless security on your router—with WPA2 being the strongest protection.

- To further protect against unwanted identification and intrusion, change your router's default name (SSID) and password, and perhaps even hide the SSID.

- To protect against malware, install anti-virus and anti-spyware utilities on each of your networked computers.

CONNECTING HOME COMPUTERS

The wireless router is the central hub of a home network. To that router, you can connect any number of wireless devices—chief of which, for many people, are personal computers of both the desktop and notebook variety.

Just how do you connect your specific computer to your wireless network? Can you connect Windows and Mac PCs together? How can you configure your computers to share files and folders with other devices on the network?

These are all good and common questions, and this chapter answers them.

Connecting Computers to the Network

If you're connecting your computer via Ethernet, the process is as simple as plugging one end of an Ethernet cable into the Ethernet port on your computer and the other into a free Ethernet port on your router. After a few seconds, your computer recognizes your router's network and that's that; nothing else is required on your part.

Connecting wirelessly, however, is a tad more difficult. Not a big deal, but there is some interaction required on your part. And, to make things more challenging, that interaction differs, depending on what type of operating system your computer is running.

Connecting Windows 8 Computers

Windows 8 is the latest version of Microsoft's ubiquitous operating system. You can use touch gestures (if your PC has a touchscreen display) or good old mouse-based points and clicks to select the wireless network you want to use. Just follow these steps:

1. Display the Charms Bar and click or tap Settings to display the Settings panel.

2. Click or tap the Wi-Fi icon (typically labeled Available if you're not yet connected to a network) to display a list of available networks, as shown in Figure 11.1.

FIGURE 11.1

Selecting a wireless network in Windows 8.

3. Click or tap your wireless network.

4. To connect to this network automatically in the future, check the Connect Automatically option, and then click or tap Connect.

5. If prompted, enter the password (network security key) for your network, and then click or tap Next.

6. When prompted to turn on sharing and connect to other devices, select Yes.

That's it. You're now connected to your home network.

Connecting Windows 7 Computers

Windows 8 uses the new Start screen to access all apps and functions. Older versions of Windows use the traditional desktop with its Start button, Start menu, and taskbar—and on the taskbar, the aptly named Notification Area on the far right. This is where you go to connect to a wireless network in Windows 7.

1. Click the Network icon in the Notification Area of the taskbar; this displays a Jump List of available networks, as shown in Figure 11.2.

2. Select your network from this list and click the Connect button.

3. If prompted to enter your password or network key, do so.

FIGURE 11.2

Selecting a wireless network in Windows 7.

NOTE   If prompted to select a network location, click Home. Learn more about this in the section, "Setting a Network Location."

Connecting Windows Vista Computers

Connecting to a wireless network is slightly different if your computer is running the older Windows Vista operating system. Follow these steps:

1. Right-click the wireless network connection icon in the Notification Area of the taskbar, and then select Connect to a Network.

2. Windows displays the Connect to a Network dialog box, shown in Figure 11.3, which lists all wireless networks in the immediate vicinity. Select your new network, and then click the Connect button.

3. When prompted, enter your password or network key.

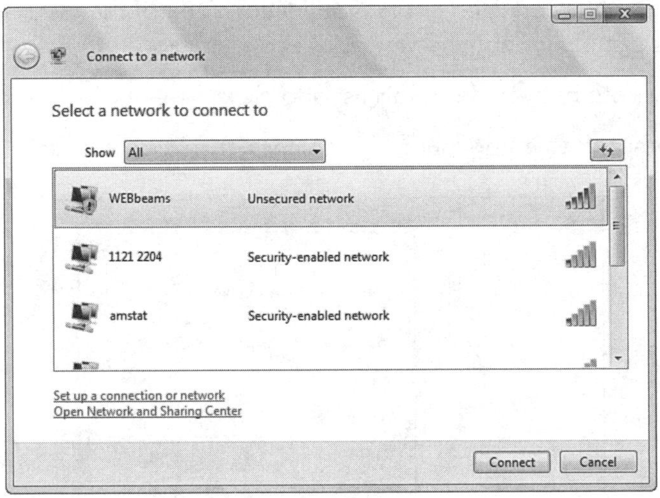

FIGURE 11.3

Selecting a wireless network in Windows Vista.

Connecting Windows XP Computers

Believe it or not, almost half of all PC users are still running Windows XP, even though that operating system is more than a decade old. If you're using an XP PC, selecting a wireless network is similar to how it works in the newer Windows Vista OS.

Follow these steps:

1. Right-click the wireless network connection icon in the Notification Area of the taskbar, and then select View Available Wireless Networks.

2. When the Connect to Wireless Network dialog box appears, go to the Available Networks section and click the network to which you want to connect.

3. When prompted, enter your password or network key, and then click Connect.

Connecting Macs

If you have a Mac, you know that Apple often does things differently than Microsoft. Fortunately, connecting your Mac to your wireless network is just as simple as connecting a Windows PC. Just follow these steps:

1. Click the Wi-Fi symbol on the toolbar at the top of the screen to display a list of available wireless networks.

2. Select your network from the list, as shown in Figure 11.4.

3. When prompted, enter the password for your network, and then click OK.

FIGURE 11.4

Selecting a wireless network on a Mac.

  NOTE   If your network is not password protected—and shame on you!—you'll be automatically connected without prompting for a password. Learn more about password protecting your network in Chapter 10, "Securing Devices on Your Network."

That's it—pretty much as simple as possible.

Dealing with Network Locations, Workgroups, and HomeGroups in Windows

Microsoft Windows has some networking options that are unique to that operating system. In particular, you'll need to set a network location and workgroup.

Setting a Network Location

When you're connecting to a wireless network in Windows, you're prompted to select a *network location*. This is important, because the option you select determines various file sharing and security settings for this particular network connection.

In this instance, "location" doesn't refer to an actual physical location, but describes a type of network—Home, Work, or Public. Each type of network has its own default security settings appropriate to the needs of that network type. Table 11.1 describes the three network location types.

TABLE 11.1 Network Location Types

Type of Location	Used For	Public or Private	Description
Home	Home networks	Private	Enables Network Discovery so you can see other network computers
			Enables file and folder sharing
			Configures Windows Firewall to allow programs and other communication
Work	Office networks	Private	Enables Network Discovery so you can see other network computers
			Enables file and folder sharing
			Configures Windows Firewall to allow programs and other communication
Public	Wi-Fi hotspots	Public	Disables Network Discovery
			Disables file and folder sharing
			Hides computer name from other nearby computers
			Configures Windows Firewall to block certain programs and services and protect your PC from unauthorized access

If you're connecting to a home network, choose Home; this configures all the settings necessary for normal home use. If, on the other hand, you're connecting to a small office network, select Work. (Both Home and Work use the same settings, for what it's worth.) You should only choose Public if you're connecting to a public Wi-Fi hotspot, such as those you find at coffeehouses and restaurants.

Selecting a Workgroup

In the world of Windows, a *workgroup* is a group of computers, all on the same network, that share common resources and functions. You can create multiple workgroups on a single network; not all computers on a network necessarily belong to the same workgroup.

By default, Windows assigns your computer to the workgroup that is imaginatively named **WORKGROUP**. It's easy enough to change to another workgroup, however. In older (pre-Win8) versions of Windows, open the Start menu, right-click the Computers item, and select Properties. (In Windows 8, go to the All Apps screen and right-click Computers.) Go to the Computer Name, Domain, and Workgroup Settings section, and click Change Settings. When the System Properties dialog box appears, select the Computer Name tab and click the Change button. The resulting dialog box lets you enter a new workgroup name.

 NOTE In Windows XP, the default workgroup name was MSHOME.

It's easy enough to access computers within your current workgroup; these PCs will automatically appear when you select Networks in Windows Explorer. You can also access computers in other workgroups, as all available workgroups should also be displayed in the Networks section of Windows Explorer. Just double-click a workgroup name to display all the computers within that workgroup.

Creating a Windows HomeGroup

In Windows 7 and Windows 8, you can create a special type of network called a *HomeGroup*. A HomeGroup is kind of a simplified network that lets you automatically share files and printers with other computers in the same HomeGroup.

To create a new HomeGroup in Windows 8, follow these steps:

1. Display the Charms Bar and click or tap Settings to display the Settings panel.

2. Click or tap Change PC Settings to display the PC Settings screen.

3. Scroll down the list on the left and select HomeGroup.

4. Click or tap the Create button.

5. When the next screen appears, go to the Library and Devices section and click or tap On those items you want to share with other computers. You can choose to share your Documents, Music, Pictures, Videos, or Printers and Devices.

6. If you want non-computers, such as network-connected TVs or video game consoles, to be able to access the content on this computer, scroll to the Media Devices section and click or tap "on" this option.

7. Scroll to the Membership section and write down the password. You need to provide this to users of other computers on your network who want to join your HomeGroup.

Creating a HomeGroup in Windows 7 is done from the Network and Sharing Center. Click Choose HomeGroup and Sharing Options, and then click Create a HomeGroup. On the next screen, check those types of items you want to share across your network, and then click Create New. Make sure that you write down the password, and then click Finish.

NOTE   Only PCs running Windows 7 and Windows 8 can be part of a HomeGroup. Your HomeGroup cannot contain PCs running Windows Vista or XP, nor any Apple Macs. Because most people have more of a mixed network, this makes the HomeGroup feature, while well intentioned, somewhat useless.

Configuring File and Printer Sharing

If your intent is to share the files and folders on a given computer with other PCs on your network, you'll need to enable file and folder sharing. Likewise, if you want to share a printer or other peripheral connected to a given computer, you'll want to enable printer sharing on that computer.

CAUTION   Be cautious about enabling the file-sharing feature on a given computer. When you allow a folder to be shared, any-one accessing your network can access the contents of the folder.

Enabling File and Printer Sharing in Windows 8

If your computer is running Windows 8, you had the opportunity to enable file and printer sharing when you first connected to your home network. If you didn't do it then, or need to change these settings later, you can manually configure Windows' sharing options.

Here's how to do it:

1. Right-click on the Start screen to display the Options bar.

2. Tap or click All Apps.

3. When the Apps screen appears, tap or click Control Panel (in the Windows System section).

4. When the Control Panel opens, click Network and Internet.

5. On the next screen, click Network and Sharing Center.

6. From the next screen, click Change Advanced Sharing Settings.

7. When the next screen appears, as shown in Figure 11.5, click the down arrow to open the Private section.

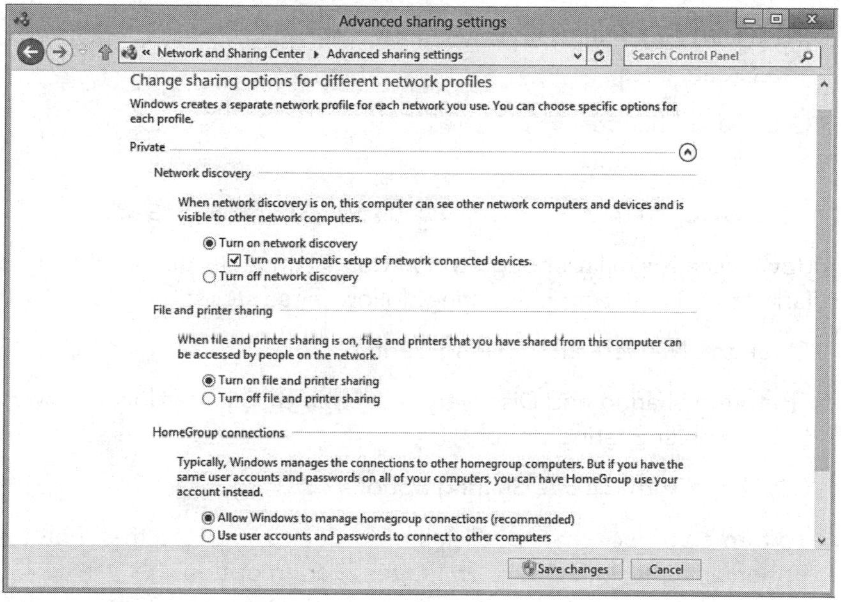

FIGURE 11.5

Enabling file and printer sharing in Windows 8.

8. Click Turn On File and Printer Sharing.

9. Click Save Changes.

 NOTE You only have to enable printer sharing for the computer to which the printer is physically connected. Once printer sharing is enabled on that PC, the printer will be visible from all other computers connected to your network.

Enabling File and Printer Sharing in Windows 7

For machines running Windows 7, activating file printer sharing is actually a little simpler, if only because it's easier to get to the Network and Sharing Center. Here's what you do:

1. Click the Network icon in the taskbar's Notification Area and select Open Network and Sharing Center.

2. From the Network and Sharing Center, click Choose HomeGroup and Sharing Options.

3. In the next window, click Change Advanced Sharing Options.

4. On the next screen, click the down arrow next to Home or Work.

5. Click Turn On File and Printer Sharing.

6. Click Turn On Sharing So Anyone with Network Access Can Open, Change, and Create Files.

7. Click Save Changes.

Enabling File and Printer Sharing in Windows Vista

Windows Vista is similar enough to Windows 7 that file/printer sharing activation is similarly easy. To turn on file sharing, follow these steps:

1. Open the Network and Sharing Center.

2. Go to the Sharing and Discovery section and click the down arrow next to the Public Folder Sharing option.

3. Check the Turn On File Sharing option.

4. To turn on printer sharing, click the down arrow next to the Printer Sharing option and check the Turn On Printer Sharing option.

Enabling File and Printer Sharing in Windows XP

Activating file and printer sharing on older Windows XP computers is a different process. With Windows XP, you can share files stored in the Shared Documents folder or in any other folder you specify. By default, file sharing is turned on for the Shared Documents folder; you have to manually activate file sharing for any other folder you want to use. You do this by following these steps:

1. Open My Computer and navigate to the folder that contains the file you want to share.

2. Right-click the folder icon and select Sharing and Security from the pop-up menu.

3. When the Properties dialog box appears, select the Sharing tab.

4. Check the Share This Folder on the Network option.

5. Click OK.

Enabling printer sharing is a completely different process. To do so, follow these steps:

1. Open the Control Panel and double-click Printers and Other Hardware.

2. Select View Installed Printers or Fax Printers.

3. When the Printers and Faxes window opens, select the printer that you want to share.

4. Click Share This Printer in the Printer Tasks panel.

5. When the printer Properties dialog box appears, select the Sharing tab and check the Share This Printer option.

6. Edit the name of the printer if you want, and then click OK.

Enabling File and Printer Sharing on a Mac

File and printer sharing on a Mac is equally easy to configure, even if that's a somewhat different experience than on a Windows PC. For example, to enable file sharing, follow these steps:

1. Open the System Preferences app from the dock.

2. From the System Preferences window, click Sharing.

3. When the Sharing dialog box appears, as shown in Figure 11.6, go to the Service list and click On the File Sharing option.

4. Below the Shared Folders list, click the Add (+) button.

5. You now see a list of devices and places. Find and select the folder(s) you want to share, and then click the Add button. (To select multiple folders, press and hold the Shift key while selecting folders with the mouse.)

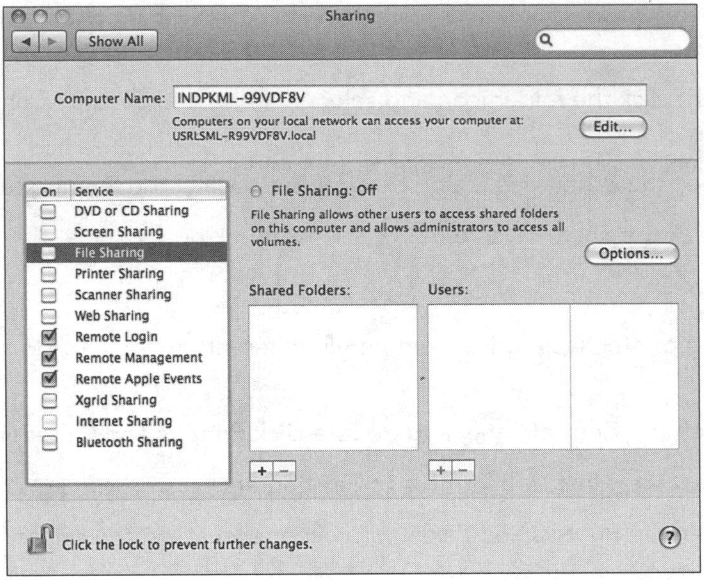

FIGURE 11.6

Enabling file sharing on a Mac.

To enable printer sharing, follow these steps:

1. From the Apple menu, choose System Preferences.

2. From the View menu, choose Sharing.

3. When the Sharing dialog box appears, go to the Service list and select Printer Sharing.

4. Click On the Printer Sharing option.

5. By default, your computer automatically shares all the current printers connected to your Mac. To select specific printers for shared printing, check or uncheck printers in the Printers list.

Accessing Other Computers on Your Network

After you have your home network set up, you can access shared content stored on other computers on your network. How you do so depends on which operating system you use.

Accessing Computers from a Windows PC

It doesn't matter which version of Windows you're using: You connect to other computers on your network using Windows Explorer (which is called File Explorer in Windows 8, for some reason).

 NOTE   You can only share content that the other computer's owner has configured as sharable.

From within Windows Explorer, click the Network section in the navigation pane. This displays all the computers connected to your network, as shown in Figure 11.7. (If you have more than one workgroup connected to your network, double-click a workgroup name to view the computers in that workgroup.)

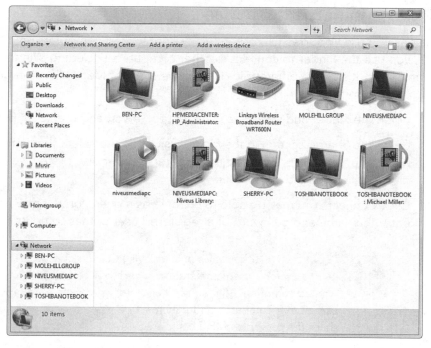

FIGURE 11.7

Accessing network computers in Windows 7.

Double-click the computer you want to access, and Windows displays the shared folders on the selected computer. Double-click or tap a folder to view that folder's content.

TIP On most older computers, shared files are stored in the Public folder. Look in this folder first for the files you want.

Accessing Computers from a Windows HomeGroup

If you set up a Windows HomeGroup, you can also access your HomeGroup computers from Windows Explorer/File Explorer. Click the HomeGroup section of the navigation pane to display all of your HomeGroup computers. You can then click the name of the user whose computer you want to access.

Windows now displays the shared libraries on the selected computer. Double-click a library to access that particular content.

Accessing Computers from a Mac

Just as you use Windows Explorer to access networked computers on a Windows PC, you use the Finder to connect to other computers (including Windows PCs) from a Mac. It's a little different in different versions of Mac OS, but in general, you should do the following:

1. Open the Finder and select Go, Connect to Server, and then click Browse.

2. Go to the Shared section in the Finder's sidebar and select the computer to which you want to connect. If the computer you want isn't listed, select All to display all networked computers.

3. Click Connect. You may be able to connect as a guest, or you may have to enter the name and password of a registered user of that computer.

NOTE On either Macs or Windows PCs, you may be prompted for a username and password to access a specific networked computer. This is the ID and password used for a given user of that computer, and they must be entered before you can share the contents of that computer.

Managing a Windows Network

On Windows computers, all network functions can be monitored and managed via the Network and Sharing Center. As you can see in Figure 11.8, this utility lets you configure all manners of network-related settings, including network discovery (to see other PCs on your network), file sharing, public folder sharing, printer sharing, password-protected sharing, and media sharing (for music, video, and picture files). In some versions of Windows, you can even display a map of all the computers and devices connected to your network.

You can open the Network and Computer Center from the Windows Control Panel. You may also be able to open it by clicking or right-clicking the network icon in the Notification Area of the taskbar.

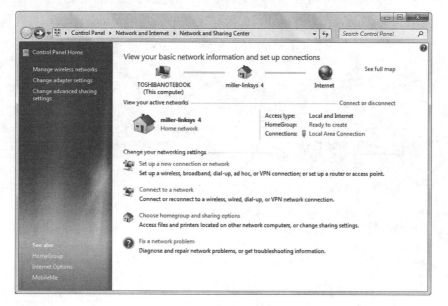

FIGURE 11.8

The Windows 7 Network and Sharing Center.

THE ABSOLUTE MINIMUM

Here are the key points to remember from this chapter:

- To connect a computer to your wireless network, you must select your network from a list of available networks, and then enter the necessary password.

- Windows 7 and 8 let you create a special type of network, called a HomeGroup, that greatly simplifies the connection and configuration process.

- To share files and printers on a given computer, you must first enable file and printer sharing on that machine.

- To access other computers on your network from a Windows PC, use Windows Explorer or File Explorer. From a Mac, use the Finder.

- On a Windows PC, you can manage most network functionality from the Network and Sharing Center.

12

CONNECTING A HOME SERVER

Chances are you have multiple computers connected to your wireless network. You also probably have lots and lots of media files—digital photos, music, and videos—stored on each of these computers.

Although one of the advantages of a home network is sharing media files of this sort, it's difficult to do when those files are scattered across multiple computers. Even though all of your computers are connected, finding, sharing, and streaming those files takes some work; heck, it's hard enough just figuring out what's stored where.

The solution to this storage conundrum is something called a *home server*—a separate, low-cost computer connected to your network for the sole purpose of storing and serving media (and other) files. Installing a home server may be the solution for all of your media storage needs.

What Is a Home Server, and Why Do You Need One?

A home server is nothing more than a computer dedicated to storing and serving files of all types. This computer typically doesn't have a monitor or keyboard; it's a storage device, not a computer you use for traditional computing. The server is connected to your home network, either via Ethernet or wirelessly, from where it can serve its files to any other computer or device connected to the network.

Why do you need another computer on your network? Don't you already have enough computers, all with their own internal storage?

The problem is, just connecting a bunch of computers together in a network doesn't necessarily offer a practical way to share those files that all of you want to access. I'm talking media files, primarily—digital photos, music, and videos that everyone wants to watch or listen to. The more connected devices you have in your household, the less practical it becomes to store your media files on individual computers. What do you do when you want to listen to a song that's on your wife's notebook PC—and your wife and her notebook aren't around? Can you even find the photo or video you want—do you know which PC the thing is stored on?

Enter the home server. Instead of storing your photos, music, and videos on all of your computers willy nilly, you store all those media files on the home server. The home server is then connected to your home network, of course, and any other computer connected to your network can easily access and play those media files, in real time. With a home server, you know where all of your media files are and have immediate access to them from any computer on your network.

Exploring the Many Uses of a Home Server

The point of a home server is to put all of your various media files in one place. Instead of having some photos and music on your PC, other photos and music on your spouse's machine, and still more photos and videos on your kids' computers, you put all of your photos, music, and videos in a centralized location, where all of your PCs can access it. One place for all of your media, so that it can be accessed by all the computers and mobile devices in your household.

Imagine this scenario: You're working in your office while listening to some digital music. Your spouse is posting some photos to her Facebook page while listening to different music. Your son is watching a TV show he recorded the previous evening, while your daughter is listening to her own music in her bedroom. With a home server, all these files—your music, your wife's music and photos, your son's recorded video, and your daughter's music—is all served and stored from the central home server. In fact, if your son had a friend over who wanted to listen to some tunes on his iPhone, you could grant him access to the music stored on your home server, too. No more hunting for files, no more missing files; with a home server, everything is one place, served when needed.

Your home server can also be used to serve music and video to a home theater system. Instead of storing all the files on a big PC in your living room, you instead connect a small media player device to your TV and audio system, and have that device pull music and video from your home server, itself tucked away unobtrusively in another room in your house. It's a more elegant and less conspicuous way to feed digital media to your home theater system.

In addition, a home server can serve as a centralized backup device for all the computers on your home network. Just schedule the backup routine for each computer individually, and have them all back up to the hard drive on your home server. (Even better, many home servers can schedule backups on all network-connected computers, remotely.) The backup takes place automatically, over your network, with all the backup files stored on the home server. If a computer ever fails, all you have to do is restore the backed-up files from your server. It's hard to get any easier than that.

In other words, you use a home server to store all those files you need to share in your household, as well as to store backups from all of your other computers. It puts all of your important information in one place and provides backup security.

Home Server or NAS: What's in a Name?

Before we go much further, we need to address a variation on the server theme called *network attached storage* (NAS). At one point in the past, home servers and NAS devices were two separate things—although that's not the case today.

Originally, a NAS was kind of a dumbed-down cousin of the more fully featured home server. A NAS unit was primarily for data storage with no other extras, such as media streaming and data backup. It was kind of like an external hard drive that could be accessed over a network. If you wanted more than just storage, you had to spend additional bucks for a home server.

Today, however, NAS units have been beefed up to include most, if not all, of the functionality of a traditional home server. In fact, the terms NAS and home server are often used interchangeably. Computer manufacturers tend to call their offerings home servers, whereas networking and storage companies tend to use the NAS nomenclature.

Beyond the name thing, a NAS is a home server, and a home server is a NAS. It doesn't matter what you call it, it does pretty much the same thing.

 NOTE   Some manufacturers fuzz the difference by calling their NAS offerings NAS servers or just network storage servers.

Shopping for a Home Server or NAS

With its role as centralized media storage, you might think a home server or NAS would be something big, costly, and complex. Just the opposite is true; most of these devices are small enough to fit on or under a normal office desktop, and cost far less than a traditional desktop PC.

As you can see in Figure 12.1, the typical home server doesn't even have a keyboard or mouse or monitor. You access and monitor the server via the other computers on your network. In day-to-day operation, it just sits there—and works.

FIGURE 12.1

A NETGEAR ReadyNAS device. (Photo courtesy of NETGEAR.)

CAUTION Don't confuse a home server or NAS with a *network hard drive*. A network hard drive is nothing more than a single external hard drive that can be connected directly to a network, without first connecting to a PC. Network hard drives do not have all the added functionality found on a modern NAS or home server.

Determining Storage Capacity

As to what to look for in a home server, the hard drive is the main thing. You want no less than 1 terabyte (TB) of storage, more if you have a lot of digital media.

You may even want to consider units that include multiple swappable hard drives; this lets the unit combine multiple hard drives into a single virtual drive and provide some drive redundancy (using RAID technology). A home server with multiple hard drives can also serve as its own backup (going from one hard drive to another) and enables you to quickly swap out one drive for another if one goes bad or you need to add more storage.

 NOTE RAID stands for *redundant array of independent disks* and describes a way of storing data across multiple hard disks. Depending on the type (level) of RAID array, identical data is written to more than one drive, essentially "mirroring" the data so that if one drive fails, the data also exists elsewhere in the array.

Choosing Networking and Backup Functionality

Obviously, your home server needs some sort of network connection. While some home servers offer wireless connection via Wi-Fi, I prefer connecting a server via Ethernet; it's faster and more reliable. So, look for an Ethernet port when you're shopping.

You'll also want to consider what software comes with the home server. Some home servers offer their own backup software that will back up data from all connected PCs. Without such software, you'll have to schedule backups on the individual machines.

Selecting an Operating System

A home server or NAS is more than just a hard drive in a case; it also offers media streaming and data backup, as well as networking functionality.

All these non-storage functions have to be managed by an operating system of some sort, much as a traditional computer uses Windows or the Mac OS to manage all of its operating functions.

Most NAS units and many home servers use some variation of Linux as their operating system. Some higher-end servers use a variation of Windows, such as Windows Server. Still other devices run other stripped-down operating systems, such as FreeNAS, an open-source NAS solution designed for commodity PC hardware.

 NOTE The Windows Server OS is targeted more at businesses than home users. Microsoft used to offer a Windows Home Server OS, but it discontinued that in 2012.

For most users, however, which operating system you get really doesn't matter. Because you're not using the server the same way you use a traditional computer—you're not opening and running programs or even doing web browsing—you don't need anything too fancy. Your interaction with the server will typically be via some sort of browser-based configuration utility. After that, it's just a matter of grabbing the stored files you want to use.

Making the Purchase

NAS devices are available from most networking and storage companies, such as Cisco/Linksys, D-Link, NETGEAR, Seagate, and Western Digital. Home server machines are available from many personal computer manufacturers, such as Acer and Lenovo.

You should be able to find NAS or home server units for home use priced as low as $200 up to $500 or so. Your local consumer electronics store is as good as any place to buy one.

 TIP If you're a techie tinkering type, you don't even have to purchase a new home server or NAS unit. It's easy enough to convert an old desktop PC into a home server with little additional investment required. You may want to upgrade the machine's hard disk to something a little larger, but the fact that you're using an older and presumably slower machine won't matter; a server doesn't have to be as fast or as powerful as a desktop machine that you use to run real-time apps. If you can save a few bucks by reusing an old PC, more power to you.

Configuring Your Server

Most home servers connect to your network independently. That is, you can connect a home server unit directly to your router via Ethernet (recommended, if they're in the same room) or via Wi-Fi. The home server or NAS does *not* have to physically connect to another computer on your network.

Once connected, you need to configure the server. Because these units do not have their own keyboards or monitors, you do this from another computer on your network. Follow the manufacturer's instructions on how to run the configuration program on your PC; in many instances, you perform configuration operations using your PC's web browser. (Figure 12.2 shows the Setup Wizard for a NETGEAR ReadyNAS device.)

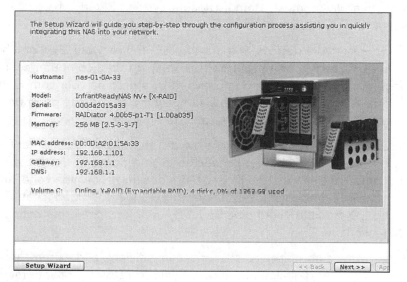

FIGURE 12.2

Configuring a NETGEAR ReadyNAS unit.

Although you can probably accept most of the server's default settings, you will have to do things like set the date and time, activate security settings, and (if you like) change the server's default name and administrator password. You'll probably also need to configure the server's file sharing and media serving functions, as well as any included file backup functionality.

Once everything is configured, you can then access the server from any device connected to your network. It should appear as any other device on a network map; if you've properly configured file sharing, you should be able to access files on the server and save new files to the device.

Using Your Server for Media Storage

Home servers are great for storing and serving digital media files of all sorts: music, videos, and photos. It's really simple; you store all of your media in one place, and then serve them to whatever computers and other devices you have connected in your home.

The key here is that just about any type of device can access your media library stored on a home server. Of course, you can do this with a desktop or notebook computer, but you can also access your server with an Apple TV box, a Sonos media player, and any other network media player device you have connected to your network. Many A/V receivers can connect over your network to your home server, as well, and play back your digital music without need of an additional device. In addition, most Internet-capable TVs and Blu-ray players can play back videos you have stored on your server.

As to your portable devices, you may be able to sync your iPod or iPhone directly to your home server, or it may be easier to sync it to a computer connected to your server. Your music files don't have to be stored on your computer for iTunes or Windows Media Player to access and play the files; these programs work just fine by grabbing the files stored elsewhere on your home server.

You can download new music and movies directly from the Internet to your home server by using any computer connected to your network. Use the most convenient computer to access the iTunes Store or similar download site, and then choose your home server (over the network) as the download location. You can even rip CD music to your home server by using any computer connected to your network.

In short, using a home server is an effective, efficient, and extremely convenient way to store your digital media library. It lets you store all of your media files in one place and then access them from any device connected to your network.

Backing Up to a Home Server

Here's another practical use for a home server. You can back up over your network from any computer to your home server. In fact, many people purchase home servers just for the purpose of backing up data from their other computers.

The process is just as easy as backing up from a computer to an external hard drive. You schedule the backup within the backup program, and then let the bits and bytes fly over your network connection at the designated time. In fact, many home servers and NAS devices come with backup functionality preinstalled. Just set it once and forget it; all of your data will be automatically backed up.

TIP   How do you back up data stored on a home server? Well, some would say that RAID redundancy is good-enough backup, but I prefer to back up from the server to an external hard drive. Better safe than sorry in case the entire server goes up in flames.

Connecting to Your Server from the Internet

It's a no brainer to use a home server or NAS to serve media files to all the networked devices in your home. But, what about when you're away from home—is there any way to access your media files from outside your network?

With a home server's default configuration, the answer is no; it's designed purely for LAN access. But, there's a way to turn some home servers into web servers, which you can then access from any device connected to the Internet, anywhere in the world. This way, you can play your music library from your iPhone while you're traveling or view your photo collection from your office PC.

It's all a matter of installing the proper web server software on your home server or NAS unit. There are several different options, including the following:

- Abyss Web Server (www.aprelium.com/abyssws/)

- Apache (www.apache.org)

- Dekoh Desktop (www.dekoh.com)

 NOTE   Some NAS devices come with software preinstalled that enables remote access without the need to install or configure a standalone web server.

There are other configuration issues to consider. You may need to open holes in your firewall software/hardware to allow access to the server, configure the directory structure to be mapped on the server, and set up individual access accounts on the server. You'll need to follow the instructions that come with your server software to make sure everything that needs to get done gets done.

Once the software is installed and configured, you can access the server from the web browser of any device connected to the Internet. Just enter the URL of your server into your web browser (which is provided when you configure the server software), and you can browse the files on your server.

 TIP   If all you're interested in is streaming music from your server to another computer or smartphone, check out Audiogalaxy (www.audiogalaxy.com) or Subsonic (www.subsonic.org). Both of these applications turn your home server into a music-streaming service that lets you listen to your music, in real time, from any Internet-connected device.

THE ABSOLUTE MINIMUM

Here are the key points to remember from this chapter:

- A home server or network attached storage (NAS) device is like a big hard disk connected directly to your network router and accessible from any networked device.

- You can use a home server to store all of your media files in a single location or to back up data files from other networked computers.

- Look for a home server or NAS with at least 1TB of storage; many servers let you swap in additional hard drives to increase capacity.

- Because a home server or NAS doesn't have a keyboard or monitor, you configure it from another computer connected to your network, often from within that PC's web browser.

- Many home servers and NAS devices come with built-in backup functionality to help you schedule automatic backups from other computers on your network.

- If you like, you can install additional software on your home server to turn it into a full-fledged web server. This lets you access your files from any device connected to the Internet.

CONNECTING VIDEOGAME DEVICES

Chances are that you or someone in your household likes to play videogames. There are more than 75 million videogame consoles in use in the U.S. today, which means there are a lot of folks out there playing games—and using their game consoles to connect to the Internet.

That's because every game console sold today is Internet compatible and offers a raft of additional features (both game-related and not) when connected to the Internet. To connect a game console to the Internet, of course, means first connecting it to your home network—either via Ethernet or Wi-Fi.

Why Would You Want to Connect a Videogame Device to Your Network?

If you have a Wii, Wii U, Xbox 360, PlayStation 3, or newer videogame system, your console has all the necessary connections to connect to your home network. Which begs the question, why should you do that?

It's for the Internet, dummy.

Every game console today offers its own namesake Internet service for online games and other functionality. You can connect to your manufacturer's service to download additional features and updates for your favorite games, play those games with gamers around the world, and access a ton of other web-based content and services.

What kind of additional content and services? Today's modern videogame consoles let you send instant messages and email to other gamers; watch streaming video; listen to streaming audio; access the latest news, sports, and weather; and browse and post to Facebook, Twitter, and other social networks.

And it's not just web-based stuff. Most consoles let you connect to your network to listen to music, watch movies, and view photos stored on other computers elsewhere on your network. This lets your game console function as the centerpiece of your home entertainment system; just power it up, point to the console's Internet features, and you're online to do just about anything you want to do.

For example, Microsoft offers the Xbox LIVE service for Internet-based play and content on its Xbox 360 console, as shown in Figure 13.1. When you log into your LIVE account, you can opt to engage in the following activities:

- Purchase and download new Xbox games

- Update your existing Xbox games

- Play multiplayer Xbox games online with other members

- Purchase, download, and stream movies from the Xbox Video store

- Purchase, download, and stream music from the Xbox Music store

- Watch streaming movies and TV shows from Hulu and Hulu Plus, Netflix, Amazon Instant Video, Crackle, EPIX, HBO GO, ESPN, YouTube, and other services

- Listen to streaming music from Last.fm, iHeartRadio, and other services

- Keep in touch with online friends via Facebook and Twitter

- Send and receive instant messages to/from other users via Xbox Social instant messaging

- Browse the web with Internet Explorer

FIGURE 13.1

The Home screen for the Xbox LIVE service.

That's a lot of options—the majority of which really aren't game related. And you don't get any of them if you don't connect your Xbox console to your home network for Internet access.

 NOTE   Basic Xbox LIVE membership is free, but doesn't include much more than game downloads and updates. For more complete entertainment options, you need a Gold membership, which runs $5 per month (U.S.).

Along similar lines, Sony offers the PlayStation Network for PS3 and PSP devices, and Nintendo offers the Nintendo Network for its Wii, Wii U, and Nintendo DS units. Both of these networks offer similar content and services to Microsoft's Xbox LIVE network. The basic PlayStation Network is free, although the more feature-laden PlayStation Plus network costs $49.99/year; the Nintendo Network is free.

Wi-Fi Versus Ethernet: What's Best for Gaming?

When it comes to connecting your videogame console to the Internet (via your home network), the first question you have to answer is whether to connect via Wi-Fi or Ethernet. There are advantages and disadvantages to either type of connection.

Connecting via Wi-Fi

All game consoles today have built-in Wi-Fi, which means there's no additional equipment to purchase if you want to connect wirelessly. The Xbox 360 and PlayStation 3 also offer built-in Ethernet; the Nintendo Wii does not.

Since Wi-Fi is built-in, setting up a Wi-Fi connection is fairly simple. Just select your home network from the menu of available wireless networks, enter your network's password, and connect. Naturally, there's the advantage of connecting without having to run a (possibly long) Ethernet cable from your console to your network router.

Unfortunately, wireless connections can sometimes be a tad unstable. (Some might say flaky.) Speeds might fluctuate, packets might get dropped, your entire connection might even get disconnected. Although this sort of thing might be unnoticeable when doing web browsing and such, it's game changing (literally) when playing games in real time. If your connection freezes for even a fraction of a second, gameplay will be interrupted; your game may lag, smear, or freeze. Not a good thing.

Connecting via Ethernet

Connecting via Ethernet (at least on a Xbox 360 or PS3) is equally simple. Just connect an Ethernet cable and you're up and running—not much more to it than that.

The primary benefits of connecting via Ethernet are reliability and speed. With Ethernet, you don't have to worry about the stability of your connection; plus, you get anywhere from 100Mbps (for the Xbox) to 1Gbps (for the PS3) speed, which is great for when you're playing games in real time and watching streaming video.

It's the stability, however, that matters. When connected via Ethernet cable, you don't have to worry about latency issues, temporary disconnects, and the like. Everything's there and everything stays there, which means much more reliable gameplay.

 CAUTION When playing an online game, latency is the lag between initiating an action and seeing that action played onscreen. Even the smallest amount of latency can affect gameplay.

For the best possible gameplay, then, Ethernet is the way to go. That said, for most players, a Wi-Fi connection is just fine and a heck of a lot easier to set up. (No cables to run, that is.)

Connecting an Xbox 360 Console

How, exactly, do you connect and configure your videogame console for network and Internet use? It differs from console to console, of course, so we'll look at all three of the major videogame systems today—starting with Microsoft's Xbox 360.

Is Your Xbox Wireless?

Remember when I said that all videogame consoles sold today include wireless connectivity? That's certainly true of the Xbox 360; all current models have Wi-Fi built in. Older models, however, did not include built-in wireless, and thus need an optional wireless adapter to add Wi-Fi functionality.

For these older consoles, Microsoft sells an official Xbox 360 Wireless Networking Adapter, like the one shown in Figure 13.2. This little device offers 802.11n connectivity and sells for around $60. The Wireless Networking Adapter connects to the Xbox via USB and snaps onto the back of the console for easy placement.

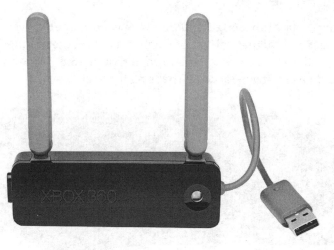

FIGURE 13.2

Microsoft's official Xbox 360 Wireless Networking Adapter. (Photo courtesy of Microsoft.)

This official wireless adapter is a little on the pricy side, however—especially when you consider that you can use *any* USB wireless adapter with your Xbox. You can find wireless adapters from other networking manufacturers for $20 to $40 or so, and they should work fine.

Connecting via Wi-Fi

Connecting your Xbox 360 console to your home wireless network is relatively easy. It works something like this:

1. Press the Guide button on your Xbox controller to display the main screen.

2. Go to Settings and select System Settings.

3. Select Network Settings.

4. All available wireless networks should be listed here. Select your home network from the list.

5. You're prompted to select the security type. Enter the password for your wireless network.

That's it. You're now connected and should have full Internet access.

Connecting via Ethernet

Connecting your Xbox 360 to your network via Ethernet is even simpler. Just run and connect an Ethernet cable from your network router to the Ethernet port on the back of the Xbox console, as shown in Figure 13.3. Once that's connected, you should have network access. That's all there is to it.

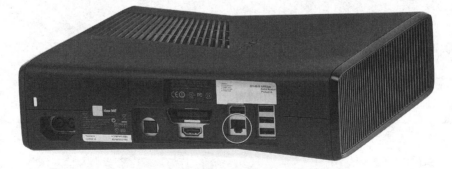

FIGURE 13.3

The Ethernet port on the back of the Xbox 360 console.

Connecting a PlayStation 3 Console

Like the Xbox 360, Sony's PlayStation 3 (PS3) console has built-in Wi-Fi, so no external adapter is necessary. It also has an Ethernet port on the back, should you decide to go that route.

NOTE Actually, there's one PS3 model that *doesn't* have built-in Wi-Fi; that's the low-end 20GB model, of which few are sold. If you have this model and want to connect via Wi-Fi, you need to purchase a wireless adapter that connects to the device via Ethernet (sometimes called a wireless Ethernet bridge), because the PS3 doesn't have USB ports, either.

Connecting via Wi-Fi

To connect to your PS3 to your home wireless network, follow these steps:

1. From the XrossMediaBar (XMB) menu, select Settings, Network settings.

2. Go to Internet Connection and select Enabled.

3. Scroll down to and select Internet Connection Settings.

4. When you see the notice about being disconnected from the Internet, select Yes.

5. On the next screen, select Easy.

6. When prompted for which type of connection method, select Wireless.

7. Under WLAN Settings, select Scan.

8. The PS3 now displays a list of nearby wireless networks, as shown in Figure 13.4. Select your home network from the list.

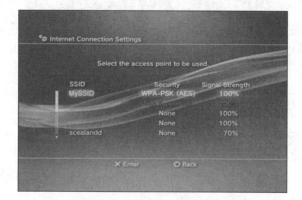

FIGURE 13.4

Selecting a wireless network on the PS3.

9. On the next screen, confirm your network's name (SSID) and press the right direction button to continue.

10. Select the type of security your network uses.

11. Enter your password (security key).

12. The PS3 now displays a list of your network settings. Press the button to save these settings.

Connecting via Ethernet

Connecting your PS3 via Ethernet is considerably easier. Just connect an Ethernet cable from your network router to the LAN port on the back of your game console, shown in Figure 13.5. Your PS3 now automatically connects to your home network.

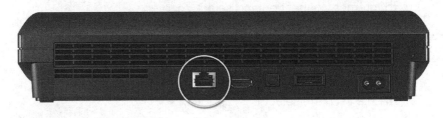

FIGURE 13.5

The LAN port on the back of the PS3 console.

Connecting a Nintendo Wii Console

The Nintendo Wii has been around for a half dozen years; its successor, the Wii U, shipped just in time for Christmas 2012. We'll focus our attention on the original Wii, as there are so many of them out there.

Connecting via Wi-Fi

The Wii console comes with built-in Wi-Fi, and Nintendo assumes this will be the way you connect to your home network. Here's how to do it:

1. Press the A button on the Wii Remote to display the Wii's main menu.

2. Select the Wii button from the main menu.

3. Select Wii Settings to display the Wii System Settings menu.

4. Scroll to page two and select Internet.

5. Select Connection Settings.

6. Select Connection 1: None.

7. Select Wireless Connection.

8. Select Search for an Access Point.

9. The Wii now displays a list of nearby wireless networks. Select your home net-work from this list.

10. You are prompted to enter a password or key for your network, as shown in Figure 13.6; do so, and click OK.

11. Select OK, Save Settings, and then Yes to save your wireless configuration.

Connection 1

BTHomeHub-A016	🔒	📶	▲
BTHomeHub2-RQZ7	🔒	📶	
BTOpenzone		📶	
BTHomeHub-AF12	🔒	📶	▼

Back	Try again

FIGURE 13.6

Selecting a wireless network on the Wii console.

Connecting via Ethernet

Unfortunately, the Wii console doesn't have an Ethernet port. This makes connect-ing via Ethernet somewhat problematic.

If you want to connect the Wii via Ethernet, you'll have to purchase a LAN adapter—that is, an adapter that has an Ethernet port on one end and a USB con-nector on the other. Connect an Ethernet cable to the LAN adapter, and then plug the LAN adapter into one of the Wii's USB ports. Your Wii should recognize the connected network and work fine from there.

 NOTE   I'm writing this before Nintendo has shipped the new Wii U, but initial specs indicate similar connectivity to the original Wii—802.11n wireless, but no Ethernet.

Connecting a Portable Videogame Device

All of today's portable videogame devices include built-in Wi-Fi. This means you can connect your PlayStation Portable (PSP), Nintendo 3DS, and even your iPod Touch (not solely a game device, but used by many for that purpose) to your home network and thus to the Internet for online game play.

For example, to connect a Nintendo 3DS to a wireless network, follow these steps:

1. Tap the wrench icon to display System Settings.

2. Tap Internet Settings.

3. Tap Connection Settings.

4. Tap New Connection.

5. Tap Manual Setup.

6. Tap Search for Access Point.

7. The 3DS now displays all available wireless networks. Tap your network from this list.

8. Enter your network password when prompted.

Other portable game systems have similar processes for wireless setup. Follow the instructions for your specific game device.

Once connected, you can use your game player not only to play games, but to access a variety of web-related content. As you can see in Figure 13.7, for example, the 3DS lets you watch videos from Netflix, browse the web, and more. Other devices offer similar Internet functionality.

FIGURE 13.7

Watch Netflix movies on a Nintendo 3DS connected to your home network.

Configuring Your Network for Optimum Gameplay

As you've just seen, connecting your videogame console or portable device to your home network is usually a piece of cake. Once you're connected, you can then use your game machine for all sorts of web-based viewing and listening and browsing—as well as for playing games online with other gamers, in real time.

It's this last function that can be somewhat demanding on a home network. Many routers, in their default configurations, can lag or lock up during fast real-time high-resolution gameplay. If you're a big-time online gamer, you may need to reconfigure your router for the best possible gameplay.

Getting Faster Broadband

So, what do you need for optimal real-time gameplay? First, you need as fast an Internet connection as possible. I'm assuming that you have a broadband connection (not dial-up), but there are often different levels of broadband. Chapter 7, "Connecting to the Internet," discussed the relative benefits of various types of broadband; for gameplay, I recommend either cable broadband or FiOS. (DSL is slow enough to make this decision easy.)

 CAUTION Satellite Internet is a non-starter for online game playing, because of its excessive latency rates, caused by all that uplinking and downlinking from the distant orbiting satellite. Typical two-way latency is around a second; although this may be unnoticeable when browsing web pages, it's totally unacceptable for real-time game playing.

But, even within cable broadband, you may have different levels of service available. Take XFINITY by Comcast, for example. Its standard broadband service (dubbed Economy Plus) promises download speeds of 3Mbps and upload speeds of 768Kbps. For an extra $20 or so per month, you can upgrade to the Performance plan, which promises 20Mbps downloads and 4Mbps uploads. Another $10 or so per month gets you the Blast! Plan, with 30Mbps downloads and 6Mbps uploads. The Extreme 50 plan ($60 or so per month) gets you 50Mbps downloads and 15Mbps uploads, while the Extreme 105 plan (a whopping $200 or so per month) promises 105Mbps download speeds and 20Mbps uploads.

The point is that you'll probably experience better gameplay (faster loading, fewer pauses and delays) with a faster connection. Now, 105Mbps may be substantial overkill, but paying a little more each month for a 20Mbps or 30Mbps connection may be worth the expense, especially if you're a heavy gamer.

Upgrading Your Router

Some network routers are better suited for demanding gameplay than others. Many networking manufacturers offer so-called "gaming routers" that they incorporate a quality of service (QoS) technology called StreamEngine. This technology gives priority to time-sensitive traffic (packet prioritization), resulting in lower latency and lag-free gaming sessions.

If you have a router with StreamEngine technology, you'll want to go into the advanced configuration screen and identify the port used by your videogame console. You can then assign priority to that port, ensuring that your gaming comes first, as far as the router's traffic is concerned.

 TIP Most of these gaming routers also offer dual-band 802.11g Wi-Fi, so you can allocate the less-crowded 5GHz band to your videogame consoles.

Most manufacturers offer gaming routers, typically at a premium price. For example, D-Link's Xtreme N Gaming Router, shown in Figure 13.8, sells for around $200. Pricey, yes, but it's worth it if you're a hardcore gamer who wants the best possible performance.

FIGURE 13.8

Enhance your wireless gaming performance with D-Link's DGL-4500 Xtreme N Gaming Router. (Photo courtesy of D-Link.)

THE ABSOLUTE MINIMUM

Here are the key points to remember from this chapter:

- All videogame consoles today offer Internet-based services for watching movies and TV shows, listening to music, and playing real-time games online with other gamers.

- Connecting via Wi-Fi is the easiest way to go, although an Ethernet connection is both faster and more stable for hardcore gamers.

- The Xbox 360, PlayStation 3, and Nintendo Wii consoles have built-in Wi-Fi.

- The Xbox 360 and PlayStation 3 consoles have built-in Ethernet.

- For optimal gameplay, invest in a fast Internet connection and gaming router with StreamEngine technology.

14

CONNECTING OTHER ENTERTAINMENT DEVICES

Today, many people like to get their entertainment fix from the Internet. Not from cable or satellite or DVDs or CDs, but from music, movies, and TV shows streamed over the web.

It's easy enough to watch a streaming movie on your notebook computer or tablet, but the picture's a little small. Likewise, listening to music over your PC's speakers leaves a lot to be desired, fidelity wise. If you want the best possible picture and sound, you want to watch your streaming media not on a personal computer, but rather in your living room, on your wide-screen TV and home theater or home audio system.

The challenge, then, becomes choosing the best way to get that streaming web content to your TV and audio system. Naturally, whatever you choose has to be connected to your home network, to access the Internet. But, you have many choices in terms of how you go about it.

The Many Ways to Consume Web-Based Media in Your Living Room

All of your streaming media is delivered over the Internet, through your wireless router and home network. Thus, any compatible device you connect to your network can access and play streaming audio and video.

Not every device can provide an acceptable playback experience, however. For example, you can certainly watch streaming movies on your iPhone, but that's hardly a theater-like experience. iPhone movies might be fine for when you're commuting or standing in line, but they're somewhat underwhelming compared to what you're used to watching on your living room TV and home theater system.

One approach is to connect one of your personal computers to your TV and home theater system. While that certainly works (assuming your PC has an HDMI output, which is what you need to connect to most widescreen TVs and audio/video receivers), not everyone is comfortable putting a computer in their living room. There's the esthetic issue, of course, plus PC operation isn't as user-friendly as pointing a handheld remote at the TV screen. (Can you imagine having to reboot your TV as often as you do your PC?)

If you don't want a computer in your living room, what about a videogame console? As you learned in Chapter 13, "Connecting Videogame Devices," most game consoles have built-in Internet functionality, including access to streaming media services. It's easy enough to fire up the old Xbox, log into the Xbox LIVE network, and then navigate to Netflix to watch your movie of choice.

Then, there's the network media player option. A network media player is a small-ish box with the appropriate consumer-friendly outputs (typically HDMI and analog or digital audio) to connect to a TV and A/V receiver. Media players connect to your home network, typically wirelessly, and feed streaming media content to your living room devices. Most network media players include functionality for the major web-based streaming services (Hulu, Netflix, and Amazon Instant Video) and can play media files stored on computers elsewhere on your network.

You may not even need a separate device. Many high-end TVs today are Internet-capable, meaning they can connect to your network (and thus to the Internet) and stream movies and TV shows from the major streaming services. Some of these Internet-capable TVs have built-in wireless connectivity; others require an Ethernet connection or some sort of wireless adapter. Still, having that connectivity built into your TV may be the easiest way to go.

Likewise, many Blu-ray players are also Internet-capable. Many early Blu-ray players had Ethernet ports on the back, primarily to connect to sites that offered enhanced content for specific discs. More recent machines, however, build on that basic connectivity to offer streaming media from Netflix, Hulu, and the other usual suspects. Connection can be via Ethernet or Wi-Fi, depending on the unit.

Finally, many high-end A/V receivers have network connectivity, either wirelessly or via Ethernet. Although some of these receivers offer access to streaming media services, others are strictly designed to pull music (and sometimes photo) files from other networked PCs. This way, you can store your music on an office PC or home server and play that music through your A/V receiver and home audio system via your network.

Which option is best for you? It depends on how you like to do things. If you already have a videogame console connected to your TV, you might as well use that. If you want full PC functionality in your living room, then by all means, connect your PC to your TV. If you want something more consumer friendly, go with an inexpensive network media player or (if you're in the market for a new TV) an Internet-capable TV or Blu-ray player. If music is your main thing, you can't beat the convenience of a networked receiver.

 NOTE   Learn more about playing music and videos over your network in Chapter 18, "Streaming Audio and Video."

Connecting an Internet-Capable TV to Your Network

Although there are still a lot of low-end, inexpensive TVs sold today, there's a growing trend to include Internet connectivity in high-end TVs. These TVs offer network connectivity either via built-in Wi-Fi or Ethernet, and then provide access to various streaming media services via onscreen gadgets or apps that connect to the websites in question. Figure 14.1 shows how an Internet-compatible TV fits within your home network.

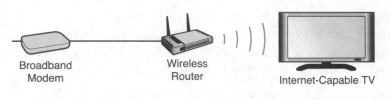

FIGURE 14.1

An Internet-compatible TV connected to a wireless network.

For example, the Sony LCD TV shown in Figure 14.2 has both built-in Wi-Fi and Ethernet connectivity. Once connected to your home network, the set can access the Sony Entertainment network, an online gateway to Netflix, Pandora, and other streaming services.

FIGURE 14.2

The Ethernet connection on a Sony LCD TV; there's also built-in Wi-Fi. (Photo courtesy of Sony.)

Many of these so-called *smart TVs* also support a technology called Digital Living Network Alliance (DLNA). Any device that's DLNA certified can discover, access, and play media stored on any computer or network storage device connected to the same home network. So, for example, you could use your DLNA-compatible TV to view digital photos, watch home videos, or listen to ripped music stored elsewhere on your network. Pretty nifty.

Configuring an Internet-capable TV can be as simple as connecting an Ethernet cable to the back-panel Ethernet port. Depending on the manufacturer, you may also have to enter your TV's setup menu and select Wired Connection.

If you want to connect wirelessly, you need to go through the setup menu, select wireless setup, select your wireless network from a list, and then use an onscreen keyboard to enter your network password. (Figure 14.3 shows one of the setup screens for a Toshiba TV.) It's a one-time setup; after that, your TV stays connected, so you can access web-based content at any time.

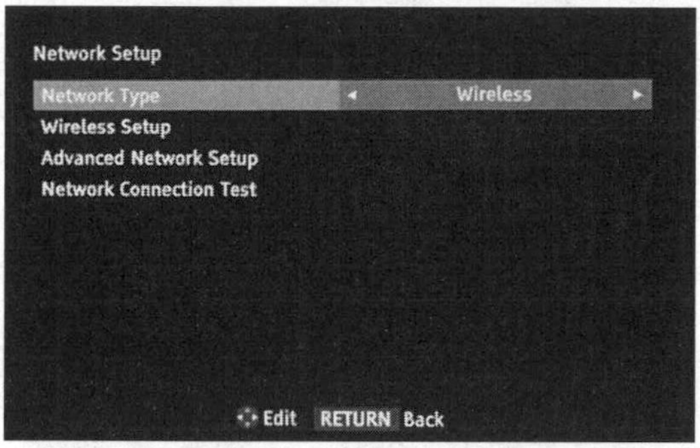

Network Setup

Network Type ◄ Wireless ►
Wireless Setup
Advanced Network Setup
Network Connection Test

Edit RETURN Back

FIGURE 14.3

Configuring a Toshiba TV for a wireless network. (Photo courtesy of Toshiba.)

Connecting a Blu-ray Player to Your Network

Just as many LCD and plasma TVs are coming with Internet connectivity, so are many Blu-ray players. This may be a better choice for many folks, as an Internet-compatible Blu-ray player is much less expensive than a comparable Internet-capable TV. (Figure 14.4 shows how to connect a Blu-ray player to your TV and home network.)

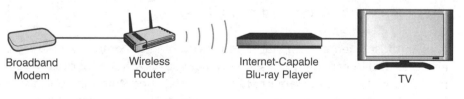

Broadband Modem   Wireless Router   Internet-Capable Blu-ray Player   TV

FIGURE 14.4

An Internet-compatible Blu-ray player connected to a wireless network.

Most Internet-compatible Blu-ray machines have an Ethernet port on the back; about half of these units also have built-in Wi-Fi. Obviously, going the wireless route is going to be easier for most users, because you don't have to worry about stringing an Ethernet cable between your player and your network router. You may have to pay an extra $20 or so for a Wi-Fi unit.

Blu-ray players use the network connection to connect to the Internet. Many Blu-ray discs have optional web-based features that cinemaphiles tend to like;

in addition, manufacturers can update the players' firmware over the Internet to keep things up to date.

But, the biggest reason to connect your Blu-ray player to the Internet is to access streaming video service, such as Hulu and Netflix. It might seem strange, purchasing a device designed to play physical discs and then using it to stream virtual media over the Internet, but that's the way the game is played these days.

For example, the Sony BDP-S390 is a mild mannered Blu-ray player until you connect it to the Internet—which you can do either wirelessly or via Ethernet. (Figure 14.5 shows the back-of-box connections for this unit.) Once connected, you have access to Netflix, Hulu Plus, Amazon Instant Video, CinemaNow, Crackle, and other online video services. You can also use this player to connect to Pandora, Slacker, and other streaming music services; read and post messages to Facebook; and use the included Opera web browser to surf the web. And, if you do a little shopping, you can get all this for just a little over $100. Not a bad deal.

FIGURE 14.5

The back panel connections on Sony's BDP-S390 Blu-ray player; there's an Ethernet port, along with built-in Wi-Fi. (Photo courtesy of Sony.)

As with those Internet-compatible TVs, most Internet-compatible Blu-ray players also offer DLNA capability. This means that you can stream photos, videos, and music from elsewhere on your network and play them through your disc player. That puts a lot of entertainment power in one thin little device.

Connecting your Blu-ray player to your network is similar to connecting an Internet-compatible TV. If it's an Ethernet connection, just connect the Ethernet cable and select Wired from the setup menu. If it's a Wi-Fi connection, you need to select your network from the list of available networks, enter your network password, and so forth. (Figure 14.6 shows the wireless setup menu from a Sony Blu-ray player.)

Internet Settings - Access Point Scan

Select the access point to use.

SSID	Security	Signal Strength
Charter WiFi	WPA2-PSK (AES)	100%
Network 1	WPA-PSK (TKIP)	78%
Network 2	WPA-PSK (AES)	45%
Network 3	WEP	20%

Not selected. Select and go to the next screen.

FIGURE 14.6

Configuring a Sony Blu-ray player for a wireless network. (Photo courtesy of Sony.)

Connecting an Audio/Video Receiver to Your Network

If you have a home theater system in your living room, chances are everything runs through some sort of audio/video (A/V) receiver. You might not know this, but even mid-range receivers these days include some sort of Internet connectivity—probably via Ethernet, although some models also have built-in Wi-Fi. (Figure 14.7 shows how to connect an A/V receiver to your home network.)

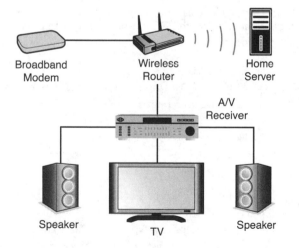

FIGURE 14.7

An A/V receiver connected to a home network.

What you get from most connected A/V receivers is the ability to play digital music stored elsewhere on your home network. For example, you may have a bunch of downloaded or ripped music stored on your home server or desktop PC. A DLNA-compatible receiver connects to your network, locates your digital music files, and lets you play those files through the receiver's onscreen menu.

For example, the mid-priced ($650 or so) Denon AVR2112CI audio/video receiver connects to your home network via Ethernet, as shown in Figure 14.8, and then plays back MP3, WAV, and WMA-format audio files—and displays your JPG digital photos. (It can also stream AAC-format music from your iPod or iPhone via Apple's AirPlay technology, which is similar to DLNA but for Apple-manufactured devices, such as your iPod or iPhone.)

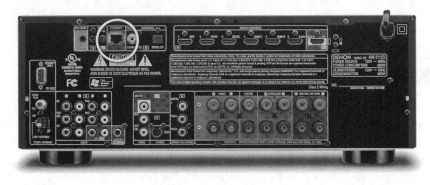

FIGURE 14.8

Use the Ethernet connection on this Denon A/V receiver to connect to your home network for audio playback. (Photo courtesy of Denon.)

 NOTE   DLNA-compatible A/V receivers are mainly for playing music across your network; some also provide access to web-based streaming music services, such as Pandora, Spotify, and the like. While some of these units also offer the ability to display digital photos, few—if any—offer network-based video streaming.

 CAUTION   Not all DLNA devices can play back all file formats, even if they're covered in the DLNA standard. For example, my Onkyo A/V receiver can play back MP3 and WMA compressed music files, but not WMA Lossless files—which is a pain, since my entire library is ripped in WMA Lossless. (Some other DLNA devices can play WMA Lossless, so there's a lack of consistency there.)

Connecting a Network Media Player to Your Network

Then, there are those "black boxes" that connect to your TV or home theater system and provide access to streaming video and music services, as well to digital media stored elsewhere on your home network. These devices have lots of different names—network media player, home media player, streaming media player, and so forth. Whatever the name, these devices all let you watch a variety of online programming in your living room without having to connect a PC to your TV.

The concept is simple. The network media player (or whatever you want to call it) sits in your living room, next to your existing audio and video equipment. It connects to your flat-screen TV or A/V receiver, typically via HDMI. It also connects to your home network, either wirelessly (via Wi-Fi) or via Ethernet cable. (Figure 14.9 shows how this works.) Using your home network, the network media player accesses the Internet for streaming video and music, as well as grabbing music, movies, and photos stored on any PC connected to your network.

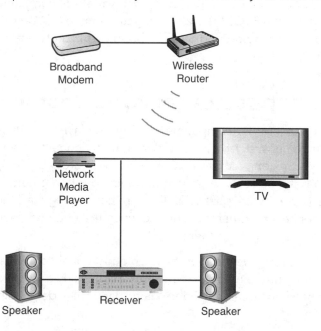

FIGURE 14.9

A network media player connected to a wireless network.

Most of these network media players are smallish boxes, much smaller than a similar PC or piece of audio equipment. They're small because they can be—there's not a lot inside, no hard disk or CD/DVD drive or the like. You have the expected connections on the back (HDMI, analog audio, maybe digital audio and USB), but not much more than that. (Figure 14.10 shows the simplified connections on the back of D-Link's MovieNite Plus media player.)

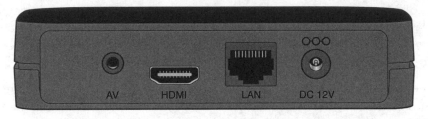

FIGURE 14.10

Connections on the back of the MovieNite Plus media player—LAN (Ethernet), HDMI, and AV, which connects to an audio/video adapter cable. (Photo courtesy of D-Link.)

You can find network media players from a variety of companies, including Apple, D-Link, Logitech, NETGEAR, Roku, Seagate, Sony, and Western Digital. Most of these units are priced around $100, although you can typically find some on special for less than that.

Configuring Your Router for Streaming Media

Connecting an Internet-compatible TV, Blu-ray player, or network media player to your home network isn't much different than connecting a PC or other similar device. If you're connecting via Wi-Fi (which you probably are), all you have to do is call up the device's setup menu, select your home network from the list, and enter your network password. If you're connecting via Ethernet, it's even simpler; just connect an Ethernet cable between the unit and your network router. Everything else flows from there.

That's not to say, however, that there isn't additional configuration you can do to optimize your entertainment experience—particularly for wireless connections. This is important when streaming video, particularly HD video, which requires a lot of bandwidth.

Connecting at 5GHz

First, if both your networked device and your wireless router are compatible with dual-band 802.11n Wi-Fi, connect your device to the router using the less-trafficked 5GHz band. By default, you'll connect in the busier 2.4GHz band; by going with the higher band instead, you'll have a cleaner pipe from the router to your streaming device with less network congestion.

You do this by creating a separate SSID for each of the bands on your router. You might call the normal 2.4GHz band MYDATANETWORK and the 5GHz band MYMEDIANETWORK. Then, when you go to connect your media player or TV or other streaming media device, just select MYMEDIANETWORK from the list of available wireless networks. It's that easy.

Enabling WMM

Many newer routers include a technology called Wireless Multimedia (WMM). WMM sets streaming video and similar network traffic a higher priority level. This is a good thing; if there's any network congestion at all, you want your streaming video and music to keep playing, even if other network data has to slow down or pause.

Consult your router's instruction manual to see if it offers WMM and how to configure it. It's somewhere on your router's advanced configuration screen; exactly where depends on the manufacturer and model.

Giving Priority to Streaming Media

Even if your wireless router doesn't include WMM technology, you can still configure it to give higher priority to your streaming media by using a technique called quality of service (QoS). There are a number of ways your router might utilize QoS.

As previously noted, WMM is a form of QoS. So, if your router offers a simple Enable WMM setting, use it.

Another approach is to let you select a network priority for different categories of traffic. For example, when you open your router's advanced configuration utility, you might see a list of categories, such as Voice, Gaming, Video, Applications, and the like. For each item, you then might be able to select Normal or High priority. Find the categories associated with streaming media and set them at the highest priority. Job done.

Some routers, especially older ones, may require more work on your end. You may have to identify the particular device in the router's configuration utility, either by its network name or IP address, and then set the traffic priority for that device. It's a little more work, but it provides essentially the same results.

 TIP   This same sort of priority setting can be done for any videogame consoles connected to your network to ensure more consistent real-time gameplay.

THE ABSOLUTE MINIMUM

Here are the key points to remember from this chapter:

- Many web-based services, such as Hulu and Netflix, offer streaming movies and TV shows.

- To enjoy streaming media in your living room, connect an Internet-compatible device to your TV and audio/video receiver.

- Many high-end TVs have Internet connectivity built in and can access streaming media services without the need for additional devices.

- Most Blu-ray players have either Ethernet or Wi-Fi capability and offer access to streaming media services, in addition to playing back movies on disc.

- Standalone network media players connect your TV to your home network to access Internet-based streaming media.

- When streaming media across your network, use the 5GHz 802.11n band and configure your router to assign higher priority to your streaming devices.

15

CONNECTING SMARTPHONES AND TABLETS

Just about everybody has a mobile phone, and most folks have so-called smartphones—phones like the iPhone that let you connect to the Internet to do all sorts of fun and useful stuff. Most smartphones can connect to the Internet via the service provider's cellular data network, or via any nearby Wi-Fi network. Because you have a Wi-Fi network in your home, that's probably how all your smartphones will connect.

It's not just your personal smartphone. Chances are your spouse has one, too, and some or all of your kids. Plus your kids' friends when they visit (which is all the time—admit it), as well as any visitors you welcome to your humble abode. At any given time, you might have a half-dozen or more smartphones connecting to your home network, which probably makes the smartphone the most commonly connected device in your home.

Then, there's all the tablets. Whether you're a iPad, Kindle Fire, or Microsoft Surface user, you need to connect your tablet to your home network to do all the stuff you want to do.

Handheld devices. Wireless network. It may be a marriage of convenience, but it's certainly a necessary conjunction. Read on to learn more.

Connecting to a Wireless Network

Connecting any handheld device to your wireless network should be relatively easy and relatively similar. Your device has to find your network, you have to select your network from a list of available networks, and then you have to enter your network password. Once that's done, your device should recognize your network whenever it's nearby, and do all subsequent connections automatically.

Connecting Your Smartphone

Most smartphones automatically recognize Wi-Fi networks and hotspots when they're in range. It's up to you, however, to determine just *which* network your phone connects to.

This is typically done from your phone's setup or settings menu. On the iPhone, you tap the Settings icon to display the Settings screen. From here, tap Wi-Fi to display the Wi-Fi screen shown in Figure 15.1. Make sure that Wi-Fi is enabled (that's the top setting, which should be On), and then you see a list of nearby networks. Tap the name of your home network and, when prompted, enter your network password. Pretty easy.

Now, if you want to automate this process in subsequent settings, tap the right-arrow next to your network name. The next screen contains settings for this particular wireless network; the operative one is Auto-Join, which you should switch On. Your iPhone remembers your settings and password for this network and connects automatically whenever it's in range.

The process is similar if you have an Android phone. Tap the Settings icon to display the Settings screen, and then tap Wireless Controls. On the next screen, tap Wi-Fi settings, and then tap your network from the list of available networks, as shown in Figure 15.2. When prompted, enter your network password and tap Connect. That's it.

FIGURE 15.1

Connecting to a Wi-Fi network from an Apple iPhone.

FIGURE 15.2

Connecting to a Wi-Fi network from an Android phone.

Same thing if you have a Windows phone: Display the App list, tap Settings, and then tap Wi-Fi. When the Wi-Fi screen appears, as shown in Figure 15.3, make sure that Wi-Fi is turned on and tap the name of your home network. When prompted, enter your network password. Again, it's easy.

FIGURE 15.3

Connecting to a Wi-Fi network from a Windows phone.

 NOTE Most mobile device will default to Wi-Fi reception when near a Wi-Fi hotspot. You'll see your device switch to the 3G data network only when Wi-Fi reception gets too weak or disappears entirely.

Connecting Your Tablet

Connecting a tablet to your home network is just like connecting the related family smartphone.

For example, if you have an iPad, follow the exact same steps as connecting an iPhone, starting by tapping the Settings button. Same thing with most Android tablets; go to the Settings screen and proceed from there.

That said, some Android tablets have their own proprietary interface. For example, the Kindle Fire requires you to open the Home screen, tap the Quick Settings icon, and then tap Wi-Fi. Make sure that Wireless Networking is switched on, and then you'll see a list of all available networks, as shown in Figure 15.4. Tap your network from the list, enter the network password when prompted, and you're in. It's pretty much the same steps as with other tablets, just ensconced within the Kindle Fire ecosystem.

FIGURE 15.4

Connecting to a Wi-Fi network from a Kindle Fire tablet.

If you're at all in doubt, consult your device's instruction manual or relevant help file. The wireless settings shouldn't be too hard to find or configure.

 NOTE   Apple's iPod touch is kind of a like a very small iPad, or maybe an iPhone without the phone functionality. In any instance, it's fully Wi-Fi capable and connects and configures just like an iPhone or iPad.

Using a Guest Network for Visiting Friends

Everybody has a smartphone these days, and they're always tap, tap, tapping on them. Whenever there's a down moment in the conversation, it's time to check your Facebook feed, consult the local weather forecast, or do some web surfing.

That means that most visitors will pull out their smartphones while they're there. Although they could use their cellular data network to connect to the Internet, it's less costly (and possibly faster) for them to connect to the web via your home Wi-Fi network.

For this to happen, you have to provide your guests with your network password. This may seem like an innocuous thing, until you realize that they could also use that password to connect to your network with a notebook PC—and, if they're shifty and technically savvy (certainly not mutually exclusive traits), they could hack into your network to steal your personal data.

Which is why you probably *don't* want to hand out your network password to everyone who darkens your door. You want to be hospitable and share your Internet connection with friends, but you don't want to be *too* friendly, sharing-wise.

The solution, if your wireless router allows it, is set up a guest network just for this purpose. A guest network lets anyone signing in access your Internet connection, but not access the rest of your network. That is, guests can browse the web (with their smartphones or whatever) but not browse the computers and other devices on your network. It's a pretty nifty solution.

 NOTE A guest network runs side-by-side with your normal wireless network. It typically has a different SSID, such as **myguestnetwork**.

Some routers require you to set passwords for your guest network; I suggest something short and easily remembered, such as **guest** or **password**. (You're not really worried about anyone hacking into this guest account, so the password doesn't need to be uber-secure.) Other routers let guests log in without a password, which is less secure but probably okay for just Internet browsing. The point is to allow guests limited access without fully offering the contents of your networked computers.

Switching Between Wi-Fi and Cellular Networks

All smartphones, and many tablets, also let you connect to the Internet via your carrier's cellular data network. If your device offers 4G connectivity (and you have a 4G network nearby) that connection can be pretty quick. Even a 3G device and network can provide enough speed for most web surfing and media streaming.

Why Wi-Fi Is Better Than Cellular

There are issues with connecting via your cellular provider. First, you may not have a 3G or 4G network nearby, or your connection may be flaky. (I sympathize; I lose my AT&T connection when I sit on the far end of the big couch in my living room.) If you don't have a fast and reliable cellular connection, using that connection to access the Internet is an exercise in frustration.

Second, some phone functions are only available via a Wi-Fi connection. For example, if you have an iPhone, you can only update apps from the App Store over Wi-Fi and only sync your phone to computer over Wi-Fi. These functions simply aren't enabled over a cellular connection—by the dictate of either your cellular carrier or device manufacturer.

Finally, your cellular connection costs you money. Most of us are on limited data plans, which means we pay our cellular company a set amount each month and in return receive a set amount of data we can download. If you go over that limit, you pay through the nose for additional minutes. That means that you want to minimize the surfing you do over your costly cellular network, and maximize the surfing you do via (free) Wi-Fi. When you have the option, Wi-Fi is preferable to your cellular data network.

When to Connect via Cellular

When, then, should you connect your smartphone over your carrier's cellular data network? It's really as simple as this: You should only connect via 3G/4G when you don't have a Wi-Fi connection available. When Wi-Fi is there, use it. Only go cellular when there's no other option.

That means you should connect via Wi-Fi at home, where you have access to your home wireless network. You should connect via Wi-Fi when you're out and about and near a Wi-Fi hotspot, whether that be a local coffeehouse, restaurant, or whatever. You should connect via Wi-Fi when you're at a friend's house and he lets you log onto his home wireless network.

You should only use your cellular data connection when there's no Wi-Fi nearby. So, you can connect via cellular when you're driving in your car, commuting via bus or subway, lounging in the park, or simply outside the range of any Wi-Fi network or hotspot.

 CAUTION When you do connect to your carrier's cellular data network, you want to minimize your data usage. Avoid downloading big files, watching streaming video, and other activities that use a lot of those bits and bytes.

How to Switch from Wi-Fi to Cellular

Most phones will default to a Wi-Fi connection if one's available. It's a bit more challenging to switch to a cellular connection instead of Wi-Fi, if that's really what you want to do.

In most cases, you actually have to switch off your phone's Wi-Fi to switch over to a cellular connection. For example, if you have an iPhone you need to tap the Settings icon, tap Wi-Fi on the Settings screen, and then tap Off the Wi-Fi switch. It's a similar process on other phones.

Of course, this means you need to manually turn Wi-Fi back on when you're done using the cellular network. If you leave Wi-Fi off, you'll do all your connecting via cellular, and that could become costly.

Using Your Smartphone or Tablet to Control Networked Devices

Interestingly, once you have your smartphone or tablet connected to your home network, you can do much more with it than simply browse the web. A number of useful apps let you access and control other connected devices in your home from your phone or tablet—essentially turning your phone into a remote-control device for specific functions.

Here are some of the more interesting remote-control apps I've run across:

- **Intelliremote** (www.melloware.com/intelliremote/). Turns your phone or tablet into a full-featured remote control for many PC-based media player programs, including iTunes, MediaMonkey, WinAmp, and Windows Media Center.

- **iRule** (www.iruleathome.com). A terrific little app that converts your phone into a universal remote for your TV and home theater system. Use it with an accompanying black box that converts your phone's commands into infrared signals compatible with all your audio/video equipment.

- **Remote** (www.apple.com/apps/remote/). Apple's official remote control app, shown in Figure 15.5, lets your iPhone or iPad control iTunes playback on any PC (Mac or Windows); it also controls an Apple TV box, if you have one. It's a great app if you play back iTunes media from a computer connected to your home theater system.

FIGURE 15.5

Control iTunes playback on your Mac or Windows PC with Apple's Remote app.

- **Roku** (www.roku.com). Lets you control your Roku media player from your smartphone.

- **Sonos Controller** (www.sonos.com). Controls all media players connected to a Sonos multi-zone music system.

- **TiVo** (www.tivo.com/mytivo/product-features/stay-connected/iphone/). Completely control your TiVo DVR from your iPhone. View channel guides, search for programs, schedule recordings, and more.

Many of these apps work outside as well as inside the home. For example, the TiVo app, shown in Figure 15.6, lets you program your home DVR to record selected shows, even if you're at the office, on the town, or on vacation. Just tell it what to record, wherever you are, and it contacts your TiVo unit at home (assuming it's connected to your Wi-Fi network) to schedule the recording.

FIGURE 15.6

Scheduling a recording with the TiVo smartphone app.

Using Your Smartphone to Control Things When You're Not Around

Speaking of controlling things when you're not around, there are actually lots of apps that let you run your house when you're out and about. These apps run on your smartphone and connect to the Internet from any Wi-Fi hotspot; the commands then transit the Internet to the wireless network in your home, and to the appropriate connected devices.

The most popular of these home control apps include the following:

- **Alarm.com** (www.alarm.com). If you're a customer of this security firm, you can use their app to monitor and control your home's security system—including monitoring any security cameras you have installed, as shown in Figure 15.7. This is great for when you're away from home and want to make sure everything is locked up tight. (Other security companies offer similar apps.)

- **DIRECTV.** If you're a subscriber to this satellite TV service, you can use this app to schedule recordings when you're away from home. (Other cable and satellite services offer similar DVR-recording apps.)

FIGURE 15.7

Monitoring your home's security cameras with the Alarm.com app.

- **LiftMaster Home Control** (www.liftmaster.com). Lets you control your LiftMaster-brand garage door or gate opener from anywhere in the world. Great if you think you left your garage door up or if you want to have the door open when you pull into your driveway.

- **Nest Mobile** (www.nest.com). Use this app with your Nest Learning Thermostat to control your home's heating and cooling from wherever you happen to be at the moment. (Other thermostat manufacturers offer similar apps for their units—but few are as neat as this one. See Figure 15.8.)

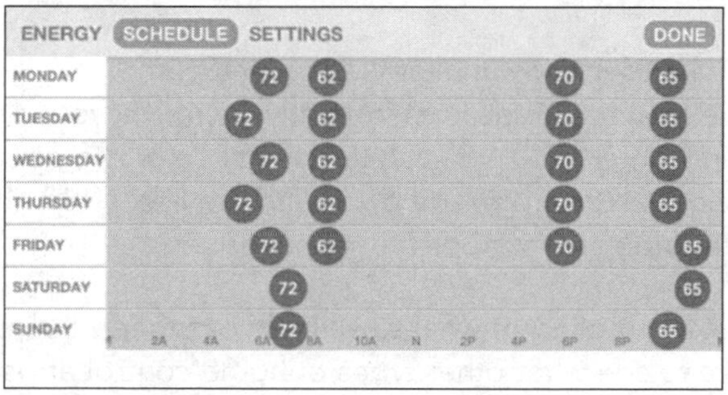

FIGURE 15.8

Controlling your home's heating and cooling—from a distance—with the Nest Mobile app.

- **Pentair ScreenLogic Mobile** (www.pentairpool.com). Helps you manage your pool from the relative comfort of your living room—or anywhere, really. You can adjust the water temperature, turn lights on and off, and even check on the levels of your chemicals. (This app works with IntelliTouch systems, but other pool system manufacturers offer similar apps.)

- **Reef Tank Pro** (www.reeftankpro.com). In conjunction with the Reef Tank Pro aquarium controller, this app lets you monitor the water quality of your saltwater or freshwater fish tanks, even when you're away from home. (Figure 15.9 shows this app in action.)

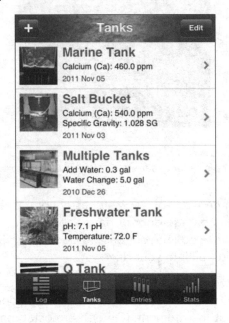

FIGURE 15.9

Keep your aquarium in tip-top shape with the Reef Tank Pro app.

- **X10 Commander** (www.melloware.com/x10commander/). Lets you control any X10 home automation devices from anywhere, via your phone or tablet. As you can see in Figure 15.10, you can turn lights on or off, open or close mechanized drapes, close an open garage door, and the like. (Other home automation companies offer similar apps for their products.)

These are just a sampling of what's available out there. Search your phone or tablet's app store to see what other types of home control apps are available to control devices connected to your home wireless network.

FIGURE 15.10

Control your home automation system with the X10 Commander app.

THE ABSOLUTE MINIMUM

Here are the key points to remember from this chapter:

- You need to connect your smartphone or tablet to either your home wireless network or your cellular data network to access the Internet.

- Any visiting friends will want to share your Wi-Fi connection to connect their phones to the Internet; consider setting up a guest network to provide Internet-only access for these visitors.

- You probably want to use your phone's Wi-Fi connection to access the Internet whenever you can to avoid costly cellular data charges.

- A number of smartphone/tablet apps let you use your device to control other networked devices, such as your computer or television set.

- Many apps also let you control home functions while you're away from home, over the Internet.

16

SHARING PRINTERS AND OTHER DEVICES

One of the primary advantages of setting up a home network is that you can share expensive equipment, such as printers and scanners, between all the computers and other devices connected to the network. You don't have to buy separate printers for each computer you own; instead, you can share a single networked printer.

There are a number of ways to share a printer over your home network. You can share a printer that's already connected to one of your networked computers. You can connect a so-called network printer directly to your network router, either wirelessly or via Ethernet. And you can use a cloud printing service, such as Google Cloud Print, to access your shared printer over the Internet when you're not at home.

Connecting a Shared Printer to Your Network

The easiest way to share a printer over a network is to connect that printer to a host PC, as normal, and then let all the other computers on the network access it via the host. This type of setup is shown in Figure 16.1.

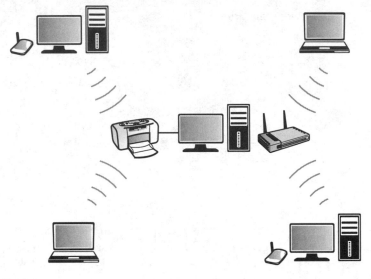

FIGURE 16.1

A single printer connected to all the computers on a network, through a host PC.

For this network configuration to work, you have to configure the host PC to activate printer sharing and that printer has to be configured as sharable in your computer's operating system. Then, each of the other computers on the network has to install the drivers for that printer as a network printer.

After you complete the installation and configuration, the printer will appear as an option when you go to print from any PC on your network. Click the Print button, and the print instruction will be sent from the current PC to the PC that hosts the printer and then on to the printer itself.

This type of setup works with virtually any type of printer—inkjet, laser, multifunction, photo, or whatever. The printer is typically connected to the host PC via USB. As long as the printer is connected to a network computer and configured for shared usage, it will be available to all other computers on the network.

 NOTE Connecting a printer to a computer is typically easy. For example, in later versions of Windows, all you have to do is connect one end of a USB cable to the USB output on your printer and the other to a USB port on your PC. Connect the printer to a power outlet and power it on, and Windows should automatically recognize the new printer and install the proper device driver automatically. Follow the onscreen instructions to finish the installation.

To share a printer that's connected to one of your networked printers, you have to configure that printer for network use. The process is different, depending on which operating system the host computer is running.

Chapter 11, "Connecting Home Computers," discussed how to configure different types of printer sharing. Turn there for detailed instructions, and then keep reading here to learn how to use your newly networked printer.

NOTE   You only have to enable printer sharing for the computer to which the printer is physically connected. Once printer sharing is enabled on that PC, the printer will be visible from all other computers connected to your network.

Connecting a Wireless Network Printer

If you're sharing a printer between multiple computers on your home network, you might want to go with a network printer. This is a printer, like the one shown in Figure 16.2, that connects to the router in your wireless network, but doesn't physically connect to any single computer. Most network printers today are wireless, with built-in Wi-Fi, although models with Ethernet connections are also available.

FIGURE 16.2

HP's Deskjet D3050A wireless inkjet printer, with 802.11b/g/n networking. (Photo courtesy of HP.)

Figure 16.3 shows how a network looks with a wireless printer installed. Any computer or handheld device connected to the network can print to this printer, no cables required.

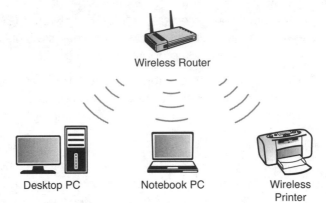

FIGURE 16.3

A wireless network with a wireless printer installed.

Benefits of a Network Printer

The primary benefit of a network printer is that you can place it anywhere in your home. Because it's not tethered to a given PC, it doesn't have to sit next to any single computer.

A wireless printer can also make sense if you only have a single computer connected to your network, and you don't want to (or can't) connect the printer directly to the PC. You can keep your wireless printer in your office while you use a notebook PC in your living room or bedroom. When you opt to print a document from your PC, wherever it may be, that document prints on the printer in your office. Physical constraints to printing are eliminated.

Setting Up a Network Printer

In general, the setup goes something like this: You turn on your printer and do the normal printer setup stuff, such as inserting the ink cartridge. You then connect the printer to your network router either via Wi-Fi or Ethernet.

In most instances, the printer automatically detects and connects to your network. With some models, however, you may need to run an installation utility from one of your network computers, and input the printer's IP address (which should appear on the printer's display screen) when prompted. You may also be prompted to enter your network's security password on the printer's keypad.

After the printer is properly configured, it should appear as a printing option for all computers connected to your network.

Connecting a Printer via a Print Server

What do you do if you have an older printer that you'd like to convert for wireless network use? When you want to disconnect a printer from a specific PC and connect it to your network router, you need a device called a *print server*.

A print server is a small device, like the one in Figure 16.4, that connects your printer directly to your network router and lets all the computers on your network access the printer. You can find both wireless and Ethernet print servers, although most units these days are hard wired—that is, the printer connects to the print server via USB, and then the print server connects to your router via Ethernet. Units are typically priced in the U.S. $50–$100 range.

FIGURE 16.4

D-Link's DP-301U print server for USB printers. (Photo courtesy of D-Link.)

NOTE Because of the profusion of printers with wireless-networking functionality built in, the popularity of print servers is waning—although you can still find these devices at most consumer electronics outlets.

Setup and configuration differs from model to model, but typically is a little more involved than setting up other network equipment. For example, you may need to assign a dedicated IP address to the print server. Make sure that you follow the instructions that come with the print server and consult the manufacturer's website if you run into difficulties.

Installing a Shared Printer on Other PCs

To print to a shared or network printer, device drivers for that printer will probably need to be installed on each of the other computers on your network. As you might suspect, the details differ slightly different for different operating systems, although the general process is similar.

On a Windows computer, open the Control Panel and navigate to the Printers section. From there, click Add a Printer and then opt to add a network printer (*not* a local printer). Select the printer from the list provided, enter a name for that printer, and finish the installation. Windows will then search for and install the device drivers for that printer onto this computer.

The steps are similar if you have a Mac. Open Print & Scan and click the + or Add button to add a new printer. Your networked printer should appear in the list of available printers, perhaps within a specific workgroup (if the printer is connected to a Windows computer). Select this printer, pick the correct printer driver, and you should be ready to print.

Printing to a Network Printer

Once you have one or more printers connected to your network, you can print a document from any connected computer to any of the network printers. It's easy.

When you click the Print button to print a document from just about any application, you typically see a Print dialog box, like the one shown in Figure 16.5, or a Print panel, like the one in Figure 16.6.

All the printers connected to your network are accessible from this dialog box or panel, just as if they were physically connected to the current PC. Select the printer you want from the Printer list and click the Print button.

 NOTE In most Windows applications, network printers have a little green connector at the bottom of the icon.

The print instructions are now sent from the open application on the current computer across the network to the shared printer. The printer prints the document, indifferent to which PC it came from.

 NOTE Print functionality differs from program to program. Make sure that you consult a given app's help files if you need assistance in configuring various print options.

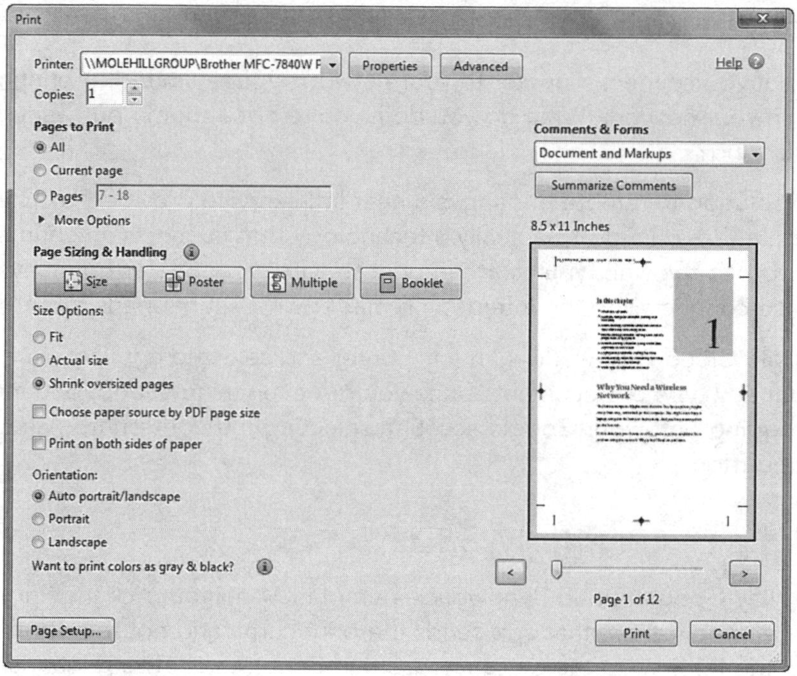

FIGURE 16.5

Using the Print dialog box to print to a network printer.

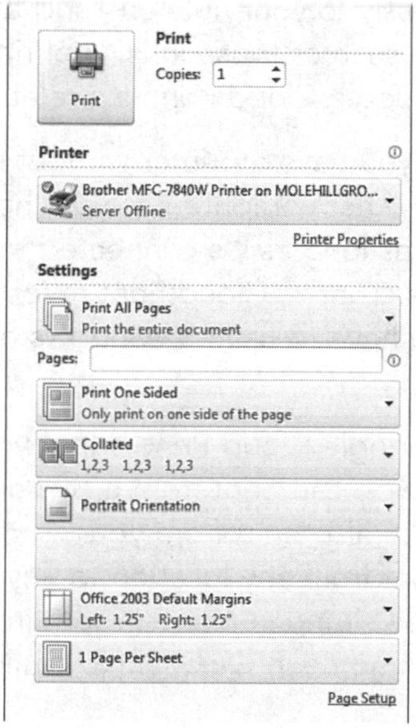

FIGURE 16.6

The Print panel in Microsoft Word, printing to a network printer.

Using Google Cloud Print

Even if you connect a printer to your network, you're limited to printing from within your network. What do you do if you're not at home but want to print something?

The solution to remote printing is a neat little service provided by Google, called Google Cloud Print. It's actually a technology that connects any printer on your network to the web; you can then print to a network printer from any computer or device connected to the Internet, no matter where it happens to be.

Google Cloud Print works with any printer and selected applications to print just about any type of document. Once you get everything set up, printing is as simple as logging onto your Google account, selecting the right printer, and clicking the Print button.

How Google Cloud Print Works

The way Google Cloud Print works is simple. When you click the Print button in a given application, that app sends the print command not to a local printer, but over the Internet to the designated Cloud Print printer. The printer isn't physically connected to your current computer or network; the entire process is web-based.

Of course, you now have the issue of finding an Internet-ready printer that's compatible with Google Cloud Print. Some are, but many aren't. You need a printer that can connect wirelessly to your network, and thus connect over the Internet to the Cloud Print service, such as those in HP's ePrint line. Configuring one of these printers to work with Google Cloud Print is a relatively easy operation.

But, what do you do if you have a printer without built-in Cloud Print capability? Here, Google relies on other computers in your household. Cloud Print can print to any existing printer, as long as it's connected to a Windows or Mac computer that has Internet access. That is, Cloud Print relies on the PC for the connection—which means you have to have a Windows or Mac computer handy (and powered up).

The nice thing about Google Cloud Print is that you can use it to print from just about any device. Yes, you can print from a computer on your network to a Cloud Print printer, but you can also print from your iPhone or Android smartphone or tablet. And you can print from any location to any configured Cloud Print printer, which means you can be sitting in a hotel room in New York City and print to your Cloud Print printer back home in Omaha. No cables or printer drivers necessary.

Cloud Print Utilities

Unfortunately, not every application lets you print directly via Google Cloud Print. You can print web pages from the Google Chrome web browser, but beyond that, you won't find a Cloud Print option in Microsoft Word or PowerPoint.

For all other apps, you need to install a "virtual printer" utility on your computer that enables cloud printing. This utility installs a Cloud Print option in your list of printers in your operating system; cloud printing, then, is as easy as selecting this virtual Cloud Print printer from the list of available printers.

A few of these virtual printer utilities are available:

- **Paperless Printer for Windows** (www.rarefind.com/paperlessprinter/, free)
- **Cloud Print for Windows** (www.swdevs.com/cps.htm, $19.95)
- **Cloud Printer for the Mac** (www.webabode.com/software/cloudprint.html, free)

 NOTE You can also install similar printing utilities for your iOS or Android portable device. Learn more at www.google.com/cloudprint/learn/apps.html.

Connecting a Cloud Print-Ready Computer

Before you can print from Google Chrome, you first must connect your printer to the Google Cloud Print service. You can connect either Cloud Print-ready printers or existing printers connected to a Windows or Mac computer.

If you're looking for a Cloud Print-ready printer, models are available from Canon, Epson, HP, and Kodak. To use one of these printers for cloud printing, you must register it with the Google Cloud Print service. Follow your manufacturer's instructions to do so. (It's typically as simple as going to a registration page on the web and entering your printer's email address.)

Connecting an Existing Printer

To connect an existing printer to the Google Cloud Print service, it must be connected to a Windows or Mac computer that is connected to the Internet. You'll also need to have the Google Chrome web browser installed on your computer and have a Google account registered in your name. You then enable the Google Cloud Print Connector, which connects this computer's printers to the Cloud Print service.

NOTE   To download and install Google Chrome (it's free), go to www.google.com/chrome/. To create a new Google account (also free), go to www.google.com/accounts/.

Here's how to do it:

1. Open the Google Chrome web browser, click the Customize and Control button at the top-right corner (shown in Figure 16.7), and select Settings.

New tab	Ctrl+T
New window	Ctrl+N
New incognito window	Ctrl+Shift+N
Bookmarks	▶
Edit	Cut Copy Paste
Zoom	– 100% + ⌞ ⌝
Save page as...	Ctrl+S
Find...	Ctrl+F
Print...	Ctrl+P
Tools	▶
History	Ctrl+H
Downloads	Ctrl+J
Signed in	
Settings	
About Google Chrome	
View background pages (2)	
Help	
Exit	

FIGURE 16.7

Getting ready to connect a printer to Google Cloud Print.

2. When the Settings page appears, scroll to the bottom of the page and click Show Advanced Settings.

3. Scroll to the Google Cloud Print section and click the Sign In to Google Cloud Print button.

4. When the Set Up Google Cloud Print dialog box opens, sign into Google Cloud Print with your Google account email address and password and click the Sign In button.

5. Google displays a dialog box that tells you Google Cloud Print has been enabled for all printers connected to this computer. Click the OK button.

Sharing a Printer

After you register a printer with the Google Cloud Print service, you can then opt to let other users share that printer. You can share a Cloud Print printer with any user who has a Google account; you just have to tell Google Cloud Print that the user has permission to print.

1. Go to www.google.com/cloudprint/ using your web browser.

2. Click the Printers tab in the left sidebar, as shown in Figure 16.8.

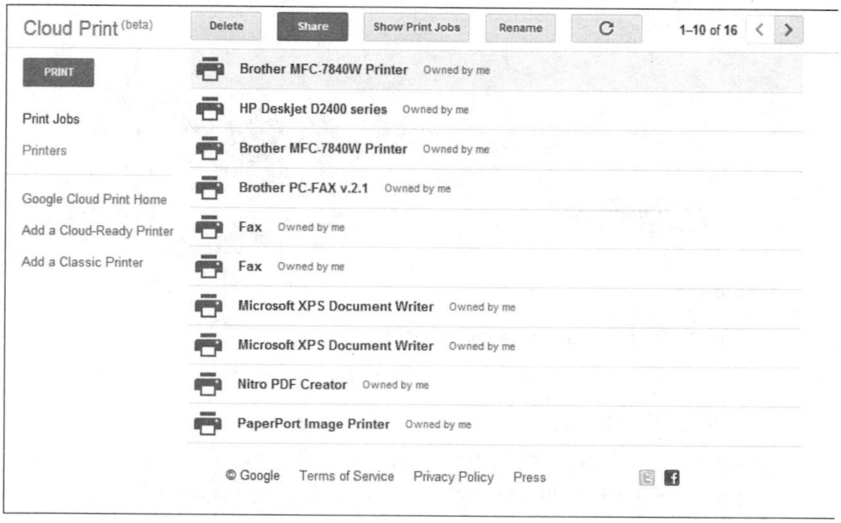

FIGURE 16.8

Managing Cloud Print printers.

3. Click the printer you want to share, and then click the Share button.

4. When the Sharing Settings dialog box appears, as shown in Figure 16.9, enter the email address of the person you want to share with into the large box at the bottom.

5. Click the Share button.

If, at a later date, you decide that you no longer want to share your printer with a particular user, you can delete that person from your approved sharing list. Just return to the Sharing Settings dialog box for that printer and click the X next to that person's name.

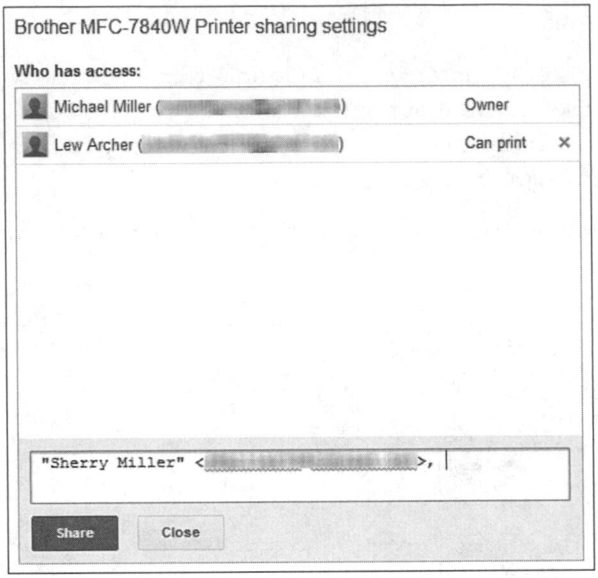

Brother MFC-7840W Printer sharing settings

Who has access:

Michael Miller ( )	Owner	
Lew Archer ( )	Can print	×

"Sherry Miller" < >,

Share   Close

FIGURE 16.9

Sharing a Cloud Print printer with other users.

TIP   You can also view all in-process and recent print jobs from the Cloud Print web page. Just click the Print Jobs tab in the left sidebar, and you'll see the status of all recent documents.

Printing via Google Cloud Print

To print from any computer to a printer connected to Google Cloud Print, that printer must be powered on and connected to the Internet. If it's a "classic" printer, it must be connected to a Windows or Mac PC that is connected to the Internet. If it's a Cloud Print-enabled printer, it just has to be turned on.

Printing, then, is as simple as clicking the Print button within your application. Select the desired printer from the Printer list, and then click the Print button.

NOTE   The desired Cloud Print printer may be listed in a Google Cloud Print section of the printers list.

Sharing Other Peripherals

Printers aren't the only peripherals you can share over a network. Just about anything you can connect to a PC can be shared with other PCs via network connections.

For example, many families and offices only have a single scanner, as this peripheral isn't used that often. It wouldn't be cost-effective to buy scanners for every PC in the building, so sharing that single scanner over the network makes a lot of sense.

Installing a network scanner is just like installing a network printer. You connect the scanner to a host PC, enable printer sharing on that PC, and then have access to the scanner from any other PC on your network.

Many homes and offices like to share big external hard drives. This type of peripheral is even easier to share than a printer or scanner. All you have to do is connect the hard drive to a host computer, enable file sharing for that computer, and then configure the drive as a shared drive. Any PC on your network can now access that shared drive via Windows Explorer or the Mac Finder.

THE ABSOLUTE MINIMUM

Here are the key points to remember from this chapter:

- Any printer connected to any computer on your network can be shared with other computers and devices on your network.

- Even better, a wireless network printer can be connected directly to your network router; it's not necessary to first connect a wireless printer to a PC.

- Older printers can be turned into freestanding network printers by means of a small print server device that connect directly to your network router.

- Printing to a network printer is as easy as selecting that printer from the list of available printers in an application.

- To print to one of your printers when you're away from home, connect that printer to the Google Cloud Print service. You can then print to that printer from any computer or device with an Internet connection.

SHARING AND TRANSFERRING FILES

One of the primary benefits of setting up a home or small business network is being able to share files between multiple computers connected to the network. You can store all of your digital photos on one computer and view them on others; work collaboratively from multiple computers on a single project file; even copy and back up files from multiple computers to a single central location.

How easy is it to share and transfer files over a small network? Easier than it used to be—and a lot easier than you'd think.

How File Sharing Works

You'd think file sharing would be an automatic thing on a network, but that isn't necessarily so. Just because you have multiple computers connected to your home network doesn't mean that the contents of each of the PCs will be automatically visible to each other. In fact, all the contents of a PC are hidden from other users by default—so you *can't* view or share files. (It's a security thing.)

If you want other users on your network to be able to view or edit a document on one of your computers, you must enable file sharing for that particular computer and folder. There are two ways to do this.

If you want to share a single document on a Windows PC, the easiest way to proceed is to save that document to the Public folder on your hard disk. This folder is, by default, accessible to every user on this computer, as well as every user on the network.

Windows also lets you configure any other folder or drive on a given computer as a shared folder/drive. That way another user could go directly to your Documents or Music folders, for example, without you first having to move the shared file to your Public folder.

Once file sharing has been enabled for a given folder, all the other computers on your network will be able to see the drive or folder you decided to share—assuming you assign permission to given users. When you open Windows Explorer, File Explorer, or the Mac Finder on another computer, you'll see the shared drive/folder displayed.

CAUTION   Although it's great to share files across two or more PCs on your network, be cautious about enabling file sharing. When you share a folder or drive, anyone with appropriate permission can access the contents of that folder or drive over your network. Make sure that you share only those folders and drives you want to share, and keep the other folders on your computer private.

You should also make sure that you have a firewall installed on your network and that you've activated adequate wireless security (if you have a wireless network). This keeps unwanted intruders from hacking into your network—and gaining unauthorized access to your private files.

Configuring File Sharing in Windows

Before you can share files and folders, even the Public folder, you first have to enable file sharing on a given computer. If file sharing is *not* enabled, no files or folders will be visible to other computers on the network.

We went through the steps to enable file sharing back in Chapter 11, "Connecting Home Computers," so I won't repeat that information. Follow the instructions in Chapter 11 to turn on file sharing for your particular computer.

Enabling Password-Protected Sharing

When you enable file sharing, any user on your network can access any shared folder on that computer, no questions asked. You may, however, want to limit access to only those users who have valid user accounts on your network. To do this, you need to enable (on a Windows PC) what Microsoft calls password-protected sharing.

With password-protected sharing, no one can access your shared folders, including the Public folder, without first providing a valid username and password. Even more stringent, the username must be registered on the same computer on which the shared folder is hosted; a user on another computer who does not have a user account on the folder's computer will not be able to gain access.

If a user tries to access a password-protected folder, he will automatically gain access if he has a user account on that computer and is signed in under that user account. If that isn't the case, the user will be prompted for his username and password; entering a valid username and password gains access to the folder. If the user does not enter a username and password that is registered on the folder's computer, access is denied.

Password protection is applied to all the shared folders on a computer, not just for selected folders. To enable password-protected sharing on a Windows machine, you need to open the Network and Sharing Center and select Change Advanced Sharing Settings. Scroll to the Password Protected Sharing section, shown in Figure 17.1, select Turn On Password Protected Sharing, and then click Save Changes or Apply.

Again, for password-protected sharing to work, each user must have an account registered on the computer that holds the shared files. For example, if a user named Bob has an account on computer 2 but not on computer 1, when he tries to access a shared folder on computer 1, he'll be denied access.

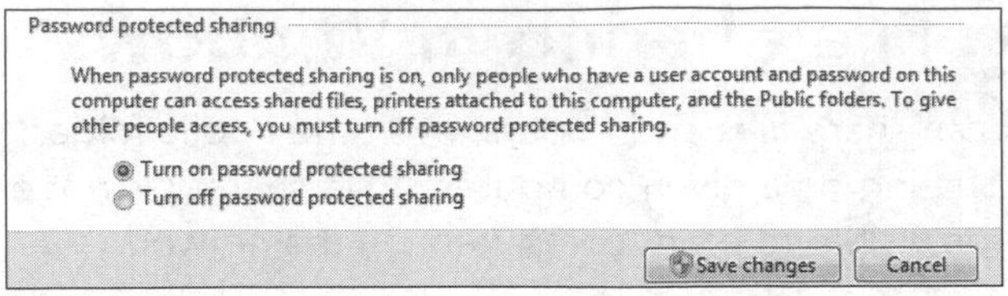

Password protected sharing

When password protected sharing is on, only people who have a user account and password on this computer can access shared files, printers attached to this computer, and the Public folders. To give other people access, you must turn off password protected sharing.

⦿ Turn on password protected sharing
⦾ Turn off password protected sharing

Save changes   Cancel

FIGURE 17.1

Enabling password-protected sharing in Windows 7.

For that reason, you probably want to create user accounts for all users on all of your computers. Back to our Bob example, you'd want to create a user account for Bob on both computer 1 and computer 2. Then, when Bob tries to access the first computer from the second, his account will be recognized and file access granted.

Sharing the Public Folder

The easiest way to share files on a Windows machine is to move or copy the files you want to share into the Public folder. Other users across the network can then access the Public folder as a shared folder and all the contents within.

For this to work, however, you first have to enable public folder sharing on each PC you want to share. To do this, open the Network and Sharing Center and select Change Advanced Sharing Settings. Scroll to the Public Folder Sharing section, shown in Figure 17.2, and select Turn On Sharing So Anyone with Network Access Can Read and Write Files in the Public Folders. (This option may be worded slightly differently in different versions of Windows.) Click Save Changes or Apply when done.

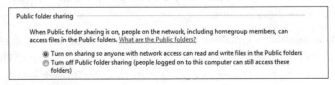

Public folder sharing

When Public folder sharing is on, people on the network, including homegroup members, can access files in the Public folders. What are the Public folders?

⦿ Turn on sharing so anyone with network access can read and write files in the Public folders
⦾ Turn off Public folder sharing (people logged on to this computer can still access these folders)

FIGURE 17.2

Enabling public folder sharing in Windows 7.

Sharing Other Folders

Using the public folder is the easiest way to share files on a Windows PC, but it's not the only way. It's a little more involved, but you can designate any specific folder in Windows as a shared folder; this lets other users on the network access the folder you specify without having to move files into the Public folder.

CAUTION For individual folder sharing to work, you still need to enable file sharing for your entire computer, as described in Chapter 11.

To enable file sharing for a specific folder, follow these steps:

1. Use Windows Explorer or File Explorer to navigate to (but don't open) the folder you want to share.

2. Right-click the folder you want to share and select Share With from the pop-up menu and then one of the following options.

3. To let other members of a Windows HomeGroup view the files within this folder, but not edit those files, select Homegroup (Read).

4. To let other members of a Windows HomeGroup both read and edit the files in this folder, select Homegroup (Read/Write).

5. To let only specific users share the files in this folder, select Specific People and continue to step 6.

6. If you have password-protected sharing enabled, the File Sharing window, shown in Figure 17.3, will list all the users on this machine in the pull-down Add list. Select one or more users from this list with whom you want to share this folder, and then click the Add button to add them to your share list.

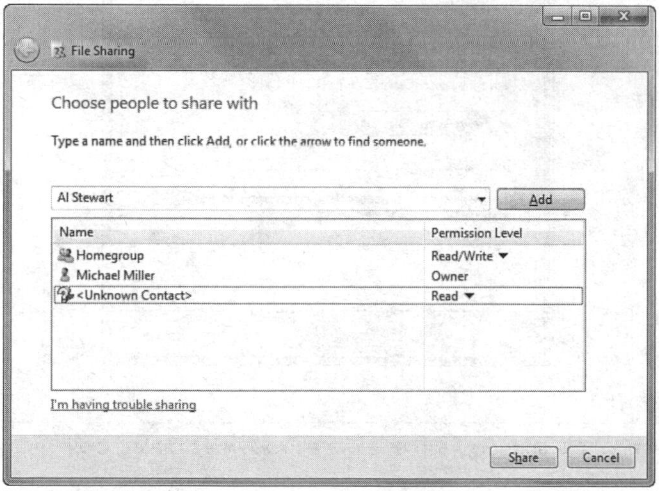

FIGURE 17.3

Selecting users with whom to share the current folder.

7. Pull down the Permission Level list next to each user and select a specific level: Reader, Contributor, Co-Owner, or (if you've created the folder) Owner.

8. Click the Share button.

 NOTE If you don't have password-protected sharing enabled, the File Sharing window Add list has only two options: the Guest and Everyone accounts. Select the Everyone account to enable sharing with all users, and then select a specific share level from the Permission Level list.

You can also enable file sharing from a folder's Properties dialog box, shown in Figure 17.4. Right-click the folder in any Explorer window and select Properties; when the Properties dialog box appears, select the Sharing tab. From here, you can click the Share button to display the File Sharing window, previously discussed, or Advanced Sharing to display the Advanced Sharing dialog box.

My Adobe Presentations Properties

General | Sharing | Security | Previous Versions

Network File and Folder Sharing

My Adobe Presentations
Shared

Network Path:
\\HP-NOTEBOOK\Users\Michael Miller\Documents\My Adobe

Share...

Advanced Sharing

Set custom permissions, create multiple shares, and set other advanced sharing options.

Advanced Sharing...

Password Protection

People must have a user account and password for this computer to access shared folders.

To change this setting, use the Network and Sharing Center.

Close | Cancel | Apply

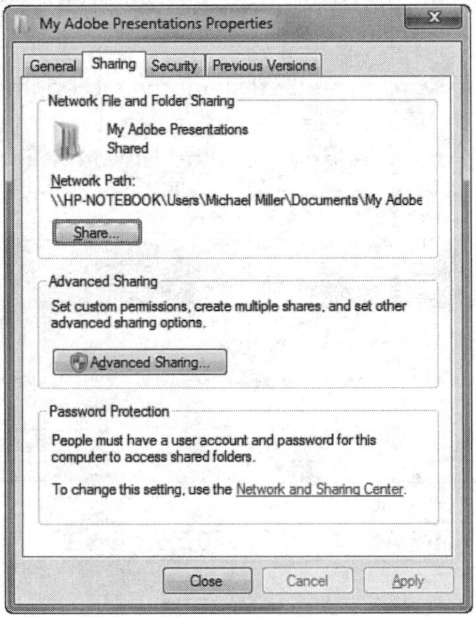

FIGURE 17.4

Enabling simple file sharing from a folder's Properties dialog box.

As you can see in Figure 17.5, the Advanced Sharing dialog box lets you do the following:

• Create more than one share for the same folder, with different share names

• Limit the number of users who can simultaneously share this folder

- Add a comment to the shared folder

- Specify who can access this folder and their permission levels (from the Permissions dialog box, shown in Figure 17.6)

- Specify whether the contents of this folder can be made available offline (via caching)

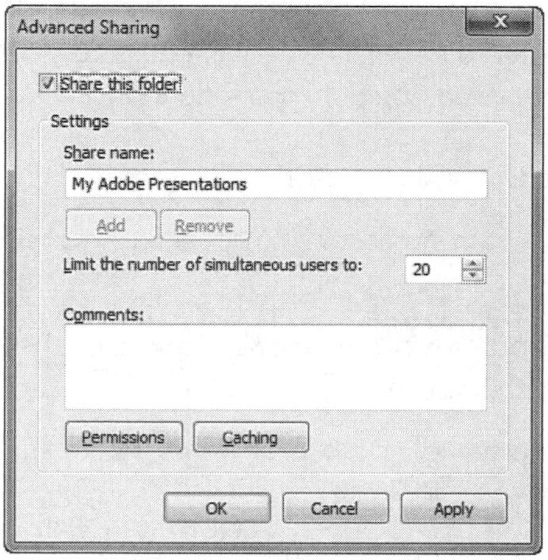

FIGURE 17.5

Configuring advanced sharing properties.

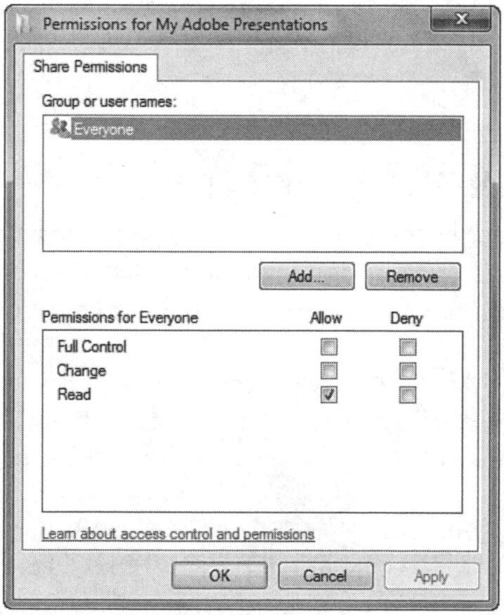

FIGURE 17.6

Setting permissions for a shared folder.

Sharing Complete Drives

Windows also lets you share complete drives on your network computers. To share a drive, you have to give that drive a distinct name; Windows won't let you share "C:", but it will let you share "Drive C" or "My Drive C."

 CAUTION Sharing the complete contents of a drive—especially drive C, which contains your system files—can be risky. It's better to designate specific folders to share, rather than allow unfettered access to your entire drive.

Follow these steps to configure a drive for sharing:

1. From either the Start menu or Windows Explorer (in Windows 8), select Computer.

2. When the Computer window opens, right-click the drive you want to share and select Share With, Advanced Sharing.

3. When the Properties dialog box appears, make sure the Sharing tab is selected.

4. Click the Advanced Sharing button.

5. When the Advanced Sharing dialog box appears, check the Share This Folder option.

6. Enter a new name for the drive into the Share Name box.

7. Click OK.

Accessing Computers on Your Network

Once you have your home network set up, you can access shared content stored on other computers on your network. How you do so depends on what type of computer you're running—and how you have it configured.

 CAUTION When you first add a new computer or shared folder to your network, it may take up to 10 or 15 minutes to be discovered by your other networked computers.

Accessing Windows HomeGroup Computers

If you have a PC running Windows 7 or Windows 8, and you have a HomeGroup configured for similar PCs, you can access the content of those other HomeGroup computers via Windows Explorer or File Explorer.

All you have to do is open File Explorer (in Windows 8) or Windows Explorer (in Windows 7) and go to the HomeGroup section of the navigation pane. Click or tap the computer you want to access, and Windows now displays the shared libraries on the selected computer, as shown in Figure 17.7. Double-click a library to access that particular content.

FIGURE 17.7

Viewing shared libraries on a Windows HomeGroup computer.

Accessing Other Computers from a Windows PC

A computer doesn't have to be connected to your HomeGroup for you to access its content from a Windows PC. Windows lets you access any computer connected to your home network—although you can only share content the computer's owner has configured as sharable.

 TIP On most older computers, shared files are stored in the Public folder. Look in this folder first for the files you want.

To access other computers on your network, open Windows Explorer or Network Explorer. Go to the Network section of the navigation pane and click or tap the computer you want to access. Windows now displays the shared folders on the selected computer, as shown in Figure 17.8; double-click a folder to view that folder's content.

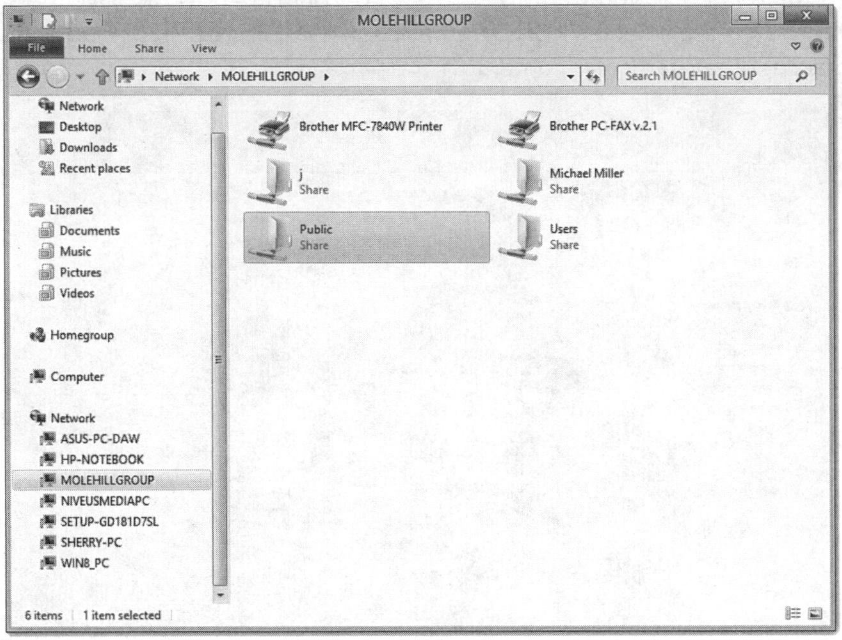

FIGURE 17.8

Viewing the contents of a networked computer from Windows Explorer.

NOTE The icons for the shared folders look like regular folders but with a green "pipe" beneath. This is supposed to signify the network connection.

If the folder is not password protected, you'll gain immediate access. If the item is password protected, one of two things will happen:

- If you're logged onto your current PC with a user account that also exists on the other PC, you'll gain immediate access to the folder or file.

- If you're not logged onto your current PC with a user account that also exists on the other PC, you are prompted for your username and password. Successfully enter those, and you'll gain access to the folder or file.

It's also possible that the shared folder has been created with a list of specific users who can gain access. If you're on the list, you'll be able to open the folder; if not, access will be denied.

Accessing Other Computers from a Mac

Accessing computers, folders, and files across a network is slightly different if you're using a Mac computer. You start by opening the Mac Finder; from there, select Go, Connect to Server, and click Browse.

Next, go to the Shared section in the Finder's sidebar and select the computer you want to connect to; both Windows and Mac computers should be listed here. If the computer you want isn't listed, select All to display all the networked computers.

With the desired computer selected, click the Connect As button. You'll be prompted to enter the name and password of a registered user of the selected computer; do so, and you now see a list of shared folders on that computer. Select the folder you want, click OK, and that folder now appears on your own desktop.

Using a Home Server for File Sharing

You can share files from any computer connected to your network to any other connected computer. The only problem with this is that it's a little scattershot; you have some files on this machine, some on that one, still more on your spouse's notebook, and so forth. When your files are scattered across multiple computers, it can be challenging to find the one specific file you want.

This type of scattershot storage is also challenging when some of the files you want are on notebook PCs that aren't always sitting at home. If you want a particular file that's on your spouse's notebook, and your spouse just happens to have that notebook with her at work today, you can't access that file; it's not available locally if the PC it's stored on isn't home and connected to the network.

The solution to this scattershot storage is to use a single computer or home server to store all your important files. With all of your files stored in this central location, it's easy enough for any computer connected to your network to find and share any specific file.

The key to this strategy is to set up a logical system of folders and subfolders on your home server. Make sure all of your music files in the Music folder; make sure all of your Office documents are in the Documents folder. And so on.

Then, make sure you properly share the key folders on your home server, and grant access (or provide user names and passwords) to everyone on your network who might want to access those files. Give everyone the appropriate read/write access so they can store their new files on the server, as well as access existing files. Then, let everyone have at it.

Backing Up Your Data Across a Network

Another advantage of network-based file sharing is being able to back up your valuable data across your network. Obviously, you want to back up data to a different drive than where it normally resides; this way, if the drive fails, you can restore the data from the backup drive. This backup drive can be an external hard drive connected to a PC on the network, or a home server or network attached storage device connected directly to your network router.

You can then back up data from any connected computer to this connected drive or server. Use the backup software that came with the external disc drive or server, or backup utilities installed on individual PCs. How you do it isn't as important as actually doing it; the more frequently you back up your data, the more you'll be protected if something bad happens to any of the computers on your network.

Sharing Files in the Cloud

What do you do if you want to access a given file on another networked computer, but you're not currently at home? You may want to consider something called *cloud computing*, where instead of storing your files on a networked PC, you store them elsewhere on the Internet—out in what we call the "cloud" of connected computers.

What Is Cloud Storage?

Many companies—including both Microsoft and Apple—offer cloud-storage services. When you subscribe to a cloud-storage service, you effectively lease storage capacity from the cloud-storage service. (Although many companies offer a small amount of storage space for free.) You then have access to the contracted amount of storage space, which you access via the Internet, typically using your web browser.

When you access a cloud-storage service, what you see in your browser window looks like a single server or hard disk on your computer, but it's really just a virtual storage device. In reality, your data may be stored across multiple physical servers, sometimes spanning multiple physical locations (or even continents!) that then appear to be a single server in your storage dashboard.

Still, you save and retrieve files from a cloud storage service much the same way you do on any networked computer. It's just that your files aren't saved on your current computer or, for that matter, anywhere on your physical network. The files are uploaded to the Internet, to your own designated storage space on the service's cloud servers. It may look like you're saving your files locally, but in reality, they're out there, somewhere, in the cloud.

Why Use Cloud Storage?

Cloud storage offers many benefits for today's computer users. Here are just a few of the reasons you might want to use a cloud-storage service:

- **Scalability.** When you rent cloud-storage space, you can opt to use as much or as little space as you need. Many services offer a basic amount of storage space for free, but let you purchase additional storage as you need it. If your storage needs are minimal, you may be able to get by with the basic storage plan. If you need to store more or larger files, you can pay extra for the additional space you need. In other words, your storage space easily "scales" to your current needs.

- **Reliability.** If you've ever had a computer hard drive fail, you know how important it is to have access to backup data. Well, cloud storage can be used as giant online backup drive; it's easy enough to mirror your existing computer drives in the cloud. Even if you rely on cloud services for your primary data storage, you still have the peace of mind that comes from knowing your data is duplicated on multiple servers, all owned by your cloud-storage provider.

- **Remote access.** Let's return to the scenario where you want to access a particular file you have stored on your home network, but you're not at home—you're on vacation, at work, or just down the street at the local coffeehouse. In any case, you don't have access to that file because you're not physically connected to your home network. This is where cloud storage excels; your files are stored on the Internet, and are thus accessible from any computer that's connected to the Internet. All you have to do is use your web browser to connect to the cloud-storage service and you have access to those files you want. It doesn't matter where you are—your files are always accessible.

- **Collaboration.** This worldwide accessibility is great if you need to collaborate on a given project with people who live in other locations. Let's say you're collaborating on a work project with people in offices around the country, or on a community project with others in your neighborhood. In either case, everyone connected to the project has access to the exact same files, no physical transfer required, just by logging into the shared cloud-storage service. With most cloud-based storage services, multiple people can work on the same file in real time; any changes one person makes is immediately reflected in what other users see onscreen. If you do a lot of collaboration, professionally or personally, cloud storage is the way to go.

Popular Cloud-Storage Services

Several services let you store your files on their proprietary corporate cloud. Some are more suited for larger corporate clients, but there are a number of services ideal for individual consumers, including the following:

- **Apple iCloud** (www.apple.com/icloud/). iCloud is a cloud-storage service for any Mac computer or iOS device, which includes iPhones and iPads. (In fact, it's built into all new Apple devices.) It's not designed for Windows PCs, so that's an issue. You get 5GB of storage for free, with an additional 10GB of storage running $20/year.

- **Box** (www.box.com). Box works on both Windows and Mac computers, and it offers 5GB of storage for free. A 25GB plan runs $9.99/month.

- **Dropbox** (www.dropbox.com). Dropbox is a popular service that easily syncs file versions between a given computer and the cloud storage. It works on both Windows and Mac computers, but only offers 2GB of storage for free. (The Dropbox Pro service offers 100GB of storage for $9.99/month.)

- **Google Drive** (drive.google.com). Google has been at the forefront of consumer-based cloud computing, so it's not surprising that the company offers its own cloud-storage service. Google Drive, shown in Figure 17.9, provides 5GB of storage for anyone with a Google account; you can upgrade to 25GB of storage for $2.50/month. You can access Google Drive from any Windows or Mac computer by using your web browser.

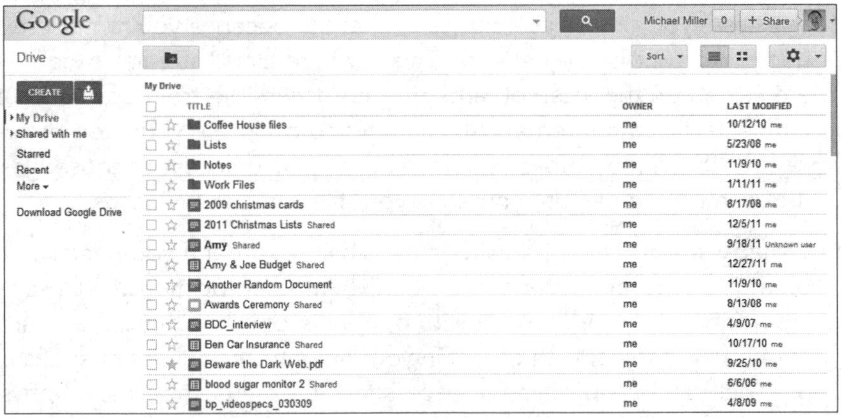

FIGURE 17.9

Accessing files stored on Google Drive.

- **Microsoft SkyDrive** (skydrive.live.com). This is Microsoft's cloud-storage service, well integrated into Windows 8. (In fact, SkyDrive uses the same tile-based interface as the Windows 8 Start screen.) You get 7GB of storage for free; a 20GB plan runs $10/year. The nice thing about SkyDrive is that you can access the service from any Windows or Mac computer, or any Apple, Android, or Windows phone or tablet. SkyDrive offers seamless integration with both desktop and web-based versions of Microsoft Office, which should appeal to business users. Sign in with your existing Microsoft Live or Hotmail account.

If your sharing needs are minimal, any of these services' free plans should fit the bill. If you need to share more or larger files, compare the monthly costs for higher capacity plans; some are more affordable than others.

Myself, I like both Google Drive and Microsoft SkyDrive. Google Drive is great if you use other Google services, where SkyDrive is ideal for Microsoft Office users. (SkyDrive is also the default cloud storage if you're using Windows 8; it's pretty much baked into that operating system.)

Sharing a File with SkyDrive

Most of these cloud-based storage services work in similar fashion, so let's look at Microsoft as an example. You log into your SkyDrive account using your web browser and point to skydrive.live.com to get started.

As you can see in Figure 17.10, SkyDrive uses a series of folders (Documents, Favorites, Photos, Public, and the like) to store your shared documents. You can also store documents in the main directory; these files are displayed as tiles beneath the main folder tiles. To display the contents of any given folder, just click its tile.

To upload a new file, begin by opening the folder where you want to store the file. (If you don't open a folder first, the file will be uploaded to the main directory.) Click the Upload button at the top of the screen and, when prompted, select the file to upload. That's it; the selected file is now stored on SkyDrive.

To open a stored file, simply navigate to it within a given folder and then click it. The appropriate app should launch with this file open within.

To download a given file, mouse over the file and then select (check) it. Click Download at the top of the window and, when prompted, select a location for the downloaded file.

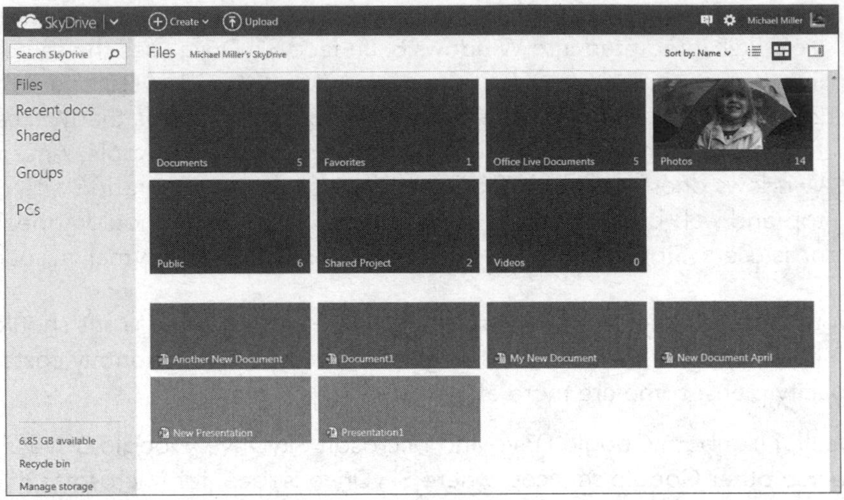

FIGURE 17.10

Microsoft SkyDrive's nifty tile-based interface.

To share the contents of a given folder with another user, open that folder and click Share Folder at the top of the window. When prompted, as shown in Figure 17.11, enter the email address of whom you want to share with into the To box, enter a personal message if you like, and—if you want the file to be editable—check the Recipients Can Edit box. Click Share to enable sharing and send your message.

All in all, it's fairly easy and intuitive to use. Also, it lets you access your files from any computer or device connected to the Internet.

FIGURE 17.11

Sharing the contents of a SkyDrive folder.

THE ABSOLUTE MINIMUM

Here are the key points to remember from this chapter:

- Before you can share files from a given PC with other computers on your network, you must enable file sharing on that computer.

- You opt to share only specific folders and require a password for access.

- Accessing files stored on another computer is easily done from Windows/File Explorer or the Mac Finder; the other computer should appear as another computer in the browsing window.

- Many users opt to store all of their important files in a central location, such as a home server, for access from other devices. You can also use a home server as a central backup device.

- To access your files when you're outside the home, consider using a cloud-storage service, such as Google Drive or Microsoft SkyDrive.

18

STREAMING AUDIO AND VIDEO

More and more regular folks are satisfying their entertainment needs over the Internet. Instead of watching broadcast or cable TV, they're watching streaming TV shows and movies on Hulu or Netflix. Instead of listening to CDs or downloading music from the iTunes Store, they're streaming music from Spotify or Pandora. It's all coming from the Internet, over their home networks, to their TVs, audio systems, and other viewing and listening devices.

What's the best way to access streaming media on your home network? What are the best streaming media services? And how can you optimize your network for best streaming media playback?

Good questions, and they all are answered in this chapter.

How Streaming Media Works

Streaming media is the Internet equivalent of broadcasting audio and/or video from one central point to multiple listeners. It works by sending multiple packets of data from the broadcasting server. Playback starts as soon as the first packet is received from a connected computer or handheld device; other packets follow in a continuous stream. The process is much faster than waiting for a traditional audio or video file to download.

A good way to think of streaming media versus normal file downloads is to envision a glass placed under a faucet. Normally, you'd turn on the faucet, fill the glass with water, and then take your drink. This is the way normal file downloads work; you can't access the file (drink the glass of water) until the file is completely downloaded (the glass is completely full).

With streaming media, however, you can access the stream immediately. This is the equivalent of placing your head under the faucet and drinking directly from the tap; there's no glass to fill up first.

Streaming media can be either live or on demand. The former is used to broadcast concerts and other live performances; the latter is used by most streaming services for music, TV shows, movies, and the like. In most instances, all you have to do is connect your computer or other device to the Internet (if you're at home, via your home network), sign into the desired streaming service, and then select what you want to view or listen to. Streaming commences within a few seconds.

 NOTE   Unlike traditional file downloads, nothing is really downloaded when you're streaming audio and video. There are no files saved on your computer.

What's Good—And What's Bad—About Streaming Media

Streaming media is becoming increasingly popular, especially among younger consumers, and for good reason. Whether you're talking streaming TV shows, movies, or music, you get a lot of selection for a low price—and, oftentimes, for free.

What's Good About Streaming Media

Compare a typical streaming music service, such as Spotify, with the old-school approaches of buying CDs or downloading tracks from an online music store. With the streaming music service, you pay anywhere from zero to $9.99 per month and, for that, you get access to 15 million or so songs to listen to, as often as you want, anytime you want, anywhere you want, on any device you want. Just dial up your favorite music from your smartphone or tablet, notebook or desktop PC, or network media player. It's an "all you can eat" (really, an "all you can listen to") scenario, at a fraction of the cost most people spend on purchasing CDs or tracks for download.

Let's say that you typically purchase two CDs a month. At current prices, that means you're spending $25 each and every month and, for that, you only get two new albums to listen to. With a $9.99 top-end subscription to Spotify Premium, you can listen to those same two new albums as well as 15 million other tracks.

It's the same thing if you're into music downloading. For the same $9.99 you spend to listen to 15 million tracks on Spotify, you can download 10 tracks from the iTunes Store. That's 15 million versus 10, which makes a streaming service sound like a pretty good deal.

This type of comparison gets even more attractive when we're talking about streaming TV shows. If you're like me, you spend big bucks every month on cable or satellite TV. When I opened my cable bill last month, the damages came to just over $250. (Yeah, I have too many TVs in too many rooms, and too many of them with the cable company's DVRs.) That's real money, right there.

Here's the thing. I could have gotten most of that programming online, via a streaming video service, such as Hulu. I'd probably have to go with the $7.99/month Hulu Plus subscription (the free basic Hulu doesn't have all the programs my wife and I like to watch), but that $7.99/month is a *lot* less expensive than the $250 I pay to the cable company every month. All of those programs stream over the same Internet connection, over the same home network, to multiple PCs and other devices connected to all the TVs in my home. (And, as an added bonus, I get to watch all the programs on my schedule; I'm not limited to when they're initially broadcast.)

Let's not forget streaming movies. How much does a movie ticket cost these days—$10, $12, maybe more? Buy two tickets and some popcorn, and you're out $25 or so for a single movie. Compare that to the $7.99 you pay each month to stream all the movies you want, to TVs throughout your home, via a subscription to Netflix. You get the picture.

What's Not So Good About Streaming Media

Streaming media lets you save big bucks in your entertainment budget. That's great.

But, it isn't all milk and roses in the land of streaming media. To get all that cheap entertainment, you may have to make some compromises in quality.

Consider the limited bandwidth available on both your home network and the Internet pipeline coming into your home, and contrast it with the large bandwidth needed to transmit audio and (especially) video files, and you see the issue. In order to fit your favorite music, movies, and TV shows into the narrow Internet and network pipeline, the quality of what you listen to and watch is likely to suffer.

When listening to streaming music, that means that what you hear isn't going to be CD-quality. Heck, a lot of times, you can't even consider it high fidelity. I'll go so far to saying that some (but not all) streaming music isn't much more listenable than a bad AM radio.

It's the same thing with streaming video. Instead of getting Blu-ray quality high-definition (HD) video, you often get a noticeably lower resolution picture. The typical streaming video looks more like watching a DVD than a Blu-ray, if that means anything to you.

To get all technical about it, streaming audio quality depends on the format and bitrate of the stream. Without going into a lot of technical detail, know that most streaming music services want a smaller packet size so that the streaming music can play back as smoothly as possible. You end up sacrificing some degree of quality to ensure a faster streaming playback.

 NOTE Bitrate describes the number of data bits processed in a given period of time, typically referred to as the number of bits per second (bps). The higher the bitrate, the better the quality.

In addition, the speed of your Internet connection can affect streaming quality. As you might suspect, the faster your Internet connection, the smoother the streaming playback. If you try to experience streaming media on anything less than a broadband connection, you'll likely experience herky-jerky playback and frequent pauses and freezes. It's definitely not for dial-up.

Streaming media also isn't for those with inconsistent Internet connections. If your connection goes down (or if you don't have Internet access), you can't listen to any streaming music or watch streaming movies. Sigh.

So, streaming media won't give you the best picture or sound, and might be a little finicky on a slow or inconsistent Internet connection. Then again, you don't pay much for it. That might be an acceptable compromise.

CAUTION   You probably don't want to watch much streaming video on your smartphone or tablet, unless you're connected to a Wi-Fi network. If you stream audio or video over your cellular provider's data plan, know that streaming media eats up a lot of bandwidth—and may incur excess data usage charges. Overdo the 3G or 4G streaming, and you'll end up paying by the minute for the excess.

Choosing a Streaming Media Device

There are lots of ways you can watch and listen to streaming media. In fact, just about any device that can connect (through your home network) to the Internet can play streaming media. It's really a matter on how you want to view or listen to it.

Streaming Media on an Internet-Capable TV

Many newer TVs, especially higher-end models, come with built-in Internet capability. That is, they connect to your home network (either wirelessly or via Ethernet) and then to the Internet. Once connected, you can access selected streaming media services from the TV's onscreen menu—no other devices necessary.

If you're in the market for a new TV, one of these so-called *smart TVs* may be the ideal solution. All you have to do is plug in your TV, make a quick connection to your home network, and then navigate to the onscreen app or gadget for the streaming service you want to use. It's probably the simplest way to go, in terms of both connection and navigation; the all-in-one nature of this type of device is very appealing.

For example, Figure 18.1 shows a Samsung Internet-cable TV. You access the set's SmartHub screen, and from there click the appropriate app to launch Netflix, Hulu, or whatever streaming service you want to watch or listen to. It's easy to set up and easy to use.

FIGURE 18.1

Accessing streaming media via the SmartHub on a Samsung LCD TV. (Photo courtesy of Samsung.)

Streaming Media on an Internet-Capable Blu-ray Player

If you don't have an Internet-capable TV, the next-best solution may be to purchase an Internet-capable Blu-ray player. This is certainly a less costly approach; you can find Blu-ray players with streaming media functionality in the $100 price range.

Most Blu-ray players have an Ethernet connection to facilitate firmware updates and the BD Live extras found on may Blu-ray discs. Many players are now offering Wi-Fi connectivity as well, which can make it easier to connect to your home network. (No long Ethernet cables to run.)

What you also get with most of these connected players is onscreen access to various streaming media services. Just connect your Blu-ray player to the Internet and to your TV or home theater system, power it up, and switch to the onscreen media menu, like the one shown in Figure 18.2. Click the app for the streaming service you want, and you're off to the races.

TIP You don't even have to use your Blu-ray player to play Blu-ray discs if you don't want to. The Internet streaming functionality is separate from Blu-ray playback.

FIGURE 18.2

The streaming video menu on a Sony Blu-ray player. (Photo courtesy of Sony.)

Streaming Media on a Network Media Player

There's another way to get streaming media in your living room, and that's by connecting some sort of network media player to your TV or home theater system. A network media player is little black box that connects to your network, via either Wi-Fi or Ethernet, and streams media from the Internet to your TV.

These are small and simple devices to set up and use. A network media player is designed to play back music and videos, and nothing else. They're also relatively inexpensive, typically priced at or under $100 or so.

All the functions of a media player are accessed via remote control, which is typically included in the price of the unit—although some also have iPhone or Android apps for control via your smartphone. You sit across the room in your comfy chair or couch and press the appropriate buttons to browse through and play your favorite music, movies, and TV shows.

For example, Western Digital's WD TV Live, shown in Figure 18.3, sells for $99 and can play back music, movies, and photos from any computer connected to your home network. It also lets you play streaming media from Netflix, Hulu Plus, Pandora, Spotify, and other web sources. It has built-in Wi-Fi and Ethernet connectivity, and sports a variety of audio and video connectors, in addition to the expected HDMI output.

FIGURE 18.3

The affordable and extremely versatile WD TV Live network media player, complete with stylish remote control. (Photo courtesy of Western Digital.)

If you like Apple products, check out the Apple TV media player, as shown in Figure 18.4. It also sells for around $100 and has built-in Wi-Fi, plus an Ethernet connection if you want to go that route. As you might suspect, it's great for playing all the media you've downloaded from the iTunes Store or have stored on your iPod or iPhone.

FIGURE 18.4

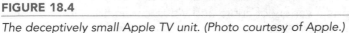

The deceptively small Apple TV unit. (Photo courtesy of Apple.)

NOTE Most network media players stream both audio and video. But, if all you care about is streaming your digital music from room to room, consider the Sonos system. It's essentially a series of audio-only media players that stream digital music files from a central location across your network.

There are actually lots of options when it comes to choosing a network media player. Table 18.1 details some of the more popular units.

TABLE 18.1 Network Media Players

Unit	Website	List Price	Outputs	Network Connection
Roku HD	www.roku.com	$59	HDMI, composite video, R/L analog audio	Wi-Fi
Roku 2 HD	www.roku.com	$79	HDMI, composite video, R/L analog audio	Wi-Fi
D-Link MovieNite Plus	www.dlink.com	$79	HDMI, composite video, R/L analog audio	Wi-Fi, Ethernet
Sony SMP-N200	store.sony.com	$79	HDMI, component video, composite video, optical digital audio, RCA R/L analog audio	Wi-Fi, Ethernet
Apple TV	www.apple.com/appletv	$99	HDMI, optical digital audio	Wi-Fi, Ethernet
Western Digital WD TV Live	www.wdc.com	$99	HDMI, composite video, optical digital audio, RCA R/L analog audio	Wi-Fi, Ethernet
Seagate FreeAgent GoFlex TV HD	www.seagate.com	$129	HDMI, component video, composite video, optical digital audio, RCA R/L analog audio	Ethernet
Netgear NTV550	www.netgear.com	$199	HDMI, component video, composite video, optical digital audio, RCA R/L analog audio	Ethernet
D-Link Boxee Box	www.dlink.com/boxee/	$229	HDMI, optical digital audio, RCA R/L analog audio	Wi-Fi, Ethernet

NOTE You can also use your PlayStation 3, Xbox 360, or Wii console as a streaming media player. All these consoles connect to the Internet (and your TV) and access the major streaming video services.

Streaming Media on a Personal Computer

In spite of all these options, I'd wager that most people today consume streaming media on their computers. It's just too easy; your computer is already connected to your home network (and thus the Internet) and any streaming media site is just a click away in your web browser.

Really, that's about all you need to know. If your computer is connected to your home network, just launch your web browser and navigate to Netflix or Hulu or whichever site you like, log into your account, and then start watching.

Of course, when you watch streaming video on your computer screen, it's a fairly small picture. That 15" notebook display may be fine for composing memos and crunching numbers, but it doesn't give you the big-screen viewing experience when you're watching a movie. To that end, many people connect their computers to their big-screen TVs. It's easily done, depending on what kind of outputs you have on your PC.

If your computer has an HDMI output, just run a cable from that to the HDMI input on your TV or A/V receiver. HDMI handles both sound and picture, so you're all set.

If your PC *doesn't* have an HDMI output, the connection is a bit more difficult. Some TVs have VGA (typically labeled "PC") inputs, and almost all PCs have VGA outputs, so that'll take care of the video. You'll then need to connect a separate R/L audio cable from your PC to either your TV or your audio system, and go from there.

NOTE Because most computers don't have separate R/L audio outputs, you'll need to employ a splitter or adapter cable that connects to your PC's single mini-jack audio output and converts it to separate R/L connectors.

Once connected, you control your streaming media from your computer and watch it on your TV. That may be a little awkward, but it works.

Streaming Media on a Smartphone or Tablet

Finally, you can experience most streaming media services from most smartphones and tablets. Most of the major streaming media services have dedicated iPhone and Android apps, so it's a simple matter of installing the app, connecting your device to your home Wi-Fi network, and then tap-tap-tapping to start the streaming.

For example, Figure 18.5 shows the iPhone's Netflix app. Tap an item to start playback, and then turn your phone sideways to watch your selection. Figure 18.6 shows the playback screen, with playback controls overlaid on top of the picture. (They fade away after a few seconds; you can redisplay them by tapping the screen.)

As I said, most of the major streaming media services have apps for all the major smartphones and tablets. When it doubt, search your device's app store.

FIGURE 18.5

The Netflix app for Apple's iPhone.

FIGURE 18.6

Watching a Netflix show on the iPhone.

Streaming TV Shows and Movies

An increasing number of people are cutting the cable-company cord and moving to streaming media for their entertainment needs. Online streaming media services offer pretty much everything you have on cable, and for a fraction of the cost that the cable company charges.

It's certainly an appealing proposition. All you need to do is obtain some sort of streaming media device, as we've just discussed, and connect it to your home network. You don't even have to run an Ethernet cable; Wi-Fi is perfectly fine, in most instances. You can then stream all of your favorite movies and TV shows over the Internet to your living-room TV.

The question, then, is where to find all this wonderful programming. A number of sites offer streaming video online, and they're all worth checking out. (In fact, you may need to visit more than one site to find *all* of your favorite programming; no one site offers everything.)

Table 18.2 details what you get from the major streaming video sites. More information follows.

TABLE 18.2 Streaming Video Services

Service	Website	Price	Featured Programming
Amazon Instant Video	www.amazon.com	$1.99–$9.99 per rental; download purchases available	Movies and TV shows
Blockbuster On Demand	www.blockbuster.com/ download	$2.99–$3.99 per rental; download purchases available	Movies
Crackle	www.crackle.com	Free	Movies and TV shows
Hulu	www.hulu.com	Free	TV shows (older)
Hulu Plus	www.hulu.com	$7.99 per month	TV shows (prime time) with some movies
iTunes	www.apple.com/itunes/	$0.99–$4.99 per rental	Movies and TV shows
Netflix	www.netflix.com	$7.99 per month	Movies, with some TV shows
Veoh	www.veoh.com	Free	Movies and TV shows
Vevo	www.vevo.com	Free	Music videos
Vudu	www.vudu.com	$0.99–$9.99 per rental; download purchases available	Movies

Before you choose a streaming video service, note that it's not all about price; it's more about selection. Each service has its own unique selection of movies and TV shows, and not every service may have the programming you want. Some services have more selections than others; some specialize in newer programming and some in older stuff. It behooves you to check out what's available on a given service before you sign up.

 TIP Take advantage of the free offers that many streaming media services provide. You can get a taste of what's there before you have to start paying for things.

Hulu and Hulu Plus

When it comes to finding TV shows on the Web, Hulu (www.hulu.com) should be your first stop. You'll find Hulu apps and gadgets on just about every connected device available today.

Hulu offers two services: a free one and a paid one, called Hulu Plus. The free Hulu service, shown in Figure 18.7, offers a lot of current and classic programming; think basic cable or broadcast television, plus the vintage stuff. Hulu Plus costs you $7.99/month, but adds all the other TV shows not available on the free service. Between basic Hulu and Hulu Plus, you should find just about everything you want to watch.

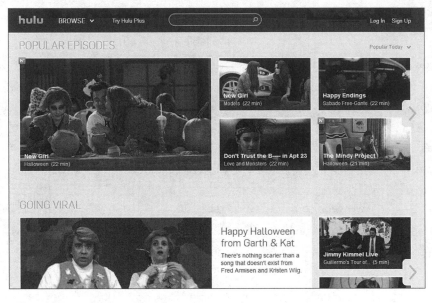

FIGURE 18.7

Hulu, your one-stop-shop for TV programming online.

 TIP One nice thing about Hulu is if a particular program isn't available on its own service, it will provide a link to where the program is located elsewhere on the web.

Watching a TV program on Hulu or Hulu Plus is a snap. Just log into your account and click the TV tab. You can click Browse TV to browse through programming (by series name, network, or genre) or use the search box to search for specific shows. When you find the show you want, click its title or thumbnail.

You now see the page for this series. Scroll down the page to see specific episodes; click an episode to begin viewing. Playback of the selected episode begins automatically, as shown in Figure 18.8.

FIGURE 18.8

Watching a Hulu program in your web browser.

Hulu also offers some streaming movies, but it's primarily for TV viewing. I'd say it's a must-have for your streaming media needs; for $7.99 per month, you get pretty much all the television programming you want to watch.

Netflix

If Hulu is the big dog for streaming TV programs, Netflix (www.netflix.com) is the go-to player for streaming movies. As you can see in Figure 18.9, Netflix offers a mix of both classic and newer movies, as well as classic television programming.

Like Hulu, Netflix is an all-you-can-eat service; you get access to all available streaming content for just $7.99 per month.

 NOTE Netflix also offers a separate DVD-by-mail rental service, with separate subscription fee.

Once you log onto the Netflix home page, you can scroll through Netflix's suggestions or use the search box to find something you want to watch. Click a given item, and Netflix begins streaming the movie or television episode. It's really that simple.

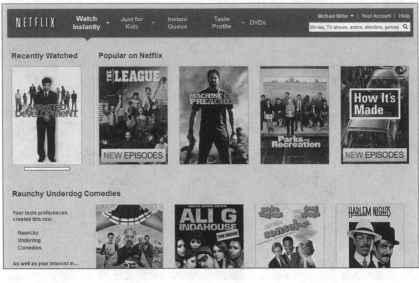

FIGURE 18.9

Viewing the programming on the Netflix site.

 TIP   Netflix analyzes your past viewing to suggest new movies you might like to watch. It also organizes programming by genre.

If you're an avid movie watcher, Netflix belongs in your streaming media mix. In fact, most users are perfectly happy with a combination of Hulu, Hulu Plus, and Netflix; those services cover most of the bases.

Amazon Instant Video

One of the newer streaming services out there is Amazon Instant Video (www. amazon.com). As you can see in Figure 18.10, Amazon offers a large number of movies and TV shows for limited-time streaming rental or purchase and download. This is not a subscription service, so you pay by the selection.

 NOTE   Amazon Prime is Amazon's free shipping service, to which Prime Instant Video is attached. You pay $79/year to become a Prime member.

If you want a subscription service, sign up to the Amazon Prime service. If you're a Prime member, you're also a subscriber to Prime Instant Video, which offers a number of selections for free streaming each month. It's a nice perk for all Prime members.

FIGURE 18.10

What's available from Amazon Instant Video.

Blockbuster On Demand

Blockbuster's neighborhood video stores may be defunct, but the brand name lives on in the Blockbuster On Demand video service. Blockbuster On Demand (www.blockbuster.com/download) offers a mix of streaming movie rentals and movies available for purchase and download.

You won't find many (if any) TV shows on this service, but Blockbuster does offer a decent selection of new and older movies. Like Amazon Instant Video, it's an a la carte service, so you only pay for what you want. Rental rates run $2.99 to $3.99.

iTunes

If you own an iPhone, iPod, or iPad, you're probably familiar with Apple's iTunes Store. Well, the iTunes Store isn't just for music downloads; Apple also offers a large selection of movies and TV shows for streaming rental and download purchase. You pay by the selection, and access the Store from the iTunes software, as shown in Figure 18.11. You can stream and download your purchases to both Mac and Windows PCs, as well as other iOS devices.

FIGURE 18.11

Viewing movie selections in the iTunes Store.

 TIP   I think iTunes is a viable option if you have an Apple TV media player or if you want to watch movies and TV shows on your iPad or iPhone. Otherwise, Hulu and Netflix offer more programming at a more affordable monthly rate.

Vudu

Vudu (www.vudu.com) is looking to be a competitor to the big streaming media services, while charging by the selection instead of offering a monthly subscription rate. They offer a decent selection of new and older movies (no TV shows), for both streaming rental and paid download. Rental rates run from $.99 to $9.99, depending on the movie.

Veoh

Veoh (www.veoh.com) is a free streaming service. While free is nice, you get what you pay for—which in this instance is mainly older and lesser-known movies and TV shows.

Crackle

Crackle (www.crackle.com) is one of the newer contenders in the streaming video space. Like Veoh, it's a free service. It offers a lot of older and lesser-known movies—lots of grade B and C (and D and F) stuff.

 TIP Crackle and Veoh are probably worth checking out; it won't cost you anything. But, I doubt that you'll find enough newer programming to make either site your go-to service.

Vevo

Vevo (www.vevo.com) is an odd bird in that it doesn't offer movies or TV shows, but rather music videos—and, as you can see in Figure 18.12, lots of them. The site is actually a joint venture between the major music labels; as such, the selection of music videos is first class. It's a totally free site, so if you're into music videos, it's worth checking out.

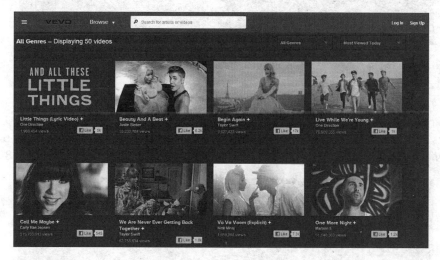

FIGURE 18.12

Browsing the music videos on the Vevo site.

Other Sites

Finally, you can watch a lot of TV shows for free from the networks' own websites. Whether you're talking NBC and CBS or The Food Network and The Hub, just about every major broadcast and cable network has a variety of programming available for your streaming pleasure.

For example, the CBS News site (www.cbsnews.com) features all sorts of videos on its Videos page. As you can see in Figure 18.13, you get all the hottest news clips for immediate viewing; you can also watch the most recent broadcasts of *60 Minutes*, *CBS This Morning*, and the *CBS Evening News*, along with individual segments from each program and special web-only newscasts.

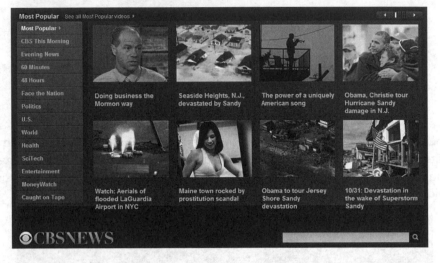

FIGURE 18.13

Watch news broadcasts for free at the CBS News website.

Similarly, you can go to the NBC website (www.nbc.com) to view full episodes of its top prime-time shows. Missed this week's episode of *The Office* or *Saturday Night Live*? They're available online, for free—as you can see in Figure 18.14.

FIGURE 18.14

Prime-time shows online at NBC's website.

Most network TV sites have similar free video offerings. Check out ABC.com (abc.go.com), CBS.com (www.cbs.com), Fox on Demand (www.fox.com), and Comedy Central (www.comedycentral.com). For your favorite music videos, both current and classic, you can't beat MTV.com (www.mtv.com) and VH1.com (www.vh1.com). And to get your daily sports fix, check out the videos on the ESPN website (espn.go.com).

 NOTE This chapter primarily talks about sites for watching TV shows and movies. There are also several websites for the uploading and viewing of non-commercial videos, such as home movies and personal video blogs. YouTube (www.youtube.com) is the largest of these video-sharing sites, although many people also like Vimeo (www.vimeo.com), which has a lot of selections from independent filmmakers.

Streaming Music

Streaming media isn't just about movies and TV shows; there's also a lot of music you can stream from the Internet. In fact, there are two types of delivery services for web-based streaming audio—you can listen to music from a streaming music service or from an Internet radio station.

Streaming Music Services

A streaming music service is typically a paid service that lets you listen to an unlimited amount of music, via streaming audio, for a flat monthly subscription fee. Even better, some of these streaming services are free; some of the paid services even offer limited-usage free plans, as well.

Most streaming music services let you browse or search for specific tracks or albums, or music by a given artist or in a given genre. Some services let you create playlists of your favorite tracks; some even create custom "radio stations" based on your listening habits. A few services are social in nature, in that they let you share your favorite music with friends on Facebook and other social networks.

Table 18.3 compares the most popular streaming music services today.

TABLE 18.3   Streaming Music Services

Service	URL	Price	Selection (Number of Tracks Available)
Grooveshark	www.grooveshark.com	$6–$9/month, plus free plan	15 million
Last.fm	www.last.fm	Free	12 million
MOG	www.mog.com	$4.99–$9.99/month, plus free plan	14 million
Pandora Radio	www.pandora.com	Free	900,000
Raditaz	www.raditaz.com	Free	14 million
Rara.com	www.rara.com	$4.99–$9.99/month	10 million
Rdio	www.rdio.com	$4.99–$9.99/month, plus free plan	12 million
Rhapsody	www.rhapsody.com	$9.99–$14.99/month	14 million
Slacker Radio	www.slacker.com	$3.99–$9.99/month, plus free plan	8 million
Spotify	www.spotify.com	$4.99–$9.99/month, plus free plan	20 million
Turntable.fm	www.turntable.fm	Free	11 million
Xbox Music Pass	www.xbox.com/music/	$9.99/month (for Xbox 360, Windows 8, Windows RT, and Windows Phone only)	18 million

Of all these services, Spotify (www.spotify.com) is arguably the most popular. With the largest library and excellent sound quality, it's hard to argue with this choice—if your device can access the service, that is. Spotify runs not from a web browser, but from its own software app, as shown in Figure 18.15. That's fine for listening from your Windows or Mac computer, but not all connected devices have comparable Spotify apps. If you're interested in Spotify, check the device's specs first.

Other popular streaming music services include Last.fm and Pandora Radio, both of which are totally free. (They make their money from advertising.) Last.fm, shown in Figure 18.16, has about 12 million tracks; while that's a little smaller than Spotify's library, it's still a pretty good selection. Pandora, on the other hand, only offers about a million tracks, but streams music at a higher bitrate (translation: it sounds better). Both services let you create online "stations" based on artists or songs you select.

FIGURE 18.15

Listening to streaming music from Spotify.

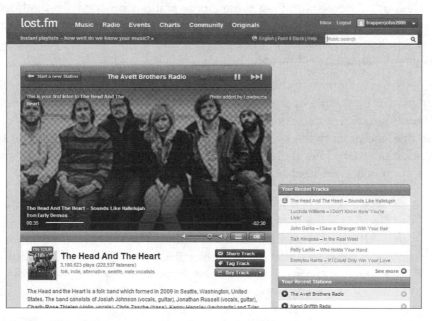

FIGURE 18.16

Listening to a user-created radio station from Last.fm.

I'm also a fan of Slacker Radio, which is both a streaming music service and an Internet radio provider. In addition to the tracks you pick to listen to, there are a variety of online radio stations programmed by in-house DJs. Slacker offers a free basic service, as well as monthly subscription plans that offer more variety and versatility. (And no ads!)

Feel free to check out the other services listed in Table 18.3, some of which you might like. As with streaming video services, you want to make sure that a given service has the music you want to listen to; not all streaming music libraries are created equal.

Internet Radio

There's a fuzzy line between streaming music services and Internet radio stations. Streaming music services let you pick your own music to listen to, whereas Internet radio stations determine which songs they broadcast. That is, streaming music services are all about you making the choice, where Internet radio stations make the choice for you.

Just as there are all different formats of terrestrial radio stations, there are also all manner of Internet radio stations. You can find stations that specialize in just about every musical genre, and then some. Some stations broadcast audio books, others news and opinion. There are even a lot of terrestrial radio stations that simulcast over the Internet, which is a great way to listen to stations that you can't pick up on your local AM or FM radio.

Tuning into an Internet radio station is as easy as clicking a link in your web browser or opening a gadget in your streaming media player. One benefit of Internet radio over traditional radio is that many Internet radio stations display the title and artist of the currently playing song, right on your computer screen. In addition, many Internet radio sites let you create your own custom "stations," based on your own listening preferences.

 CAUTION In terms of audio quality, Internet radio is typically at the low end of the fidelity spectrum. That is, you're likely to experience much lower bitrates with Internet radio than you are with other forms of streaming music. That might be fine when you're listening to an all-talk station, but if you're in it for the music, be prepared for an aural disappointment.

A large number of sites create their own original radio programming and beam it over the Internet. This programming is typically genre-specific music; many of these sites offer dozens (or hundreds) of channels, each devoted to a specific type of music. So, whether you're interested in 1970s pop hits or classic polka tunes, one of these sites probably has a channel just for you!

Table 18.4 details some of the most popular Internet-only radio sites. Most of these sites offer some, if not all, of their stations for free. (They're ad supported.)

TABLE 18.4 Internet Radio Sites

Service	URL	Description
AccuRadio	www.accuradio.com	Listen to programmed stations (typically by genre) or create your own custom stations.
AOL Radio	music.aol.com/radioguide/	A large number of genre-specific radio stations, created specifically for online listening.
Goom Radio	www.goomradio.us	A variety of genre-specific Internet radio stations, as well as user-created stations.
iHeartRadio	www.iheart.com	Presents more than 850 terrestrial and web-only stations, plus user-created custom stations.
Jango	www.jango.com	A mix of genre-based stations and user-personalized programming.
Live365	www.live365.com	One of the largest Internet radio sites, with more than 5,000 stations in more than 260 different genres.
Radio.com	www.radio.com	From the CBS Interactive Music Group, a handful of big-media channels and the ability to create your own custom channels.
Radioio	www.radioio.com	Dozens of genre-focused web-only channels.
RadioMOI	www.radiomoi.com	Features a mix of programmed channels, browsable by genre, and on-demand content.
SHOUTcast	www.shoutcast.com	Part of the AOL empire and one of the oldest and most reliable Internet radio sites. Amalgamates more than 50,000 free Internet radio stations in a single site. You can browse by genre or search by station, artist, or genre.
VirtualDJ Radio	radio.virtualdj.com	Dance music, with live mixes selected by real-life DJs.

If you're looking for a single place to start with Internet radio, you can't go wrong with Live365. As you can see in Figure 18.17, you can choose from a large number of musical genres; within each genre is a variety of different stations to listen to. For example, when you choose the Oldies genre, you see stations such as 57 Chevy Radio, Absolute Motown, All Hit Radio, Classic Oldies, Golden Oldies, Retroactive Radio, Sock Hop Oldies, That 70s Channel, and the like. Click a station to listen.

FIGURE 18.17

Browsing the musical genres at Live365.

TIP If you're an iTunes user, you can access free Internet radio via the iTunes software. Just select Radio in the Library section of the navigation sidebar, and then click a category to view all the stations available. Double-click a station to begin playback.

Terrestrial Radio, Online

Internet radio stations are fine, but what if you want to listen to your local AM or FM station online? Let's face it: Sometimes, you just want local news and views, or to listen to your local DJs, and there's no reason you should be deprived of this just because you're not near a radio. Of course, you're not limited to listening to just *your* local stations; via the magic of the Internet, you can listen to local stations from anywhere in the world, in real time.

 NOTE You're not limited to just AM and FM radio, either. If you have a subscription to Sirius/XM satellite radio for your car, you can also listen to it over the web.

A handful of sites offer direct playback of hundreds of local AM/FM stations, or links to those stations' websites. Table 18.5 details some of what's available.

TABLE 18.5 Sites for Traditional AM/FM Radio

Service	URL	Description
iHeartRadio	www.iheart.com	Offers a selection of both local AM/FM and web-only stations.
Live Radio on the Internet	www.live-radio.net	A great guide to AM/FM simulcasts from all around the globe.
Online Radio Stations	www.webradios.com	Listings of and links to local radio stations online, by location or genre.
radio-locator	www.radio-locator.com	A search engine with links to more than 10,000 AM and FM stations, searchable by city or ZIP code, country, or call letters.
Sirius/XM Radio	www.siriusxm.com/player/	Satellite radio online, with more than 130 channels of music, news and talk—including several web-only channels that aren't available via normal satellite radio.
TuneIn Radio	www.tunein.com	Lets you browse local stations in any city or state; you can also listen to local police and fire bands.

I'm a big fan of TuneIn Radio, which I use to stream live radio broadcasts from my local stations, as well as catch up on what's happening in other cities around the country. As you can see in Figure 18.18, each station shows what's currently playing, which is great when you're browsing for something interesting to listen to.

FIGURE 18.18

Listening to a local jazz station, live, with TuneIn Radio.

Cloud-Based Music Services

There's one more type of streaming music service to talk about. Instead of listening to a service's limited music library, these cloud-based music services stream your own music back to you over the Internet, on any device wherever you might happen to be.

To do this, you first have to create a cloud-based library, or upload your ripped and downloaded tracks to the service; your music is stored on a collection of Internet-based servers, dubbed the "cloud." When you want to listen, the music is streamed from the cloud servers to your Internet-connected computer or device.

As you can imagine, it can take a bit of time to upload all the tracks in a large music collection—literally days of uploading for collections of 10,000+ tracks. Once your music is in the cloud, however, it's a simple matter of streaming any individual track to any computer or smartphone or music player device that has a connection to the Internet.

Note that most cloud music services charge for this privilege—actually, for the data storage itself. It's typically not too expensive, just a few bucks a month or even a few bucks a year, depending on how much storage space you need.

Oh, and most of these services put limits on how many tracks you can upload, or how much storage space you can use. This may be a problem if you have very large music collections or tracks stored in lossless format (which creates much larger files). Check out the limitations before you sign up for any given service.

Finally, know that streaming your own music back to you might deteriorate the audio quality. When you listen to music on your own computer, you're listening at the original bitrate encoded—which can be high, if you go the lossless route. However, the music you stream back down from the cloud may not be at the original bitrate, but rather a lower bitrate determined by the cloud music service. (The download bitrate varies from service to service; some claim to stream at the original bitrate.) So, your great-sounding lossless music might come back to you with poor-sounding lossy compression.

There are a number of big players competing in the cloud music market—Amazon, Apple, and Google among them. Table 18.6 details the major players.

TABLE 18.6 Cloud Music Services

Service	URL	Price	Storage Capacity	Downstream Bitrate	Mobile Apps Available
Amazon Cloud Player	www.amazon.com/cloudplayer/	Free (up to 250 tracks); $24.99/year (unlimited)	Unlimited (with Premium service)	256Kbps	Android, iOS
Google Play Music	play.google.com/music/	Free	20,000 tracks	320Kbps max	Android
iTunes Match	www.apple.com/itunes	$24.99/year	25,000 tracks	256Kbps	iOS
MP3tunes	www.mp3tunes.com	Free (up to 2GB), $4.95/month for 50GB, $7.95/month for 100GB, $12.95/month for 200GB	200GB	Original bitrate	Android, iOS
MyMusicCloud	www.mymusiccloud.com	Free (up to 2GB), $10/year for additional 5GB	2GB free, up to 7GB paid	N/A	Android, iOS, BlackBerry

Figure 18.19 shows Google Play, which you access from any web browser. (It's free, which is another nice thing.) You can browse your library by song, artist, album, or genre; click any item to begin playback. As you can see, the ability to listen to your own library when you're away from home is appealing—it's your own music, wherever you happen to be. (Including, of course, in your own home, over your own wireless network.)

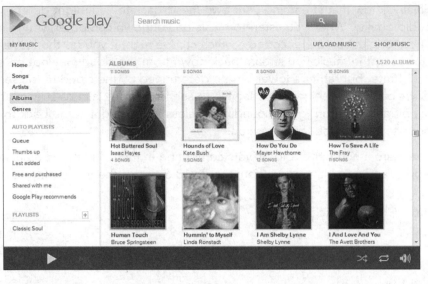

FIGURE 18.19

Google Play streams your own music back to you, over the Internet.

Streaming Media Across Your Network

Streaming movies and music from across the Internet is nice, but what about all those films and tracks you've already downloaded to your computers? Is there a way to stream your own ripped or downloaded media from one network device to another?

Of course there is. In fact, just about any computer, handheld device, or network media player can access media files stored anywhere on your network, and easily play back those files locally. All you need is for each device to be connected to your home network, and for file sharing to be enabled on the host computer, and you should be ready to go.

In fact, most Internet-enabled devices should be able to play back your local media files. Just navigate to the file you want to play and click to get started.

That sounds easy, and in fact, it is. But, there are a couple of streaming-media technologies that make network media streaming even easier: DLNA and AirPlay. It's good if your connected devices are compatible with these standards.

DLNA

As you know, many network media players, A/V receivers, Blu-ray players, and so-called smart TVs can access and play your digital music, photo, and video files over your home network. The fact that they can do so is because of a technology called Digital Living Network Alliance (DLNA).

Any device that's DLNA certified, such as the Pioneer receiver in Figure 18.20, can discover, access, and play media stored on any computer or network storage device connected to the same home network. There are many DLNA-certified devices on the market today, in all major categories. Just search out DLNA-compatibility when you're comparing equipment specs, and then you can access your video and music libraries—after a little initial setup, of course.

FIGURE 18.20

Pioneer's VSX-1122 audio/video receiver features both DLNA and AirPlay streaming media technologies.

Apple AirPlay

In the Apple universe, AirPlay is a technology similar to the more universal DLNA. AirPlay lets you stream music, movies, and photos directly from an iPhone, iPad, or iPod touch to any AirPlay-compatible device.

The good news is that there are a lot of AirPlay-compatible devices. Naturally, the Apple TV box is AirPlay-compatible, but so are most A/V receivers, network media players, and smart TVs that also feature DLNA technology. So, if you have your music library and some downloaded videos stored on your iPhone or other iOS portable device, you don't have to bother transferring those files to a computer for playback over your network. AirPlay automatically streams those files from your portable device to any other compatible device connected to your network, and it does so pretty much invisibly. It's a pretty neat technology, actually.

NOTE AirPlay also lets you "mirror" anything on your device's screen to compatible playback devices. So, if you want to show a presentation stored on your iPad on your living room TV (and that TV is either AirPlay-compatible or connected to an Apple TV device), you can do it. Same thing with gaming; AirPlay lets you see your iPhone and iPad games on the big screen.

THE ABSOLUTE MINIMUM

Here are the key points to remember from this chapter:

- When you stream audio or video over the Internet, it flows in real time through your home network to the receiving device.

- Streaming media lets you access huge libraries of movies, TV shows, and music, often for free or a low monthly subscription cost.

- You can use a number of networked devices to access streaming media services, including personal computers, network media players, Internet-capable TVs and Blu-ray players, and many audio/video receivers.

- The most popular services for streaming TV shows and movies are Hulu (and Hulu Plus) and Netflix.

- The most popular services for streaming music are Spotify, Last.fm, and Pandora Radio.

- You can also stream audio and video files stored elsewhere on your network by using DLNA and AirPlay technologies.

19

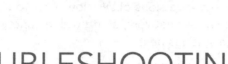

TROUBLESHOOTING NETWORK PROBLEMS

Not every home network runs smoothly, not all the time. Sometimes, you'll have trouble connecting a given device to your network. Sometimes, a previously connected device will suddenly disconnect from the network, for no apparent reason at all. Sometimes, everything will have trouble connecting to your router. Sometimes, your network will run fine, but your Internet connection won't. And sometimes, everything connects okay, but just seems slow.

When your network is hiccupping or causing you distress, you need to troubleshoot what's happening—and then fix whatever's wrong. Although it's impossible to predict and detail all possible network-related issues (a lot of them are specific to individual pieces of equipment, after all), let's look at some of the more common problems and how to deal with them.

Managing Networked Computers (Windows Version)

Before we get into a bunch of troubleshooting advice, let's examine the best ways to manage the computers on your home network. For Windows PCs, key network functions are monitored and managed via the Network and Sharing Center. This utility is the place to start when you're experienced any network-related problems—even if it differs somewhat in functionality between different versions of Windows.

To open the Network and Sharing Center, open the Control Panel and select Network and Sharing Center. Alternatively, on some versions of Windows, you can open it by clicking the Network button in the System Tray and then clicking Open Network and Sharing Center.

Figure 19.1 shows the Network and Sharing Center in Windows 7. (Like I said, it'll look a little different in other versions of Windows.) As you can see, it displays a simplified map of your current network, along with a variety of configuration settings. We discuss these settings next.

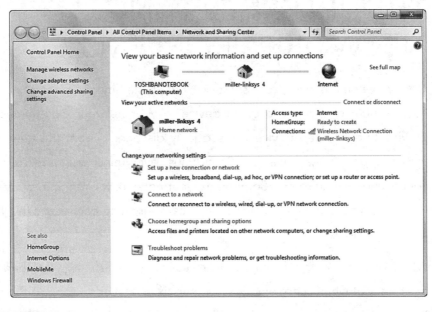

FIGURE 19.1

The Windows 7 version of the Network and Sharing Center.

Viewing a Larger Network Map

The network map displayed in the Network and Sharing Center is a basic map that shows only the immediate connections for the current computer. In some versions of Windows, you can view a larger and more complete map of your entire network by clicking the See Full Map link in the Network and Sharing Center window.

The resulting Network Map window displays all of your connected network devices. To open any network computer or device shown on the map, simply double-click its icon.

 CAUTION Computers running Windows XP or older operating systems may not automatically appear in the network map, instead appearing by themselves below the map. That's because the map displays only those computers that have Link-Layer Topology Discovery (LLTD) installed. If you have a Windows XP computer that doesn't appear on the network map, you can download LLTD for that computer from support.microsoft.com/kb/922120.

Changing the Type of Network Location

When you first connect your Windows PC to the network, you are prompted to set your type of network location: Home, Work, or Public. You can later change the network location type for a given network connection from the Network and Sharing Center, by clicking the location link beneath the name of your current network. When the Set Network Location window appears, select Home Network, Work Network, or Public Network.

Configuring Advanced Sharing Options

The Network and Sharing Center offers easy access to most key network configuration settings. These settings determine how your computer appears on the network, as well as how it shares files and devices.

To configure your network in this manner, open the Network and Sharing Center and click Change Advanced Sharing Options. This opens the Advanced Sharing Options window, as shown in Figure 19.2. From here, you can configure the following settings: Network Discovery, File and Printer Sharing, Public Folder Sharing, Media Streaming, File Sharing Connections, Password Protected Sharing, and HomeGroup Connections.

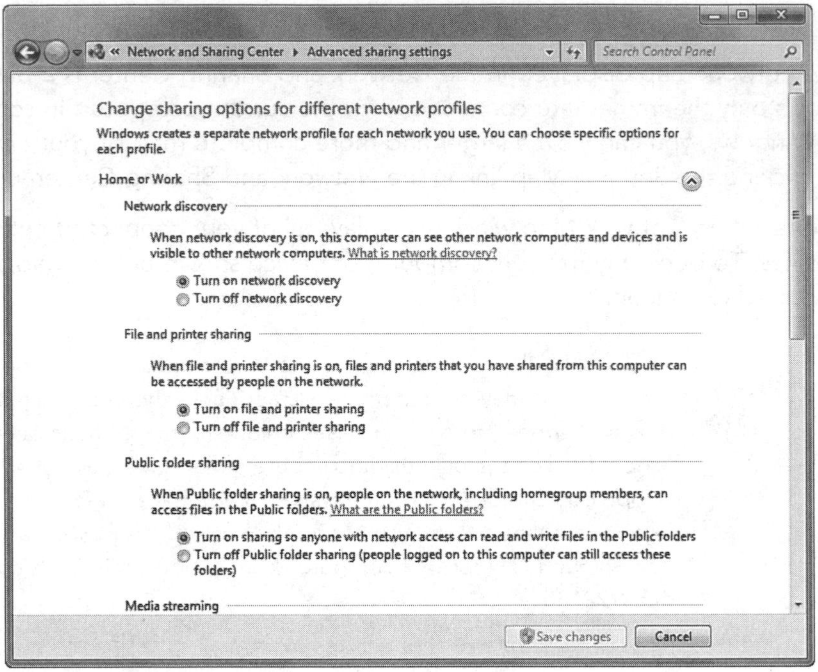

FIGURE 19.2

Configuring your network's sharing and discovery options.

These settings are available separately for all three types of connections—Home, Work, and Public. To configure the settings for both Home and Work networks, click the down arrow next to Home or Work; to configure the settings for Public networks, click the down arrow next to Public.

Viewing and Managing Network Connections

To view information about your current network connection—connection speed, amount of data transmitted, and the like—as well as to manage the connection itself, use the Network Connections folder. To access this folder, open the Network and Sharing Center and click Change Adapter Settings.

As you can see in Figure 19.3, the Network Connections folder displays icons for each available network connection on this PC. Depending on your computer and available networks, there may be an icon for both a wired and a wireless network—and, if you have a Bluetooth keyboard or mouse connected, for a Bluetooth network.

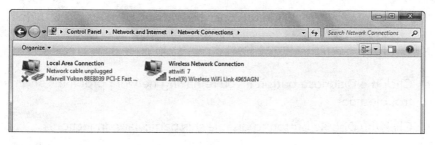

FIGURE 19.3

Managing your network connections.

To view and manage a given connection, double-click the connection's icon. This opens the Status dialog box, like the one shown in Figure 19.4. From here, you can:

- Click the Details button to view even more technical details about this connection.

- Click the Properties button to edit various technical properties for this connection, including the underlying TCP/IP protocols.

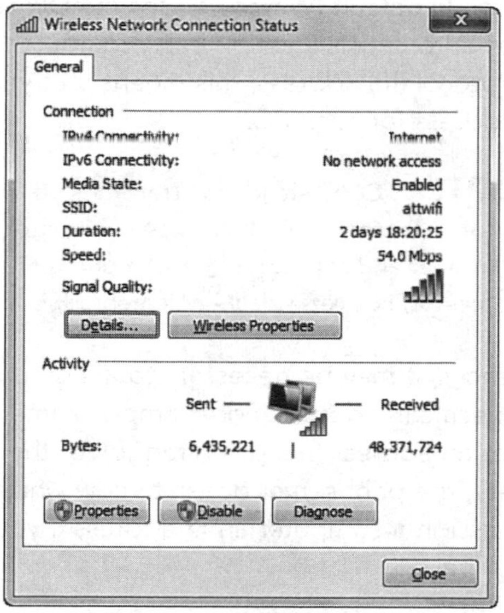

FIGURE 19.4

Viewing information about a particular network connection.

TIP You can also open the Properties dialog box by right-clicking a connection in the Network Connections folder and selecting Properties from the pop-up window.

• Click the Diagnose button if you're having network problems and need to troubleshoot.

• Click the Disable button to disable this particular connection.

TIP To rename a network connection, right-click the connection's icon in the Network Connections folder and select Rename. The connection's name is now highlighted; type a new name and then press Enter on your computer keyboard.

Changing IP Addresses

Okay, now for some technical stuff—which you probably won't ever need to use, unless you experience specific technical problems.

All computers use TCP/IP technology to enable network communication between multiple computers. By default, Windows uses the Dynamic Host Configuration Protocol (DHCP) to automatically assign each computer on your network its own unique Internet Protocol (IP) address; this means that you don't have to bother with creating an address for each PC.

NOTE TCP/IP stands for Transmission Control Protocol/Internet Protocol, which is a combination of two similar protocols. The older and still current version of the IP protocol is IPv4; its successor, not yet widely implemented, is IPv6.

In some circumstances, it may be necessary to assign one or more PCs on your network its own specific IP address. For example, some print servers require a specific address (or an address in a given range) for the host computer; without the specific address, the print server doesn't know which PC it's connected to. You may also need to assign a computer an IP address if your network has trouble recognizing that machine.

In most instances, when assigning a manual IP address is necessary, the manufacturer of the given device will indicate what address or range of addresses you should use. That said, it's good to know how to do it if you need to do it.

So, if you need to manually assign a specific IP address to the current PC, open the Network and Sharing Center and select Change Adapter Settings. When the Network Connections window opens, right-click the connection you want to change and select Properties from the context menu.

When the Properties dialog box appears, select either Internet Protocol Version 4 or Internet Protocol Version 6; then, click Properties.

If you select IPv4, select Use the Following IP Address (shown in Figure 19.5) and enter the appropriate settings into the IP Address, Subnet Mask, and Default Gateway boxes. If you select IPv6, select Use the Following IPv6 Address and enter the appropriate settings into the IPv6 Address, Subnet Prefix Length, and Default Gateway boxes. Click OK when finished.

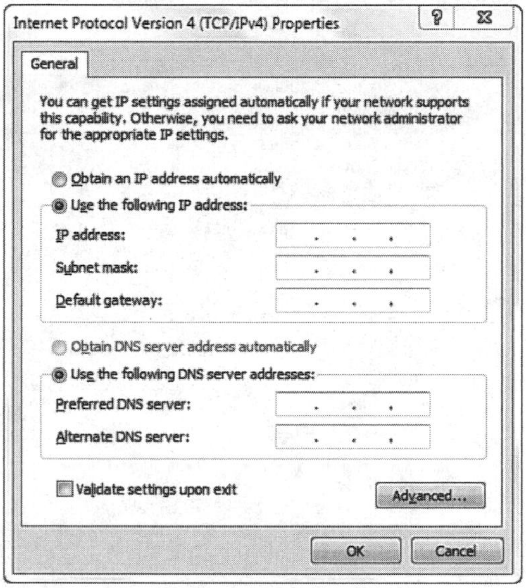

Internet Protocol Version 4 (TCP/IPv4) Properties ? ⊠

General

You can get IP settings assigned automatically if your network supports this capability. Otherwise, you need to ask your network administrator for the appropriate IP settings.

○ Obtain an IP address automatically
◉ Use the following IP address:

IP address: _ . _ . _
Subnet mask: _ . _ . _
Default gateway: _ . _ . _

○ Obtain DNS server address automatically
◉ Use the following DNS server addresses:

Preferred DNS server: _ . _ . _
Alternate DNS server: _ . _ . _

☐ Validate settings upon exit   Advanced...

OK   Cancel

FIGURE 19.5

Manually entering an IPv4 address.

TIP In some instances, you may need to indicate specific DNS server address settings to establish an Internet connection. If your Internet service provider (ISP) supplies you with this information, open the IPv4 or IPv6 dialog box, check Use the Following DNS Server Addresses, and then enter the desired addresses into the Preferred DNS Server and Alternate DNS Server boxes.

Managing Networked Computers (Mac Version)

Macs don't have a utility that directly corresponds to Windows' Network and Sharing Center. Instead, you can find most network-related settings in the Network Preferences window. To open this window, select System Preferences from the Apple menu and then click the Network icon.

Configuring Network Preferences

As you can see in Figure 19.6, all of your current network connections are listed in the navigation pane on the left side of this window. Select a given connection to see all of its settings.

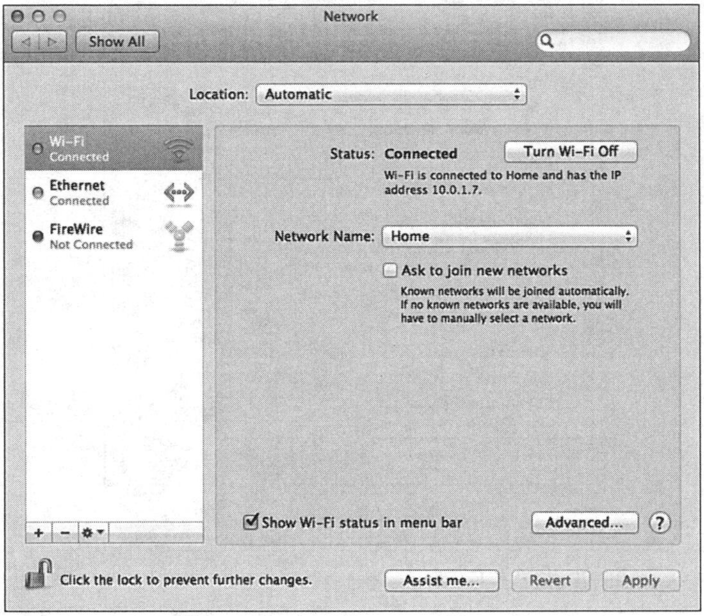

FIGURE 19.6

Managing network connections from the Mac's Network Preferences window.

For example, when you select your Wi-Fi connection, you see the connection status (and a button to turn off this connection), along with the name of the network you're currently connected to. To connect to a different network, simply pull down the Network Name list and make another selection.

To access more technical network settings, click the Advanced button. What you see next depends on the type of connection you selected, but Figure 19.7 shows the options for a typical Wi-Fi (AirPort) connection. The tabs along the top of the window let you see and configure different types of settings: AirPort, TCP/IP, DNS, WINS, 802.1X, Proxies, and Ethernet. Make the appropriate selections on the relevant tab(s) and click OK to save your changes.

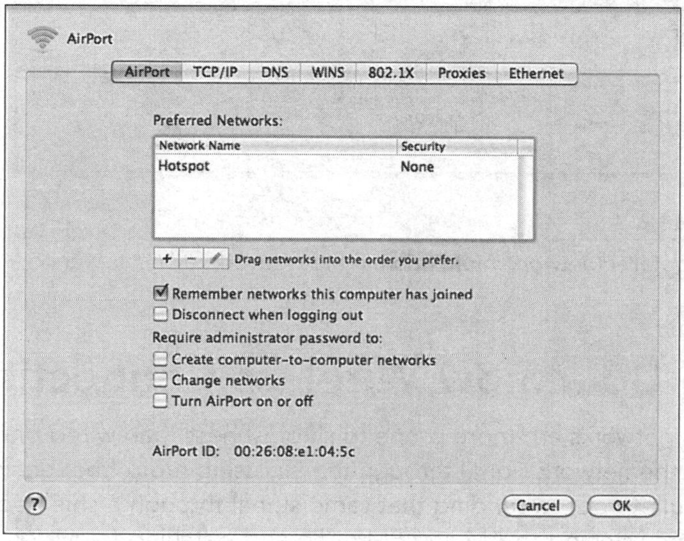

FIGURE 19.7

Configuring advanced network settings on a Mac.

Displaying Network Information

It's possible that a given network issue will be beyond your area of competence or comfort level. In this instance, a tech-support person may ask you specific information about your network connection.

In the Mac OS, most of this information is located in the Network Utility application. You launch this app from the Applications/Utilities folder.

As you can see in Figure 19.8, the Network Utility window consists of a series of tabs, each devoted to a particular type of information—Info, Netstat, Ping, Lookup, Traceroute, Whois, Finger, and Port Scan. Click a tab to view detailed information of that type.

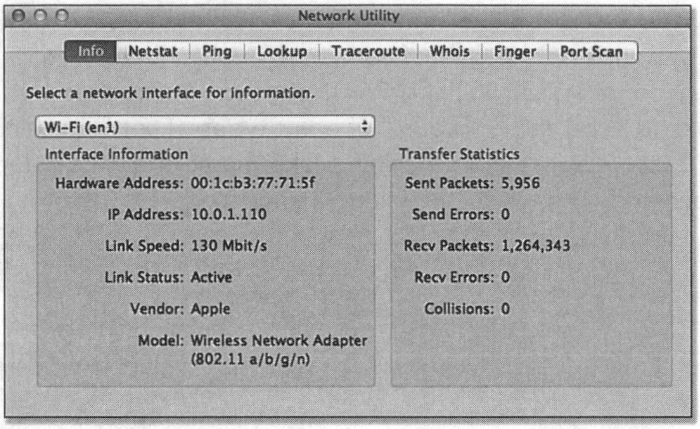

FIGURE 19.8

Viewing detailed network information in the Network Utility.

Speeding Up a Slow Wireless Connection

Wireless networks are more prone to sluggishness than wired ones. That's because sending the network signal through the air, using radio frequency (RF) signals, is not as bulletproof as sending that same signal through a shielded cable. As you know from listening to AM and FM radio and watching television via rabbit-ear antennae, lots of things can interfere with over-the-air signals.

A poor wireless connection most often manifests itself as a low signal, which provides slower data access than a faster signal. With that in mind, here are some things to look for when your wireless network starts slowing down.

Checking Your Signal Strength

First things first: How strong is the wireless signal received by your computer? It's relatively easy to determine.

If you have a Windows PC handy, you can view the strength of your current wireless signal by mousing over the wireless connection icon in the Windows system tray. This displays a pop-up information window that describes the current network's signal strength. If the signal strength is less than 100 percent, your network connection is slower than it could be.

On a Mac, pull down the Wi-Fi menu on the menu bar. The "waves" coming from the Wi-Fi icon indicate the relative strength of the Wi-Fi signal. The more waves there are, the stronger the signal.

Moving Closer to the Router

If your signal strength is low or your network connection seems sluggish, check to see how far away your computer or other device is from the wireless router. It's a simple fact: The farther away your device is from the router or access point, the weaker the signal—and the slower the connection.

A simple solution, if you can do it, is to move that computer or device closer to the router. If that sounds like it's too easy, think again. The closer a remote device is to the network router, the faster the wireless connection. If you don't believe me, position a notebook computer right next to your router and measure the wireless signal strength, then move it to the other side of the house and measure again. The wireless signal strength drops with distance, and less signal strength equals slower data transfer rates.

So, if the wireless connection on a given device is feeling sluggish, try moving it a few feet closer to the router. Alternately, you can move the router closer to the device—whichever is easiest for you. But, don't complain about slow network speeds if your sluggish computer is positioned at the extreme end of your router's range; move it closer to speed it up!

Don't Hide Your Adapter or Router

You can also increase signal strength—and speed up your connection—by not hiding your wireless router or a given networked device. Solid objects of all types can play havoc with RF signals, such as those used in your wireless network.

For example, if you have a computer that uses a USB wireless adapter, for example, it may be stuck down on the floor behind your PC, which is a perfect way to interfere with the Wi-Fi signal. Move the adapter out from behind the PC and raise it off the floor, and you'll notice a marked increase in signal strength. The same thing goes with any wireless device; get it out in the open for a better signal.

The same thing goes with your wireless router, of course. If your router is hidden behind other equipment in your office, you'll reduce its transmission range. Clear a space for it and make sure it isn't blocked in by other items. If you can't see it, that's a sign you might have problems.

 TIP Along the same lines, you may be able to improve performance by moving or redirecting the antenna on your router or wireless device, as radio signals are directional. If your router has an external antenna, swivel it around. If your router has an internal antenna, swivel the entire router.

Moving Devices That Might Cause Interference

You might not realize it, but placing a wireless router, computer, or other device too close to other electronic equipment can reduce the effectiveness of the Wi-Fi signal. The other electronic signals effectively scramble the wireless network signal, reducing the resultant signal strength—and connection speed.

For example, I once ran into problems when I placed my wireless router between a cordless phone and an old school CRT computer monitor—both devices that generate their own electronic signals or fields. Simply moving the router to the other side of these devices dramatically increased its effective signal strength.

This last point reminds us that interference from other devices can affect the Wi-Fi signal. It's never a good idea to put a wireless router or other wireless device in close proximity to other cordless devices that use the 2.4GHz frequency band. In some instances, you may need to disconnect or turn off these other devices to get a clean Wi-Fi signal.

Changing the Channel

This type of interference can sometimes be minimized by changing the wireless broadcast channel used by your router and adapter. Every router has the option of transmitting on any one of multiple channels, which use different portions of the available 2.4GHz band. If multiple devices (or multiple networks—such as yours and a neighbor's) use the same channel, interference can result.

To change the channel that your equipment uses, run your wireless router's configuration utility. Consult your router's manual for specific instructions.

Changing the Band

Another solution to 2.4GHz interference, if you have a dual-band 802.11n router (and compatible equipment), is to use the less-trafficked 5GHz band instead. There are simply fewer types of devices that use the 5GHz band, so you'll have a much cleaner "pipe" for your wireless signals if you use this band.

Upgrading to a Faster Router

If your wireless network is consistently slow, and it's old, that's probably your problem. Newer routers are faster than older ones, and that's a fact. If your router is on an older standard (802.11b or 802.11g), you'll definitely see a speed improvement by moving to an 802.11n router. Even if you have an older 802.11n router, you'll probably gain some speed by moving to a newer 802.11n router; the technology within each standard improves over time.

Given the low prices on even higher end routers today, upgrading every few years is an affordable way to put a little extra oomph in your network. You'll notice the difference.

 NOTE   Each newer Wi-Fi protocol is backwards-compatible with previous versions. So, if you buy a new 802.11n router, you can still use it with older computers that adhere to the older 802.11g standard.

Troubleshooting Bad Network Connections

What do you do if you have trouble connecting a given wireless device to your network—or if you can connect it but then not see the rest of the network from that device? What about devices that suddenly lose their connection to the network?

Well, there are some things you can do to fix all of these problems. Read on to learn more.

Letting Your Operating System Fix the Problem

Network-related problems are common enough that troubleshooting "wizards" are built into most newer operating systems. These wizards either try to fix the problem automatically or walk you through a series of steps to help diagnose the problem.

In Windows, open the Network and Sharing Center and click Change Adapter Settings. When the list of network adapters appears, select the problematic device and then click Diagnose This Connection. This launches the Windows Network Diagnostics Troubleshooter, which will try to fix the current problem, typically by disabling and then re-enabling the network adapter. Additional suggestions may also be offered.

On a Mac, use the built-in Network Diagnostics tool. You open this tool from the Network Preferences window; just click the Assist Me button and, when the next window appears, click Diagnostics. The Mac's Network Diagnostics tool walks you through the various steps of troubleshooting your current connection; follow the onscreen instructions to identify and hopefully fix the current issue.

Disconnecting the Connection

Assuming that the problem you're having is with a wireless connection, there's actually an easy solution—almost too easy. But, you'd be surprised how often it works.

If you have trouble making a wireless connection or if a connection gets dropped, just disconnect from the current network. (In Windows, you do this by clicking the Network icon in the system tray, highlighting the current wireless connection, and then clicking Disconnect.) Wait a few seconds, and then reconnect to the same wireless network. More often than not, the new connection will be better than the old one.

Rebooting the Adapter—or the Device

The next step is to go after the entire Wi-Fi adapter inside the affected device. That is, turn off the device's Wi-Fi, and then turn it back on. More often than not, this purges whatever problem was occurring and establishes a sturdy new connection.

So, for example, if you're having trouble connecting a Windows computer, open the Network and Sharing Center and disable the Wi-Fi adapter. Wait a few seconds and then re-enable it. That'll probably fix your problem.

In some instances, you may need to reboot the entire device—that is, power off the affected computer or smartphone or tablet off and then power it back on again. This will flush any problems within the device's operating system that might be affecting the wireless connection.

Rebooting Your Router

If you experience connection problems with more than one wireless device, the problem is more likely to be in your central wireless router. Again, the simplest fix is to switch off your router, wait half a minute or so, and then switch it back on again. It may take a few minutes to get the network up and running again, but when it is, you'll probably find that your connection problems are no more.

Checking the Device's IP Settings

Most wireless routers are configured so that they allow computers and other devices to join the network automatically, without having to manually set IP addresses on each device. That is, each wireless device automatically gets assigned an IP address when it connects to the network.

It's possible that a given device isn't properly configured for automatic IP addressing. Check the device's TCP/IP settings to make sure that it automatically obtains settings from the router (sometimes referred to as the DHCP server).

Manually Assigning an IP Address

Sometimes, the IP addresses that your router automatically assigns to networked devices can conflict with one another. If you keep having connection problems with one particular computer or device, you may need to manually assign that device's IP address. This gives the devices a *static* IP address that doesn't change every time it's booted up and connects to the network.

How you do this varies from device to device and from operating system to operating system. In Windows, for example, you follow the instructions in the section, "Changing IP Addresses." When you solidify your changes, this device will now be connected to your network via a static IP address—and it won't change.

Checking the Workgroup Name

If you can connect to your network but not access a particular computer on your network, the problem may be that the machines belong to two different *workgroups*. A workgroup, in the Windows world, is what Microsoft names a given collection of computers on a network. If two different computers are configured to belong to two different workgroups, they may not be able to see each other or share files or devices.

Here's the problem: In Windows XP, the default workgroup name for any Windows computer was MSHOME. In Windows Vista, Windows 7, and Windows 8, the default workgroup name is WORKGROUP. So, if you're trying to connect a Windows 7 computer to a Windows XP machine, and you haven't changed any of the default settings, the two computers belong to two different workgroups and won't be able to talk to each other.

 TIP   What is the name of your current workgroup? To find out, open the Control Panel and select System. The workgroup name is displayed in the resulting System window.

To forestall any connection issues, you need to assign the same workgroup name to all computers on your network. So, if all your computers are in the WORKGROUP workgroup except an old Windows XP machine (which is assigned to the MSHOME workgroup, if you recall), you should change the workgroup name on that old PC to WORKGROUP. Or you could change the workgroup for *all* of your PCs to something a little less generic, such as BOBGROUP, MYWORKGROUP, or whatever.

If you want or need to change the workgroup for a given computer, open the Windows Control Panel and select System. When the System window appears, scroll to the Computer Name, Domain, and Workgroup Settings section and click Change Settings.

When the System Properties dialog box appears, select the Computer Name tab and click the Change button. When the Computer Name/Domain Changes dialog box appears, enter a new name for your workgroup into the Workgroup field and click OK.

When prompted to restart your computer, do so. Upon restart, this computer now belongs to the new workgroup you designated.

Troubleshooting a Dead Internet Connection

Sometimes, your connection to the network is fine but then, for some reason, you can't connect to the Internet. Given that Internet access is one of the main reasons to assemble a wireless network, this is a situation that needs to be fixed.

Checking the Cables

This is another one of those "too good to be true" fixes, but you'd be surprised how many times the problem is a bad or loose cable. When your Internet connection goes down, there are actually two cables to check:

- The coaxial or fiber-optic cable running from the wall to your broadband modem

- The Ethernet cable running between your cable modem and your wireless router

Check both these cables. Make sure that they're firmly connected; it's easy enough for a coaxial cable to come unscrewed or an Ethernet cable to pop out of place. If everything is nice and firm, try replacing the cables; the little metal wires inside a cable can break or go bad, especially if the cable is kinked or twisted.

Rebooting the Modem

It's not unheard of for an incoming Internet signal to get off sync, so to speak. The way to address this is to reboot your broadband modem; this will clear any connection problems and start things fresh. Just unplug the power cable, wait 30 seconds or so, and then plug it back in again.

In some instances, you may have to reboot more than just your cable modem. Start by turning off your modem and powering off your wireless router. Wait about a half minute and then power up the modem. Wait for all the little lights to go green, and then power up your router. This should get everything synced properly.

Checking with Your ISP

Sometimes, your ISP is just...well, flaky. It's certainly not unheard of for an ISP to experience service outages, either system-wide or just in specific neighborhoods. When all else fails, telephone your ISP's tech support number and report your problem. Chances are, they're probably already aware of it.

Speeding Up a Slow Internet Connection

Sometimes, your Internet connection just feels slow. That may be nothing more than appearances (things seem slowest when you're in a hurry), or it may be a real problem.

Understanding Connection Speed

Unfortunately, many things can slow your web browsing. Some of these issues have to do with your browser, and others with your Internet connection itself.

Let's start with your Internet connection. Although your ISP no doubt promises blazing connection speeds, it won't always deliver on its promises. It's an unfortunate truth that the actual speed of any given Internet connection often differs from the astounding speeds promised in the promotional materials. Your distance from the nearest network node affects actual speed, as do the number of other users connecting at the same time, as do numerous other factors. So, just because your ISP promises blazing-fast 10Mbps rates doesn't mean that your connection will always be that fast.

That begs the obvious question: How fast is your Internet connection? There are several sites on the web designed to test the speed of your connection; all you have to do is access the site and click the appropriate buttons. The site will download and upload some small files to and from your PC, measure how fast it all takes, and display your current upload and download speeds.

 NOTE Most ISPs provide different upload and download speeds to their customers; download speeds are typically faster.

Some of my favorite speed test sites include the following:

- **Bandwidth Place Speed Test** (www.bandwidthplace.com)
- **Broadband DSL Reports Speed Test** (www.dslreports.com/speedtest)
- **CNET Bandwidth Meter Speed Test** (reviews.cnet.com/internet-speed-test/)
- **Speedtest** (www.speedtest.net)

NOTE   Many ISPs provide their own speed-test utilities.

Note that your connection speed may vary from day to day, or even at different hours of the same day. Test your connection a few times on different days of the week, calculate an average, and compare that to the speeds promised by your ISP.

Understanding Browser Speed

Now, let's examine your web browser, which is a software program, not much different from a word processor or spreadsheet application, designed specifically to display HTML pages on the web. Like any software program, it contains numerous configuration settings—some of which affect the speed at which web pages are displayed.

As you're probably aware, a typical web page contains a mix of text, graphics, and other elements. Text is easiest to display; not a whole lot involved with that. Graphics, however, can take longer to display, primarily because image files can be large. These large files take longer to download and thus longer to display in your web browser.

Other page elements can include audio and video files, along with bits of Java programming code. Java is typically used to insert "applets" (small applications) into a web page; these applets often contain elements hosted on other websites. For example, a page might display a clock created with Java; the code for the clock is on the web page itself, while the engine and graphics for the clock are hosted on another site. Because of this dual-hosting nature of some of this code, these applets can often take longer to display than elements hosted natively.

Naturally, the more elements on a web page, the longer it will take your browser to display them. It's not just a matter of download size; all those elements must be rendered for display by the browser, and this rendering takes computing horse-power and time. It's no surprise that bigger web pages can really slow down your browser.

Fortunately, many of these issues can be overcome by some simple configuration changes.

Cleaning Your Cache

In most cases, web browsers store a temporary copy of each web page you visit, called a *cache*. The intent is to speed up browsing by letting the browser access the local cache when you revisit a recent page.

The cache, of course, is nothing but a file on your computer's hard drive. As such, it takes up valuable disk space. And, although the cache is designed to speed up browsing, too big of a cache can slow your web browser to a crawl.

You see, over time your browser keeps adding web pages to the cache —and these pages aren't deleted automatically. So, the more web pages you visit, the bigger the cache on your hard disk—and too large a cache file puts a drain on your web browser. Simply put, a bigger cache file takes longer to load and sort through, which slows things down.

The solution to cache-based sluggishness is to clean out the cache from time to time. In essence, what you do is delete the cache file; this "empties" the cache, frees up valuable hard disk space, and makes it much easier for your browser to search for previously cached pages.

The process differs from browser to browser (and with each version of a given browser), but what you want to look for is an option, somewhere in the browser settings, to either Clear Cache, Clear Browsing Data, Delete Browsing History, or something similar. Click the appropriate button, and your browser will delete the temporary cache file—and speed up its own performance.

Changing the Size of Your Cache

In some web browsers, you can change the size of the cache. The smaller the cache, the speedier the browser will be.

For example, in Internet Explorer 9, you start by clicking the Tools (gear) button and selecting Internet Options. When the Internet Options dialog box appears, select the General tab and then click the Settings button in the Browsing History section. When the Temporary Internet Files and History Settings dialog box appears, set the Disk Space setting to the desired number.

What is the best size for your cache file? While you can set a cache as small as 8MB, I recommend something in the 50MB range. Anything much smaller is less than useful, and anything much larger just takes up disk space and slows down your browser.

Managing Your Cookies

Just as your browser stores a temporary copy of each web page you visit, it also stores information about those pages, in the form of *cookies*. A cookie is a small file, created by a website but stored on your PC, which contains information about you and your activities on that website. For example, a cookie file for a particular site might contain your username and the most recent pages you visited on that site. The cookie file created by a site is accessed by that site each time you visit in the future, and the information used appropriately.

Aside from the privacy concerns of all these websites tracking your activities, cookies can also slow down your web browser. That's because, over time, you accumulate a *lot* of cookies. These files, although small, can take up unnecessary amounts of hard disk space; in addition, your browser must sort through them all to find the cookies it needs when accessing a specific site. The more cookie files on your hard drive, the harder your browser has to work.

As with your browser's cache file, the solution to cookie-induced sluggishness is to delete all your cookies. How you do this differs from browser to browser, of course, but look for an option (typically in the advanced settings or security settings) to delete all cookies. You can also opt to not accept cookies at all, which has the added benefit of more private browsing.

 CAUTION Deleting cookies may cause some websites to not remember you on your next visit—or to not be able to access your previously entered personal data. In fact, some sites won't let you log on at all unless cookies are enabled.

Don't Display Graphics

Here's a big one that may or may not appeal to you. Many web pages are overloaded with photos and other images; these images are big files that can take a long time to download and display, especially if you have a slow web connection. You can speed up the loading graphics-intensive pages by simply turning off the graphics. That leaves you with a text-only web page, of course—but that page will load a lot faster than it did with all the images intact.

Most web browsers offer the option of not displaying images on web pages. Some browsers also let you turn off sounds and animations, which are also bandwidth hogs.

 CAUTION Turning off the display of images will speed up your browsing, but will also make many web pages less than totally useful.

Uninstalling Unnecessary Add-Ons

Some of what slows down a web browser are add-ons to the main program. These auxiliary programs require more computing power than the browser does by itself, and sometimes access third-party websites that require additional downloads. You can speed up your browsing by disabling the least essential of these add-ons, such as toolbars, apps, and gadgets.

Again, how you do this differs from browser to browser. Look for options (typically in the advanced settings) to disable add-ins, plug-ins, toolbars, and the like.

Using an Alternate DNS Service

Let's move beyond the browser to consider your actual connection to the Internet. Even the fastest broadband connection can feel slow if it takes a long time to pull up each website you want to visit. This problem is due to something called the Domain Name System (DNS) and slowness in your ISP's DNS server—and can be corrected.

You see, every website is hosted on a web server, which is a fancy type of computer connected to the Internet. To identify the millions of such servers, each server has its own unique address, called an IP address, which looks something like this: **192.111.222.255**.

Of course, you don't type this address into your web browser when you want to visit a website. What you type is the URL or website address, which looks something like this: **www.websiteaddress.com**. The URL, then, is an alias for the site's true address.

What a DNS server does is link the site's easy-to-remember URL with its hard-to-remember IP address. For example, **www.google.com** is the URL for the server located at the **74.125.224.72** IP address. When you enter the URL **www.google.com** in your web browser, that URL request is sent to a DNS server that looks up that URL's IP address and then routes the request to the server located at **74.125.224.72**. (Actually, that's just one of Google's many IP addresses; your browser might route to a different IP address.)

When you connect to the Internet via your Internet service provider (ISP), your URL requests are sent to that ISP's DNS server. That's a simple enough process—until your ISP's DNS server starts to get bogged down. When that happens, it takes longer for the DNS server to look up the IP addresses for the URLs you enter.

Unfortunately, many ISP DNS servers are notoriously slow. The result is that it takes longer to load any web page you want to visit. It's not the connection that's slow, it's the ability of your ISP to look up the web pages you want to view.

You can work around this issue by directing your URL requests to a different DNS server. To that end, several sites offer alternative DNS services, promising faster lookups and thus faster web browsing. Probably the most popular of these services is OpenDNS (www.opendns.com), which is completely free.

To use an alternate DNS service, you have to reconfigure your operating system to send all URL requests to the new DNS server. In Windows, for example, you do this from the Network and Sharing Center; click Change Adapter Settings, and when the next window appears, right-click the icon for your connection and select Properties.

When the Properties dialog box appears, make sure the Networking tab is selected, then select Internet Protocol Version 4 (TCP/IPv4) from the list and click the Properties button. When the next Properties dialog box appears, select the Use the Following DNS Server Addresses option. Enter the DNS service's preferred DNS server address into the Preferred DNS Server box, and their alternate DNS server address into the Alternate DNS Server box. Click OK, and you're all reconfigured.

You'll now access the designated third-party DNS server whenever you're web browsing—which should be slightly faster than what you're used to with your ISP's DNS server.

THE ABSOLUTE MINIMUM

Here are the key points to remember from this chapter:

- In Windows, you manage and configure your network connections from the Network and Sharing Center. On a Mac, you use the Network Preferences window.

- If your wireless network is slow, try moving your computer or handheld device closer to the router; repositioning the router or its antenna; removing other electronic devices that might be causing interference; changing the broadcast channel; changing the RF band; or upgrading to a newer, faster router.

- If a device has trouble connecting to your network, try using your computer's network troubleshooting wizard; disconnecting and then reconnecting the device from/to your network; rebooting the device or its wireless adapter; rebooting your router; checking the device's IP settings; or manually assigning a static IP address to the device.

- If your network isn't connecting to the Internet, try checking all the cables connected to your modem and router; rebooting the modem; or checking with your ISP to see if it's a system-wide outage.

- If your Internet connection seems sluggish, try cleaning your browser's cache; changing the size of the cache; deleting all cookies; not displaying graphics in your browser; uninstalling unnecessary browser add-ons; and using an alternate DNS service.

20

CONNECTING TO WI-FI HOTSPOTS

If you have a notebook PC, a tablet, or a smartphone, you have built-in Wi-Fi capability—wherever you happen to be. You're not limited to just connecting to your wireless network at home; you can also connect to your work network or any public Wi-Fi hotspot.

As you're probably aware, many coffeehouses, restaurants, libraries, hotels, and public spaces offer Wi-Fi Internet service, either free or for an hourly or daily fee. Connecting to one of these hotspots is a snap.

Where Can You Find a Hotspot?

There are literally hundreds of thousands, if not millions, of public Wi-Fi hotspots across the globe. Virtually every country in the world (save North Korea, probably) has them, as does every city in every state of the union. That doesn't mean you can stand out in the middle of a street and expect to find Wi-Fi access. Although that's possible with some municipal Wi-Fi networks, it's more likely that you'll be connecting to a privately run network with public access.

Wi-Fi Coffeehouses and Restaurants

Probably the easiest place to find a Wi-Fi connection is at your local coffeehouse. All the large coffee chains offer Wi-Fi access, as do most local independent coffeehouses.

For example, Starbucks offers Wi-Fi access through AT&T. The company used to charge for Internet access, but now it's free. (Good for me; I do my writing there almost every day!) Same thing for Wi-Fi access at competitor Caribou Coffee; you don't even have to buy anything to connect.

Other coffeehouses take different approaches. For example, Lulu's Electric Café, a local coffeehouse in Indianapolis, hands you a printed card when you make a purchase; this card includes a password good for one hour of Internet access. The only drawback to this approach is that at the end of each hour, the service stops, and you have to interrupt what you're doing to enter a new access code. A bit of a pain, but at least it's free, more or less.

 CAUTION When you find a coffeehouse with Wi-Fi access, your next challenge will probably be finding a power outlet. Not all coffeehouses offer a plentitude of easily accessible power outlets—which means that you might have to operate your notebook on battery power, as long as that lasts. (And don't get me started on the number of tables available on a busy day....)

Of course, coffeehouses aren't the only food-and-beverage establishments to offer Wi-Fi access. Many restaurant chains offer wireless Internet access, often for free. For example, the Bruegger's Bagels and Panera Bread chains both offer free Wi-Fi access, as do McDonald's, Culvers, and other burger joints. Chances are if the fast-food restaurant you're in doesn't have free Wi-Fi, the one next door will.

Wi-Fi Hotels

Most major U.S. hotel chains today offer some sort of Internet access to their paying guests. The type of access offered depends on the chain—and, in many cases, the individual location. Wi-Fi access is most common, but you may still find Ethernet connections in some locations—although if that's the case, you'll probably have to ask for a connecting cable at the front desk.

Interestingly, there's a big variance in cost between the various hotel chains. Many of the more affordable chains offer free Wi-Fi access for their guests, while a good number of the higher-priced hotels charge for the connection—typically $10/day or so. If the access is free, expect to receive an access number or password when you check in.

Wi-Fi Airports and Transportation Centers

Most airports, train stations, bus depots, and mass transportation centers offer some form of Wi-Fi access to their waiting travelers and commuters. Airport access varies wildly from airport to airport, however. Some airports offer free access throughout the entire terminal; some offer paid access only; some offer access only in kiosks or at designated gates or public areas. You also may find Wi-Fi access (typically free) in the club rooms offered by many airlines. When in doubt, turn on your PC and see what's available.

Wi-Fi in Public Places

Interestingly, many public locations today are starting to offer free or paid Wi-Fi access. For example, many big convention centers are wired for wireless, meaning you can connect to the Internet when you're attending a trade show, expo, or business conference. Ask your event organizer what type of access (if any) is available.

Libraries are also good sources for free Wi-Fi, as are other local community centers, performing arts centers, and the like. For that matter, your doctor and dentist probably offer Wi-Fi (free or paid) in their offices. You can also get a good connection at your local Barnes & Noble bookstore or FedEx Office location.

Wi-Fi Communities

Speaking of public Wi-Fi hotspots, some communities provide citywide Wi-Fi access. This type of access can be either paid or free; if free, it's typically advertiser supported. (That means you get a banner ad in your web browser when you log on.)

TIP   Still not sure where to find a Wi-Fi hotspot? Then, check out a Wi-Fi finder site before you leave home; these sites list known hotspots by location. The most popular of these include Wi-Fi FreeSpot Directory (www.wififreespot.com) and Wi-Fi Directory (www.wifidirectory.com).

Connecting to a Public Hotspot

Okay, you've found yourself a public Wi-Fi hotspot and your notebook PC or handheld device has built-in Wi-Fi connectivity. How do you connect?

First, make sure you have the Wi-Fi functionality enabled on your device. Some notebook PCs have a switch on the front or side, or use a particular keyboard key or combination of keys to turn on and off the internal wireless adapter. Read your notebook's instruction manual to find the on/off mechanism, and then turn on the PC's wireless functionality.

On a smartphone or tablet, you'll need to enable Wi-Fi from the options or settings screen. When you do, keep that screen open; you'll also use it to connect to the network.

With the internal Wi-Fi adapter working, your wireless device should automatically detect all wireless networks in the immediate area. It goes without saying that with the increasing popularity of wireless Internet, you're likely to find more than one nearby wireless connection.

Not all of these connections will actually let you connect. If a private network has wireless security enabled, you can connect only if you know the network key or passphrase, which you probably won't. Instead, you need to identify the particular public hotspot to which you want to connect—which is probably labeled as an "unsecured wireless network," sometimes with a little warning icon next to it, as shown in Figure 20.1.

You find and connect to a given wireless hotspot the same way you connect to your home wireless network. Although this differs from device to device, it's typically a matter of displaying the list of available networks and then choosing the one you want to connect to.

NOTE   We covered how to connect with different types of computers in Chapter 11, "Connecting Home Computers," and how to connect handheld devices in Chapter 15, "Connecting Smartphones and Tablets." Turn to these chapters for detailed instructions.

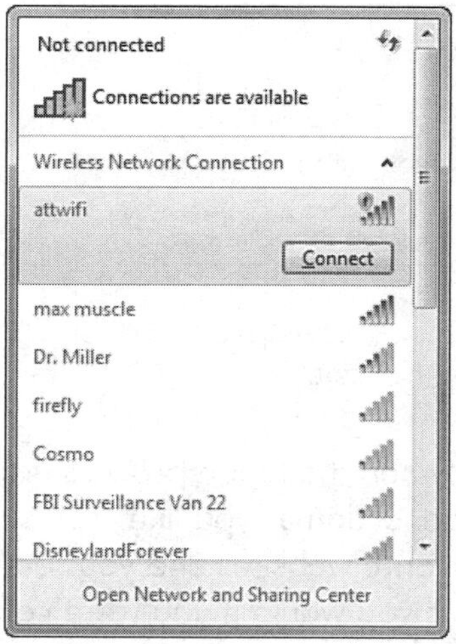

FIGURE 20.1

Connecting to an "unsecured" public hotspot with a Windows 7 PC.

Logging Onto a Hotspot

Being connected to a hotspot is not the same as obtaining full access; you may have to manually log on to the hotspot to use it. Although some hotspots don't require any logon, many do. Fortunately, it's a relatively easy process.

Typically, you do this by opening your web browser and entering any website address. You can try opening your home page, or just enter something like **www.google.com**.

What you enter is irrelevant; what's important is that you try to access a site on the Internet. The hotspot senses this and intercepts your command, instead displaying its own logon page.

Even free hotspots require you to logon, if for no other reason to agree to their terms of service. (Which no one ever reads, it's not just you.) For example, when you connect the wireless network at your local Starbucks store, you see the logon page shown in Figure 20.2.

What happens next depends on the hotspot. With the Starbucks logon page, for example, all you have to do is check the box to agree to the terms of service and then click the Connect to Wi-Fi Now button. A hotel hotspot might require you to enter your room number or the password the desk clerk gave you. Other hotspots might ask to you register or enter a user name or password.

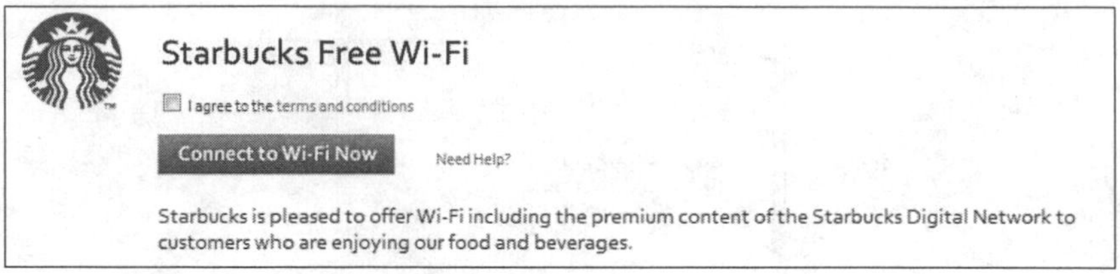

Starbucks Free Wi-Fi

☐ I agree to the terms and conditions

[Connect to Wi-Fi Now]   Need Help?

Starbucks is pleased to offer Wi-Fi including the premium content of the Starbucks Digital Network to customers who are enjoying our food and beverages.

FIGURE 20.2

Logging on to a Starbucks hotspot.

However you connect, when the logon process is complete, you can start using the wireless Internet connection as you like. You should be able to use your web browser to surf your favorite websites and your email program to send and receive email messages—just as you would if you were connecting from your home or office.

CAUTION   Some public hotspots block access to selected websites, typically those with "adult" or otherwise unsavory content. It's probably not a good idea to be browsing these kinds of sites in public, anyway.

Manually Connecting to a Hidden Network

On some occasions, an active Wi-Fi hotspot will not show up in the list of nearby available wireless networks. This happens when a wireless network or access point is configured to *not* broadcast its network name, or SSID.

Just because a network isn't broadcasting its name, however, doesn't mean you can't connect to it. In this instance, you have to establish a connection manually.

To make a manual connection, you need to know the specifics of the network. In particular, you need to know the network name (SSID), what kind of wireless security (if any) the network uses, and (if the network uses wireless security) the network key or passphrase.

This information in hand, you can display the list of available networks and then choose the Other or Other Network option, as shown in Figure 20.3. You can then manually enter the network's name and password, if you know it.

FIGURE 20.3

On an iPhone, select the Other option to manually enter a network's name and password.

Changing the Order of Preferred Networks in Windows

When you make a connection to a hotspot, Windows remembers. In fact, Windows' memory is so good that it will automatically connect to that hotspot the next time you're in the area, no intervention on your part required at all.

Although this automatic wireless connection is normally a good thing, it can prove problematic if more than one hotspot is in the immediate vicinity—and Windows chooses the wrong one to connect to. Trust me, it happens.

For example, if your hotel is located in a cluster with other hotels, you might display the list of wireless networks and see other hotel hotspots listed before yours in the list. Or imagine you're in a Starbucks on a busy Manhattan street corner and see the option of connecting not just to this Starbucks hotspot but also to a half-dozen other nearby Starbucks locations. In either situation, Windows might not connect to the network you want.

Here's a real-world example. I sometimes work out of a Caribou Coffee in Eagan, Minnesota, which happens to be right next door to a Bruegger's Bagels. I can choose to connect to the Caribou network if I want, or to the Bruegger's network. On any given day, one of the networks will likely be faster than the other, and thus influence my decision.

In situations like this, you want to control the order of which wireless networks Windows connects to, so that it doesn't just connect to the first network in the list. You do this by opening the Network and Sharing Center and clicking Manage Wireless Networks. In the next window, shown in Figure 20.4, you see a list of all the wireless networks you've successfully accessed in the past.

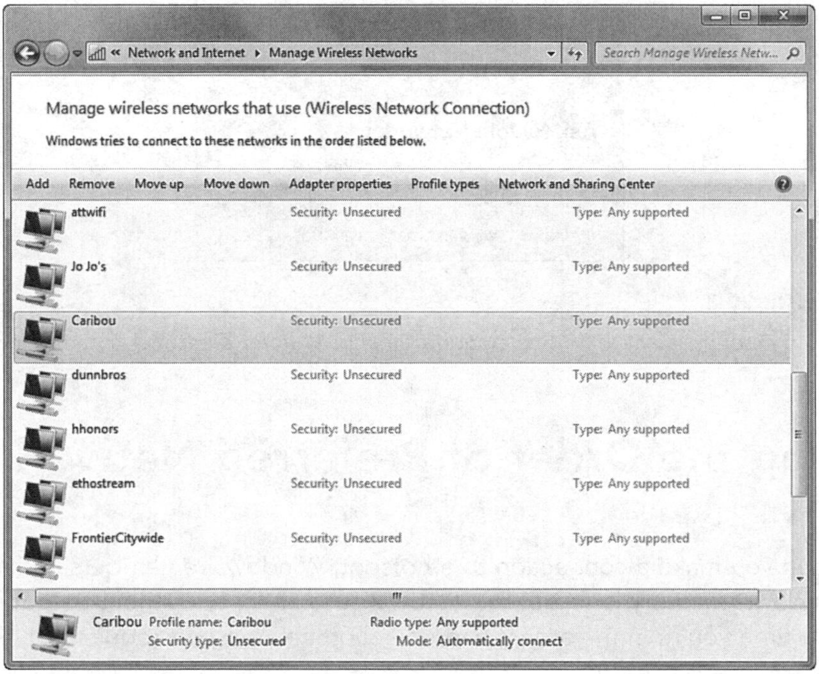

FIGURE 20.4

Managing wireless networks on a Windows 7 PC.

Windows connects to available networks in the order specified in this Manage Wireless Networks window. It attempts to connect to the first available network first; if a connection cannot be established with that network, it tries the second network in the list, then the third, and so on.

To change the connection order, select a network and move it up or down the list. You can also completely delete any selected network.

TIP   You probably want to place your own wireless network at the top of this list to make sure you automatically connect to it rather than to a neighbor's network.

Working Securely from a Public Hotspot

When you're using your computer, tablet, or smartphone at a public hotspot, you need to take special care to secure your data. You are, after all, working in public, which increases the risk of data theft.

First, know that anyone in the room can peek at what's on your screen. This is the easiest way for someone to steal personal information; they just look over your shoulder. For this reason, avoid working on or displaying personal information, such as your banking data or Social Security number. And be careful when inputting passwords; all a sneaky thief has to do is watch your fingers as you type.

Second, you should also know that it's possible for the signals you send from your wireless device to the hotspot's wireless access point to be intercepted. Hackers can use so-called "sniffer" programs to eavesdrop on the websites you visit and the emails you send. This makes your hotspot activities quite public, which isn't a good thing.

Although you won't often encounter data thieves using sniffer programs, it can happen. The only sure-fire way to protect your data on a public hotspot is to log onto encrypted sites—those that start with **https:** instead of **http:**. (For example, most online shopping checkout pages are encrypted, as are most online banking sites.) Unencrypted data, however, can be intercepted.

One solution to this problem is to use a virtual private network (VPN) for all of your public browsing. A VPN establishes a secured private network across the public Wi-Fi network by creating a "tunnel" between the two endpoints. The data sent through the tunnel (web page addresses, email, and such) is encrypted so other users can't intercept it.

TIP   Some of the more popular VPN services include GPass (www.gpass1.com), Its Hidden (www.itshidden.eu), and ProXPN (www.proxpn.com),

The takeaway from all this is when you're using your computer in a public location, most things you do online are potentially public. So, watch what you do—and avoid sending personal data (and credit-card info) to unencrypted websites.

Troubleshooting Hotspot Problems

In a perfect world, you go to your local coffeehouse, select the place's Wi-Fi hotspot on your notebook PC or mobile device, and have immediate access to the Internet.

Unfortunately, it's not always an ideal world.

When you're having difficulty connecting or staying connected to a hotspot, it's time to do a little troubleshooting. Read on to learn more.

You Can't Connect to the Hotspot

Here's the worst case scenario: You power up your PC or wireless device but don't see any hotspots listed. The likely cause of this problem is that you don't have your device's Wi-Fi enabled. If you have a handheld device, you may be able to connect to the Internet generally via your provider's 3G/4G data service, but that isn't the same as connecting to a Wi-Fi hotspot. Get into your device's settings and turn on the Wi-Fi!

What if you have your Wi-Fi enabled, see a list of nearby wireless networks, but your local hotspot isn't on the list? In this instance, try refreshing the list; often-times, this will make your particular hotspot appear. You can also try moving closer to the actual wireless router or adapter at the establishment; if you're too far away (more than 300 feet or so), you won't be able to connect.

If this doesn't do it, try disabling and then re-enabling your device's Wi-Fi func-tionality; in many instances, this will fix the connection problem. You may even want to reboot your entire computer or wireless device, which sometimes fixes all sorts of problems.

It's also possible that your local establishment is having problems with its wire-less router. Sad to say, but I've often had to prompt the guy or gal behind the counter to reboot—or, in more than one instance, just turn on—the joint's router. No kidding.

You Get Disconnected from the Hotspot

I frequently run into issues of dropped connections at public hotspots. More often than not, this is the result of some sort of router issue on the hotspot's end of things, but you still get disconnected, nonetheless.

When the connection drops, just try reconnecting; nine times out of ten, this fixes things. In some instances, you may need to manually disconnect and then recon-nect, or even disable and then re-enable your device's Wi-Fi. In any case, estab-lishing a new connection typically does the job.

Distance may also be an issue. If you're at the far end of a router's range, which sometimes happens in large hotels, moving closer to the router will establish a steadier connection.

You Connect to the Hotspot But Can't Access the Internet

You connect to a hotspot in order to access the Internet. So, what happens when you're able to connect to the hotspot but then find that there's no Internet available?

Hate to say it, but the first thing to do is disconnect and then reconnect to the hotspot. If that doesn't work, try disabling and then re-enabling your device's Wi-Fi.

Another slap-your-forehead type of solution is to make sure that you're actually logged on to the hotspot. This means opening your web browser, entering any old website address, and waiting for the hotspot's logon screen to appear. For many hotspots, you can't access the Internet unless you formally log on.

If you still can't access the Internet—if you try to go to multiple websites without success—you'll need to talk to whomever is running the hotspot. It's possible that they're having issues with their Internet connection.

You Can't Connect to Selected Websites

If you can connect to the Internet but not to selected websites, you have another issue. You can probably go to www.google.com and www.facebook.com, but some other sites keep returning a "site not found" or similar error.

This may be intentional. Many hotspots block access to certain types of sites, typically those with content best not viewed in public, but also some high-bandwidth sites, such as those offering streaming video. Check with the hotspot management to see what restrictions they may have in place.

It's also possible, of course, that a particular website is having its own individual issues. Every site goes down now and then; if your issue is with a single site, try again a little later.

You Can't Send or Receive Email

I don't know about you, but I often log onto a public hotspot just to check email. I use Microsoft Outlook, and every now and then I get a send/receive error when trying to retrieve my messages.

Sometimes, the solution is a simple one. Because many hotspots require you to log on to get Internet access, if you try to use an email program to check your email before you open your web browser, you're not connected. Open your browser, dial in any random URL, and do the log on thing before trying your email again. (This isn't a problem if you use a web-based email service, of course.)

Some public hotspots (and public ISPs) block email access from selected server ports. If your email provider uses these ports, any attempt to send or receive email on your end will be blocked. There are some potential technical solutions to this problem (such as specifying different ports in your email program), but the easiest solution may be to use your email provider's web access instead. Because most ISPs and email providers let you access your email inbox via a web browser, this is probably the way to go.

 NOTE If you're using Gmail or Hotmail, you're using web-based email to begin with, and won't experience this problem.

THE ABSOLUTE MINIMUM

Here are the key points to remember from this chapter:

- Public Wi-Fi hotspots offer wireless Internet access, often for free.

- You connect to a public Wi-Fi hotspot the same way you connect to your home wireless network—display the list of nearby networks and then select the one you want.

- Many Wi-Fi hotspots require you to sign in to get access; enter any URL into your web browser to display the login page.

- Some public hotspots may be hidden; you can access them if you know their name (SSID) and password in advance.

- Windows connects to previously accessed hotspots in a set order; you can change the connection order to avoid connecting to unwanted wireless networks.

- When accessing a public wireless hotspot, be careful of what you enter; there are data thieves out there.

21

CONNECTING IN YOUR CAR

You're used to connecting various wireless devices in your home, and away from home at public Wi-Fi hotspots. But, what about connecting those same devices while you're in-between, driving in your car?

Here's the good news. Many new automobiles let you connect your phone to your car, wirelessly, for hands-free calling. (In fact, many states now legislate hands-free calling while driving.) Some cars even let you connect your phone to your car stereo system to play your favorite tunes while on the road. And that's pretty cool.

Connecting Your Phone to Your Car for Phone Calls

Connecting wirelessly to today's automobiles is all about Bluetooth, not Wi-Fi. As you learned in Chapter 3, "How Bluetooth Works," Bluetooth is a wireless standard for short-distance ad-hoc connections—just the kind you need to make between your smartphone and your car's electronic system.

Many newer cars have built-in Bluetooth, which makes it relatively easy to connect your phone for hands-free operation. Older or less-expensive cars may not have built-in Bluetooth, which has opened the door to a lot of third-party add-on packages that do pretty much the same thing. So whether your car has Bluetooth built in or you have to go the add-on route, you can gain all the advantages of wireless connections while you're on the road.

Using Built-In Bluetooth

When you connect your phone to your automobile via Bluetooth, you go pretty much hands-free. You talk to the other party using a microphone, typically built into the driver's side visor, and listen through the speakers of your car's audio system. On most vehicles, you can even select and dial contacts using your car's dashboard-mounted controls and display. (This requires synching of your phone's contact list with your car's electronics system, which is done automatically via Bluetooth.)

For example, I drive a Volvo C70 (nice little hardtop convertible, thank you very much) and it pairs seamlessly with my iPhone via Bluetooth. Answering a call is as simple as pressing a button on the steering wheel, and making a call is done by dialing up my phone's contact list on the car's audio system.

My wife's Honda Accord also has built-in Bluetooth, and it works equally well with her iPhone. In her case, she can program the system for voice dialing by speaking the name of the contact she wants to call. The Accord has similar steering wheel-mounted buttons for dialing and answering, as shown in Figure 21.1.

To make the connection, you have to "pair" your phone with your car's electronics. Although the specifics differ from phone-to-phone and car-to-car, here's how it's done—in general terms:

1. Carry your phone to your car and turn both of them on.

2. Access the Bluetooth or phone menu on your car's dashboard display.

FIGURE 21.1

The steering wheel controls for hands-free phone operation in a Honda Accord.

3. Select the option to make your car's system discoverable by other Bluetooth devices.

4. On your phone, open the Bluetooth settings screen, enable Bluetooth, and select the option to search for nearby Bluetooth devices, if present.

5. Your phone will now search for nearby devices broadcasting a Bluetooth signal, and should find your car; select your phone from the list.

6. Your phone will now connect to your car, via Bluetooth, and prompt you to enter a four-digit passcode. This passcode is provided by your car's manufacturer and should be found in the car's instruction manual. Find and enter this passcode.

7. When prompted, tap to connect.

 NOTE With some cars, you do pretty much the opposite of what's listed here. That is, you make your phone discoverable and have your car search for your phone. It pays to read your car's instruction manual in advance, in any case.

Your phone and car should now be paired and ready to do their thing. Note that pairing is a one-time thing; you don't have to repeat the process every time you drive your car. When you enter your car, your phone and your car should recognize each other and establish a new Bluetooth connection.

Using Add-On Bluetooth Car Kits

If your car doesn't have built-in Bluetooth, you're still in luck. Many auto manufacturers and third-party companies make add-on Bluetooth kits that add Bluetooth functionality to any automobile.

Several different types of add-on Bluetooth kits are available:

- **Portable Bluetooth speakerphones**, like the Jabra DRIVE shown in Figure 21.2, have their own speakers and microphones and typically attach to your car's sun visor, the way a garage-door opener does. These devices tend to be battery-operated, so you'll have to change batteries from time to time. Some of these units have small displays for your contact list, caller ID, and the like; others rely on your phone's display for the user interface.

FIGURE 21.2

The Jabra DRIVE portable Bluetooth speakerphone. (Photo courtesy of Jabra.)

- **Hard-wired Bluetooth car kits**, which typically need to be professionally installed. These kits tie directly into your car's audio system, so you can use your car's speakers to listen to calls. They also tie into your car's power system, so you don't have to worry about battery life. There's typically a microphone that installs on your sun visor; sometimes, there's a display for caller ID, contacts, and the like, too.

- **GPS navigation devices.** This isn't a dedicated dialing solution, but an added feature found on many portable GPS navigation units. In addition to display maps and routes and such, many of these devices also have a built-in speaker and microphone for use with your Bluetooth-enabled mobile phone. If you're in the market for one of these puppies anyway, getting Bluetooth dialing is a nice plus.

- **Bluetooth-enabled in-dash stereos.** Again, added features instead of dedicated functions. If you're in the market for a new car stereo, look for one that has integrated Bluetooth. Most of these units not only feature Bluetooth-enabled hands-free calling, but also synch to your phone for wireless music playback.

Which solution is best depends on your own personal circumstances. Certainly, if you're in the market for a GPS unit or new car stereo, take the opportunity to get Bluetooth-enabled hands-free calling as an extra. If you just want a simple solution, no fancy installation required, go with a portable Bluetooth speakerphone. But, if you want the most integrated solution, and you don't mind the added cost or installation, a hard-wired Bluetooth car kit is the way to go.

Connecting Your Phone to Your Car to Play Music

Bluetooth in the car isn't just about phone calls—or at least not always. Many newer vehicles offer Bluetooth-enabled wireless music playback from your iPhone or Android phone. That's a lot more convenient (and less messy) than connecting your phone to your car stereo via some sort of connecting cable.

Listening with a Built-In System

When your car manufacturer includes built-in Bluetooth music, you can wirelessly stream tunes from your phone to your car stereo system. You don't have to connect any wires, and, in many cases, can control your phone's music playback from your car's audio system controls. Many of these systems also display track information and album art on your car's console display.

When you make this sort of wireless connection, you're not limited to playing music stored locally on your phone, either. You can connect your phone to the Internet (via your provider's 3G/4G data network) to access web-based streaming music services in real time, and then listen to them (via Bluetooth) on your car's audio system. That means you can listen to Pandora, Last.fm, or whatever service you like best while you're driving down the road—in the city or cross country.

For example, I recently had my car into the dealership for some scheduled maintenance and got the opportunity to borrow a new Volvo S60 with integrated Bluetooth audio streaming. Once I paired my iPhone with the system (took only a minute or so), I was able to control my phone's music playback from the car's dashboard-mounted controller and see what was playing on the car's in-dash display screen, as shown in Figure 21.3. It was a very neat experience, and something I'll definitely be looking for on the next car I buy.

FIGURE 21.3

Streaming smartphone music via Bluetooth on a Volvo S60.

Listening via an Add-On Bluetooth System

If your car doesn't have built-in Bluetooth music streaming, you can always add that functionality via aftermarket kits—or a completely new car stereo system.

Many third-party Bluetooth car kits, like the ones discussed previously, offer not only hands-free calling but also audio streaming. For example, the Parrot MKi9000, shown in Figure 21.4, hard-wires into your car's existing audio system and enables streaming audio from your smartphone, via Bluetooth. (Plus hands-free Bluetooth calling, of course.) You can find several kits of this sort for well under $200, which isn't much to spend for this type of convenience.

FIGURE 21.4

Add streaming music to your car with the Parrot MKi9000 Bluetooth car kit.

If you're in the market for a new car stereo, many units now come with Bluetooth streaming capability—even some lower-end models. For example, the JVC Arsenal in-dash system, as shown in Figure 21.5, sells for around U.S. $100 and includes Bluetooth music streaming and hands-free calling. Bluetooth is becoming a default feature on aftermarket car stereos these days.

FIGURE 21.5

Add streaming music to your car by replacing your existing stereo with the JVC Arsenal in-dash audio system.

Using Your Smartphone to Access the Internet While Driving

I need to be careful when discussing this next topic. I certainly don't want to encourage anyone to browse the web while driving. But, there are many reasons why you might want someone in your car to connect to the Internet while you're on the road—to generate driving directions, check email, listen to streaming music, even watch streaming movies. (That last one is great if you have kids in the car....)

The challenge is getting a good connection while you're on the road. Obviously, we're talking about connecting via your carrier's 3G/4G data service, not via Wi-Fi; as long as you're in motion, you're not going to be near any individual wireless hotspot for more than a few seconds. So, a cellular connection it is, which is probably not a big problem when you're in a major urban area, but may be more problematic when you're on the interstate between cities. But still, it's definitely doable.

You probably want to turn off your phone's Wi-Fi (just so it won't be tempted to connect to any passing wireless network) and go purely 3G/4G. You can then access any Internet-related function on your smartphone, from maps to Facebook to web browsing, just as you would normally.

Using a Wireless Router in Your Car

If you have several passengers in your car, all wanting to get online and do various Internet-related stuff, you can hope they all have phones or tablets with 3G/4G cellular data access. But, that's a lot of different (and expensive) data streams. Wouldn't it be nice if you could transform a single cellular data stream into a Wi-Fi hotspot that all of your devices could share?

Installing a Wireless Router

Your wish is granted. The Autonet Mobile CarFi Router, shown in Figure 21.6, is a wireless router for your car. It connects to your cellular data carrier of choice and then beams that single to up to 20 different devices, simultaneously. It even has a 150-foot range, so when you're in a parking spot or camping, you can wander a bit and still get reception.

FIGURE 21.6

The Autonet Mobile CarFi Router. (Photo courtesy of Autonet Mobile.)

This nifty little device mounts in your car's trunk and uses your car's power system. When installed and working, it's now easy for your spouse to fire up her notebook PC to do a little Facebooking and your kids to connect their tablet to watch a movie from Netflix, all at the same time. Heck, your kids can also connect their portable game systems to do online gaming while you're zooming along.

Unfortunately, the CarFi is not inexpensive. The unit lists for $600, plus you have to pay for that monthly cellular data plan. But, if you do a lot of long-distance traveling with your family, it may be worth it. Learn more at www.autonetmobile.com.

Using a Mobile Hotspot

If you're looking for a more affordable solution, check out one of the mobile hotspots sold by some cellular carriers. These units are small and lightweight, and can be easily moved from car-to-car, or even taken inside to create your own portable Wi-Fi hotspot. This type of unit connects to the carrier's cellular data network, and then beams that signal via Wi-Fi to nearby wireless devices—perfect for use in the car.

For example, T-Mobile's Sonic 4G Mobile Hotspot, shown in Figure 21.7, connects to T-Mobile's 3G/4G data network while you're on the road. (Or sitting in a coffee-house, for that matter.) It weighs less than 4 ounces, looks like a black bar of soap, and fits in the palm of your hand; you can easily place it on top of your dashboard for car-wide access. Even better, it only costs about $100. (Lower-priced models without 4G functionality are also available.)

FIGURE 21.7

T-Mobile's Sonic 4G Mobile Hotspot. (Photo courtesy of T-Mobile.)

If you're not a T-Mobile subscriber, Verizon, AT&T, and other carriers offer similar units. Figure 21.8 shows AT&T's Mobile Hotspot Elevate 4G, which can be had for about $50. It works just like the T-Mobile model; connect to AT&T's cellular data network and then beam the signal to other nearby devices via Wi-Fi. AT&T's unit features an LCD display that tells you how much data you have left on your monthly plan.

FIGURE 21.8

AT&T's Mobile Hotspot Elevate 4G. (Photo courtesy of AT&T.)

Looking to the Future: The Wireless Car

If you're serious about taking advantage of the Internet in your vehicle, just wait a few years. There's a coming trend of completely wireless cars—that is, cars with built-in 4G reception, no smartphone or other device necessary.

Some experts are saying that all cars will have this embedded wireless within the next five years or so. I think it may take longer than that, but it's definitely coming. AT&T says that the "connected car" is the third-fastest growing technological device today, following smartphones and tablets. (In fact, AT&T is already working with BMW, Ford, and Nissan on embedded wireless technology.)

If you want to see what this technology is like, check out the 2012 Audi A7. This luxury vehicle includes built-in 3G wireless, which powers the Audi Connect system, which turns the entire car into a giant Wi-Fi hotspot. (Up to 8 wireless devices can connect simultaneously.) You also get access to a variety of online services via the dashboard-mounted control screen, as shown in Figure 21.9, including news headlines, weather updates, gas prices, travel information, and the like. Naturally, you have a pay a monthly subscription fee for wireless access.

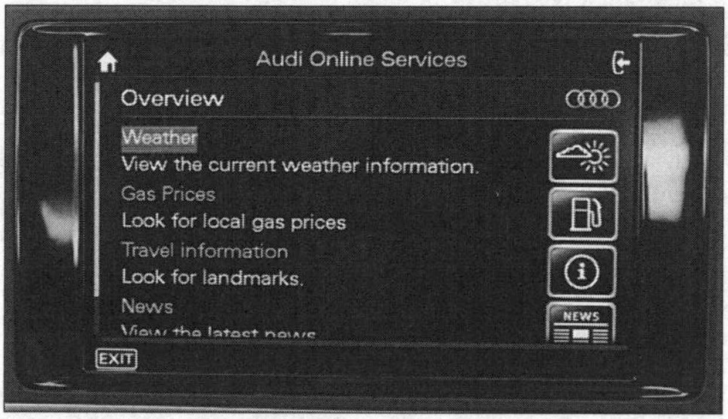

FIGURE 21.9

Accessing Audi Online Services in an Audi A7. So, how connected do you want your car to be? The options are increasing in number.

THE ABSOLUTE MINIMUM

Here are the key points to remember from this chapter:

- Many new cars come with built-in Bluetooth connectivity; connect your phone to your car via Bluetooth for hands-free calling.

- Some new cars also offer Bluetooth music streaming to wirelessly pipe music from a smartphone to the car's audio system.

- If your car doesn't have Bluetooth calling or music streaming built in, there are numerous aftermarket solutions to add this functionality.

- If you want to share a single data connection with all the wireless devices used in your vehicle, consider using a mobile data hotspot or wireless car router. These devices turn your car into a rolling Wi-Fi hotspot to which all wireless devices can connect.

- Or just wait a few years, when all new cars will come with embedded 3G/4G wireless for on-the-go Internet connections—or so they say.

Index

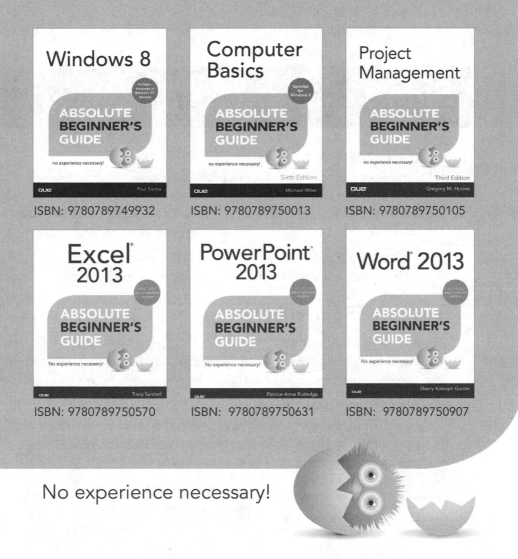